More Praise for *The Courage to Heal Workbook*

"Once again Laura Davis sensitively offers the incest and molestation survivor a path in which to heal. . . . She walks hand in hand with the survivor offering hope and validation—as survivor[s] actively participate in reclaiming their power, their self, and their life."

> —Claudia Black, author of *It Will Never Happen to Me* and *It's Never Too Late to Have a Happy Childhood*

"An invaluable guide and practical manual for those of us who are healing ourselves in an ongoing process of recovery"

> —Hank Estrada, PLEA

"Laura is a pioneer, a leader in her field. Survivors at any stage of recovery can learn from her."

> —Laurel King, therapist and coauthor of *Living in the Light*

"Laura Davis demonstrates a level of understanding of sexual molestation issues that far exceeds anything I have read or been taught."

> —Camille Caiozzo, Ph.D., clinical psychologist

"Laura Davis's work is extraordinarily powerful and insightful. Essential to child protective personnel struggling to understand and assist abused children and their families."

> —Elda Dawber, ACSW, Rhode Island Department for Children and Their Families

THE COURAGE
TO HEAL
WORKBOOK

FOR WOMEN AND MEN SURVIVORS
OF CHILD SEXUAL ABUSE

LAURA DAVIS

COLLINS LIVING

An Imprint of HarperCollins Publishers

WORKSHOPS AND LECTURES

Laura Davis offers trainings for professionals, public lectures, and groups for partners on healing from child sexual abuse. If you are interested in bringing one to your area, please contact her agent:

Denise Notzon
P.O. Box 6555
Albany, CA 94706

For a schedule of upcoming lectures, workshops, and seminars, please write to the address below. Laura welcomes any feedback, responses, suggestions, or ideas for improving or expanding upon the exercises in *The Courage to Heal Workbook* but regrets that she is unable to answer individual letters, phone calls, or requests for referrals. (Try calling the organizations listed on page 453 for referrals.) If you write in response to the workbook, please indicate whether quotes from your letter can be used in trainings or future books.

Laura Davis
P.O. Box 8503
Santa Cruz, CA 95061–8503

Designed by Laura Hough

Library of Congress Cataloging-in-Publication Data
Davis, Laura.
  The courage to heal workbook: for adult survivors of child sexual abuse/Laura Davis.
    p. cm.
  Includes bibliographical references.
  ISBN 0-06-096437-5 (pbk.)
  1. Adult child sexual abuse victims—Rehabilitation. 2. Adult child sexual abuse victims—Psychology. 3. Self-help techniques. 4. Adult child sexual abuse victims—Rehabilitation—United States. I. Title.
HQ71.D245   1990
616.85′83—dc20   89-45646

10 11 12 13   RRD H   60 59 58 57 56

To my father, Abe Davis, for always encouraging me to be myself

CONTENTS

ACKNOWLEDGMENTS

During the past few years, I have had the honor to work with survivors all over the United States. I've led workshops for survivors and partners, trained counselors, spoken at conferences, and given lectures. Everywhere I've gone, I have continued to learn from survivors, whose courage, spirit, and determination never cease to move me. They are the inspiration for this book.

I'd also like to thank the following:

The participants in the Courage to Heal workshops who first used these exercises. Their generous feedback and suggestions helped give them their final form.

The producers and volunteers who made the Courage to Heal workshops possible.

The male survivors who shared their pain and asked to be included.

Ellen Bass, Malcolm Burson, Natalie Devora, Susan Frankel, Thom Harrigan, Edith Kieffer, Sharon Koski, and Nancy Slocum, my readers, for their careful critique of the manuscript.

Janet Goldstein, my editor, for good judgment, clarity, enthusiasm, and support.

Charlotte Raymond and Denise Notzon, my agents, for paving the way.

Barbara Ohrstrom, for good humor, generosity, and technical support.

Gale Martin, Yvonne Fernandes, and Karen Barnes, for lightening my load.

My professional colleagues, for intellectual stimulation, good times, and encouragement: Lynn Bryant, Sandra Butler, Mercedes Cabral, Sahna Carmona, Clarissa Chandler, Lauren Crux, Elda Dawber, Joan Farrell, Susan Frankel, Natalie Goldberg, Thom Harrigan, Saraa Kamaria, Jaimee Karroll, Laurel King, Mike Lew, Debbie Lewis, Dan Lobovits, Robin Moulds, Padma Moyer, Starr Potts, Julie Robbins, Geneen Roth, Kathy Schulman, Ida Shaw, Maxine Stein, Gayle Stringer, Pnina Tobin, Sharon Vaughan, Judy Wilbur-Albertson, Robin Winn.

For daily sustenance and magic: Barbara Cymrot, Ruby Cymrot, Dafna Wu, Karen Zelin, Natalie Devora, Aurora Levins-Morales, Wendy Maryott-Wilhelms, Nancy Katz, Janet Gellman, Jennifer Meyer, Claire Moore, Deborah Stone, Margaret Hill, Susan Bryer, Keith Rand, Sue Elwell, Nona Olivia, Jane Scolieri, Michelle Cooper, Dotsy Berman, Jim Prall, Jamie Shaw, Kath Hartley, Sandra Haggard, Sue Estler, Paula Johnson, Leilani Miller, Maig Kennedy, and Susan Amicarelli.

My brother, Paul Davis, for opening the door.

My secret pals, Laurie White and Carol Plummer.

The members of the Wednesday night survivor's group, for inspiration and the freedom to be myself.

Ellen Bass, for being a pioneer, a colleague, and a friend.

DEDICATIONS

Since the publication of *The Courage to Heal,* I have signed thousands of books. Over and over again, I've witnessed how much it has meant to survivors to have me write a few reassuring words in the front of their book. But you don't need to wait for me to write an inspirational message on this page. You can do it yourself.

Use these pages the way you would a high school yearbook. Begin by writing a dedication to yourself. Say something that shows your faith in yourself: "I'm strong. I can do it." "I love me." "I'm determined to heal." Then go out and collect positive statements of encouragement from trusted people in your life. Ask your therapist, partner, fellow survivors, or close friends to write a few words of support. Let them remind you that it's possible to heal, that they love and believe in you, that they support your healing. If there's something in particular you want to be reminded of ("You're brave and courageous." "You can make it." "It wasn't your fault"), it's okay to ask someone to write it in your book.

You can gather dedications all at once or over a period of months or years. As your support system grows, so will your list of dedications.

SPECIAL PAGES

As you work through the exercises in this workbook, certain pages and exercises will stand out for you. A particular passage may move or inspire you; you may write something that you want to come back to over and over again. This page is a place for you to develop your own personal table of contents, so you can easily find parts of the workbook that have special meaning for you.

The sections listed below have been especially helpful to many survivors. Add any others that you want to find easily.

INTRODUCTION

Ellen Bass and I wrote *The Courage to Heal* to give hope and guidance to adults who had been sexually abused as children. When you're feeling lost, scared, and confused, you need to know that you're not the only person who has suffered. You need to be told that you're not weird or crazy, that the abuse wasn't your fault. You need to be reassured that a lot of your feelings and experiences are a direct result of being sexually abused. You need to know that healing is possible, that there is a way out, and that you're capable of finding that way. These are the basic messages we communicated in *The Courage to Heal*.

The Courage to Heal Workbook builds on many of the concepts, stories, and ideas found in *The Courage to Heal*. It is designed as a companion volume, although you can use it without having read the first book. Focusing on how-to exercises, this workbook will provide you with practical tools for overcoming the effects of child sexual abuse.

Written for individual survivors, this book can also be used by therapists with their clients. The majority of the exercises lend themselves to group participation and support, and are ideal for use in self-help or therapy groups. "The Five Building Blocks of Safety" on page 21 will help you figure out the best setting in which to use this book.

Whether you've been working with these issues for a long time or are just beginning, this workbook can be of value. If you're not sure you were sexually abused, or don't have clear memories, continue reading. Your specific needs and concerns will be addressed.

I've been told repeatedly that *The Courage to Heal* has been helpful to people who weren't sexually abused. Survivors of other kinds of abuse have said, "You know, this book has really helped me come to terms with the emotional abuse I experienced as a child." Or "This book has really helped me deal with the fact that my dad was an alcoholic." Or "My mother just died and I found parts of the book very comforting."

Healing from many childhood (or even contemporary) wounds follows a course similar to the one outlined in *The Courage to Heal* and in this workbook. Although this book is written with survivors of child sexual abuse in mind, I invite others to use it as a healing tool.

The Courage to Heal Workbook is written for women and men. This is a shift from *The Courage to Heal,* which was written for women. When Ellen Bass and I began that book in 1984, our expertise and knowledge was based on our work with women survivors. We were aware that there were a lot of men who'd been sexually abused, but we chose to keep our book focused on women since we knew their experiences best.

In the past several years, as I've had the opportunity to talk to many male survivors, I've come to learn that most of the issues faced by male and female survivors are the same. There are some significant differences, but the common ground is much greater.

At a lecture Ellen and I gave in Boston, a man stood up during the question-and-answer period and said, "You know, I really wanted to buy your book, but I felt I wasn't allowed because it said 'For women survivors of child sexual abuse.' But I really needed it, so I bought it anyway. And everything in it rang bells. And then tonight I wanted to come to this lecture, but I didn't know if I should, because it was 'for women survivors of child sexual abuse.' I came anyway, and I'm glad I did. But I want you to know it was very hard to come here. It's lonely out here. You think there aren't many resources for women—well, for men it's almost impossible."

Across the room a hand shot up. Mike Lew, author of *Victims No Longer: Men Recovering from Incest and Other Sexual Child Abuse,* stood up, holding a copy of *The Courage to Heal* in the air. He addressed the man who had just spoken. "You know what I tell men when they ask if they should read this book?" A pregnant pause. "Just change the pronouns. Women have been doing it for years."

The audience roared, but a point was clearly made. Male survivors were looking for answers, and here was information that could help them. That brave survivor, and the many men I've talked to since, have broadened my perspective. While I completely respect the need for women to heal in an environment without men (and vice versa), there are times when we can share the same resources. I decided I wanted the workbook to address all survivors.

The inclusion of men in this book will be difficult for some of you. Several women who read through early drafts of the workbook felt resentful, wishing that it was directed to them alone. So many women have been hurt and abused by men that this attitude is entirely understandable. Nonetheless, many men have been victimized and are hurting, and they need this book too.

On a broader level, women alone cannot eliminate child sexual abuse. To stop the continued devastation of children's lives, both men and women have to heal and take action in the world. The combined determination of all survivors to fight back is essential to ending this epidemic.

ABOUT LANGUAGE

I'd like to point out some specific words and phrases used repeatedly in this workbook. As you've probably already noticed, the word "survivor" refers to adults who were sexually abused as children. This is a conscious choice. Much of the early literature on abuse referred extensively to the "victims" of abuse. In *The Courage to Heal* we decided to use the word "survivor" because it gives more of a sense of strength and empowerment. "Victims" are the abused children who are murdered, who commit suicide, who end up in the back wards of hospitals. If you've made it to adulthood and are reading this book, you've already survived the worst. You're not a victim anymore; you're a survivor.

Another phrase we introduced in *The Courage to Heal* was the "healing process." We told survivors that they could heal from the long-term effects of sexual abuse, and provided a map of the journey. Although there is no easy formula, there are certain recognizable stages survivors go through as they face the impact abuse has had on their lives. These stages do not take place in a particular order, but there are universal themes that emerge: deciding to heal, remembering the abuse, believing it happened, knowing it wasn't your fault, getting in touch with anger and grief, talking about the abuse, and finally, moving on. As you heal, you experience these stages repeatedly, each time with a different perspective and a greater sense of resolution. We called this the "healing process" or the "spiral of healing."

Another term we used in *The Courage to Heal* was "partner." A partner is anyone you've made an intimate commitment to—a husband, a wife, a lover, a girlfriend, a boyfriend. We chose the word "partner" because it gave equal status to heterosexual and gay/lesbian relationships, to couples who were or weren't married. "Partner" has other connotations as well. As one woman in a workshop said, " 'Partner' gives you the feeling of two people who are working together in a cooperative relationship. A husband is someone I take for granted, someone who has power over me."

There are also certain words you *won't* see in this book. You won't find the words "dark" or "black" used to refer to the deep recesses of pain that survivors often experience. Many of us are used to describing painful feelings with these words: "I was in a black pit of despair." "There was a dark shadow over me." Although these terms have symbolic significance, they also reflect the racism of our society.

Another word you won't see is "crippled." Many survivors have talked about being crippled by abuse. Although abuse may have severely limited your options, "crippled" describes a specific physical disability, and unless I'm describing a survivor who was physically injured by abuse, I will use other language to talk about the ways abuse hurts us.

WHERE AM I RIGHT NOW?

Everyone picking up this workbook will be in a different stage in their healing. Although there is no set beginning, middle, or end to the healing process, there are points when you're closer to the beginning (when you start to wonder if you were abused, when you first recognize the effects of abuse on your life, when you're unable to think about anything else) and other points that are much further along (when you've resolved the fact that the abuse took place, when your emotions start to level out, when you start to focus more on issues in the present).

As you begin this workbook, it's good to get an idea of where you are in the healing process. Check off the statements that apply to you:

——— I have just started having memories of being sexually abused.

——— I don't remember anything specific, but I think I might have been abused.

——— I don't have specific memories or pictures, but I know something happened to me.

——— I know I was abused, but I don't know who did it.

——— I'm not sure my experience counts as sexual abuse. I wonder if this book is meant for me.

——— I've always remembered the abuse. I'm just beginning to think it affected me.

_____ I want to deal with these issues, but I don't know where to begin.

_____ I'm feeling really desperate and hopeless. I don't think a self-help book can really help me, but I'm picking this up as a last resort.

_____ The abuse happened a long time ago and I don't think it has much to do with my life today. I don't think I need this book.

_____ I've been working on these issues for a long time. I'm looking for an affirmation of how far I've come.

_____ I feel that I've dealt with most of the core issues surrounding the abuse. I just need some help around specific issues.

_____ I want to use this book as a way to chart the ups and downs of my healing process.

_____ Someone just handed me this book as a gift and thought I'd be interested.

_____ I don't think this book has anything to do with me. I just wanted to check it out for a friend.

_____ My therapist / partner / friend suggested I get this book.

_____ I've just joined a group and this is the book we're going to use.

_____ I'm a counselor and I'm thinking of using this book with clients who've been sexually abused.

_____ I want to start a self-help group with other survivors, and we want to use this book as a guide.

_____ My daughter / son / brother / sister / friend was sexually abused and I want to understand what he / she is going through.

_____ I'm the partner of a survivor. I thought this book might help my partner get over it.

_____ Buying this book terrifies me. I don't want anyone to know I have it.

If you were able to check off at least one item on the list, this workbook will have something to offer you. If you're just beginning to look at these issues, most of the material will be new to you. If you've been healing for a while, the book will deepen your understanding and affirm the healing you've already done.

Since *The Courage to Heal* was published, Ellen Bass and I have had the chance to talk with hundreds of survivors about their experiences reading the book. We fully expected *The Courage to Heal* to have an impact, but we underestimated the personal attachment survivors would form to the book itself. Some have carried it around with them, calling it their Bible. Others have slept with it at night, saying it made them feel safe in their beds. One woman made a cover for it out of one of her son's watercolors. Another came up to have her second copy signed—she'd torn the first one to shreds in a moment of frustration and despair.

These stories surprised and moved me, and sometimes they made me laugh. One woman called with the following story: "My partner and I were always fighting about sex. I kept telling him he had to read the chapter for partners, but every time he wanted to read it, I'd pull the book away from him and say, 'It's *my* book. You can't have it. I want to read it.' We tried to get him a copy of his own, but the bookstore was out. One day, when we were having yet another fight about sex, I picked up the book and tore out the whole chapter on partners and handed it to him. And you know what? Your book's made pretty well—the binding hasn't fallen apart yet."

Others have described how they found the book in the first place. My favorite story came in a letter from Peggy: "This past weekend I devoted to catching up on stuff left undone. I had weeding to do, bills to pay, furniture to move. When I got up Saturday morning, a still small voice said, 'Don't forget to go to the library because they will be closed Sunday and Monday.' As I was weeding, the voice spoke again. I was enjoying the weeding so much I didn't pay much attention. A half hour later I heard the same voice insist that I go to the library—so much so that I cut short a conversation with my niece, hopped in the car, and drove to the library.

"I have a regular routine at the library, [and I picked out a few things.] I started to check out the books when that same voice said, 'You aren't finished. Go back.' I listened even though I wanted to finish weeding before the rain set in. I turned the corner and saw *The Courage to Heal*. I knew what the book was about, just looking at the title on its spine. So I opened it at random to page 86, "Believing It Happened." I felt tears sting in my eyes. Here was a book that would tell me I wasn't crazy. . . .

"The rational part of me that manages computers and people is saying to me, 'You are crazy, writing to people you don't know about "little voices" telling you to go the library.' But the real part of myself that wants to heal is laughing at both the absurdity and the wisdom of such an act of faith."

Wherever I go, survivors tell me how deeply the book has affected them. They've talked of anger, terror, inspiration, and hope. Some have felt overwhelmed. Many survivors have read it very slowly, a section or two at a time, resting for several weeks between. Therapists have photo-copied a few paragraphs or pages to give to their clients in small doses. Many survivors have told me they haven't been ready to read it at all, but they keep it on their bedside table so they can read the title over and over.

Like *The Courage to Heal,* this workbook will evoke powerful feelings. Feelings are experienced in our bodies, so as you work through these exercises, you many experience unfamiliar feelings, body sensations, flashes of memory, or even sexual arousal. If you start to feel things you haven't felt before, or if you start to feel overwhelmed, know that you are not crazy. You are feeling. You are remembering. You are receiving images from the past. (See "Remembering" on page 204 for more infor-mation on the recovery of feelings and memories.)

If you feel overwhelmed, stop. Go to the support list on page 37 (fill it out right now). Make some calls. Get support. Don't go through it alone. You already did that once. You don't have to do it again.

Take your time, go slowly, reach out for the support you need. Feel free to skip exercises you don't feel ready for. The first section of the workbook, "Survival Skills for Healing," focuses on ways to take care of yourself. Start with those pages. They will provide a touchstone for you as you move through the rest of the book.

ABOUT THE EXERCISES IN THIS BOOK

As you begin the workbook, you'll find that most of the chapters contain both cognitive and creative exercises. Cognitive exercises ask you to think, brainstorm ideas, complete sentences, answer questions, set goals, and make assessments. The creative ones use writing and art to explore your inner thoughts and feelings. "Things to Think About" offers questions to help you absorb and expand on the key concepts of each section, to be answered alone or used as the basis for group discussion. And many of the chapters include "Activities" that give you the opportunity to do things: make collages, design rituals, work with a partner. Finally, each chapter closes with a summary section called "Reflections," which includes a set of questions to help you assess your feelings, goals, and needs as you complete the chapter.

Feel free to pick and choose among the exercises. Although each chapter follows a certain progression, there may be times when a particular exercise doesn't fit your needs. Maybe it calls for a lot of thinking, and you're having too many feelings to think clearly. Skip that exercise and come back to it later. Try a creative exercise or activity that's more geared to the expression of feelings.

As you move through the workbook, there may be moments when you feel inadequate, confused, or unable to proceed. There may be ideas that are new to you or that aren't explained adequately. That means there's a flaw in the design of the book, not in you. At other times you may find that your particular set of circumstances or feelings aren't being named or acknowledged. That's not because you don't belong; it's because of an oversight on my part.

Many of the exercises ask you to fill in blanks or answer questions, and they often begin with examples. These are intended to stimulate your own thinking and to demonstrate the way the exercise works. If the particular example given speaks to your experience, feel free to copy it down and include it as one of your answers.

On the other hand, if the specifics of a particular exercise don't pertain to you, change them. If the sample question asks about your mother but you were raised by your grandmother, substitute your grandmother's name. If you were battered but not sexually abused, adapt the material to fit your experience.

In workshop settings, survivors often want to know if they're doing the exercises the "right" way. *There is no right or wrong way to do these exercises.* They are for you. Feel free to alter them to fit your needs.

WRITING AS A HEALING TOOL

I've always used writing as a way to express myself and get in touch with my feelings, so it was natural for me to turn to writing when I began to recover memories of having been sexually abused. I wrote to quell the feelings, to deal with the panic, to express my feelings, to find answers. Writing opened up realms of information I couldn't reach with my conscious mind. It was a way to talk about what had happened to me. There was something about putting the words on paper that made me really believe they were true. In the early stages of healing, when I despaired that I wasn't getting anywhere, that all this therapy and introspection and work on myself was a cruel joke, writing was a way for me to chart my course, to mark my progress. I could go back and read my journals and see that things really had changed. And I could make commitments through my writing: "I will not give in. I will say no to sex I don't want. I won't let myself be abused anymore." Writing was a tremendous relief, and at many points my lifeline.

When Ellen Bass and I agreed to collaborate on *The Courage to Heal*, it was a perfect fit. Ellen had pioneered the use of writing in her I Never Told Anyone workshops with survivors, and had developed a series of writing exercises that were unique and powerful. She wanted to share those exercises, and they became an integral part of *The Courage to Heal*.

The *Workbook* builds on many of the writing suggestions originally made in *The Courage to Heal*. Many of the exercises use the same technique introduced in the first book—freewriting, or stream-of-consciousness writing. Freewriting helps you to get in touch with buried feelings and memories. It helps you to get past your censors.

ABOUT FREEWRITING

Try to forget everything you've ever been told about writing. Forget all the English teachers you ever had. Forget about trying to do it right. This is a new and different kind of writing.

The key to stream-of-consciousness writing is to write without stopping during the time allotted for the exercise. You put the pen down on the paper and you begin to write. Don't edit what you're saying. Don't go back and reread it. Don't censor yourself. This is not about punctuation, spelling, complete sentences, or grammar. Your words don't have to make sense to anyone else. This writing is for you.

Don't erase or cross things out or change your words. Sometimes you'll unconsciously substitute one word for another. It may not make any sense at the time, but when you go back and read over what you've written, the real meaning of the sentence suddenly pops out at you.

If you run out of things to say, just repeat the last sentence you wrote. Or write whatever thoughts are floating around in your head: "Why am I doing this stupid exercise?" "Why did I buy this workbook anyway?" "I must remember to pick up toilet paper." Whatever it is. Just repeat it until something new surfaces, taking you to a deeper level of writing.

You can do this kind of writing in any language you choose. Your native language is the one where most of your early emotional memories are stored, so if English isn't your first language, try writing in the language you spoke as a child. If your writing brings up feelings or memories from the time when you were very young, you might find your sentences getting simpler, your words getting larger (in size), your handwriting changing, and your vocabulary shrinking. Or sometimes, if your memories or feelings are preverbal, you might find yourself at a loss for words. If that happens, try drawing instead.

Continue writing (or drawing) until the timer goes off. (If you're writing in a group, someone can keep track of the time and give a five-minute warning to "Finish up.") Once the allotted time is over, stop. Stopping is important to feeling safe. It's easier to let go into the writing if you know it isn't going to last forever. If you're not finished, you'll be able to come back and write more another time.

This kind of writing can bring up strong emotions, and it's important that you build in some protection. Set a timer each time you sit down to write. That way you have a specific time frame, with a set beginning and end. (Other suggestions for creating safety can be found in "The Five Building Blocks of Safety" on page 21.)

You can also experiment with the way you write. You might want to try writing with your opposite hand. The childlike writing that results can help put you in touch with childhood feelings. I remember watching one woman do this in a workshop. After a few moments of furious scribbling, she shifted her position, grasping the pen in her fist with the point down, much as a young child would do.

Although there's ample room for writing in the workbook, you may prefer using crayons or markers on big sheets of newsprint or some double lined paper (like the kind you learned to write on). If it's too hard for you to write by hand, you can use a typewriter, a computer, or a tape recorder.

SHARING YOUR WORDS

In *The Courage to Heal* we emphasized the power of sharing your writing out loud. Frequently survivors write without any visible expression of emotion, but as soon as you read what you've written, feelings surface. You begin to absorb the things you've allowed yourself to say. It can be terrifying to share your words and deepest feelings with someone else. But it can be incredibly empowering to allow a supportive and caring person to witness your self-expression and growth. Such sharing often leads to real intimacy and affirmation.

Try to take the risk. Find someone who will respect the work you're doing (your counselor, another survivor, a trusted friend), and read some of your writings to that person. The pain you are feeling will be much less of a burden if you tell someone else. (For guidelines on how to share your experiences, see "Breaking Silence" on page 234.)

If you're not ready to talk to someone else, or if you don't yet have anyone you can share your writing with, try reading what you've written into a tape recorder and then listening to your own words. Or read to yourself out loud, perhaps while looking in the mirror. This will provide you with at least one compassionate listener—yourself.

ART AS A HEALING TOOL

If you have a block about writing or are more artistically inclined, try the collage exercises suggested throughout the book. Or try painting or drawing in response to the writing suggestions. This can be equally effective in uncovering feelings and memories. So are other creative media —music, dance, sculpture. A whole group of survivor artists are exploring their creativity and producing plays, choreographing dances, putting on art shows. Don't limit your creative expression to the exercises in this book. All creativity is healing.

ABOUT MAKING COLLAGES

You'll need a variety of magazines, a large sheet of paper, some glue, and a pair of scissors. Sit at a table. Make sure you won't be interrupted for at least half an hour (or longer if you want; you can work on your collage all in one sitting or over a period of days). Clear your mind as much as possible. Think about the subject of the collage as you leaf through the magazines. (Colorful magazines with full-page ads are the best.) Cut words, phrases, or pictures out of the magazines. Don't try to figure out why you're selecting particular things. Don't worry about what it means or whether your choices make sense. Suspend your judgment. This exercise is not about logic. It's about letting your unconscious make choices. Keep cutting things out until you feel finished. Then arrange the things you've cut out on a large piece of paper. Glue them down in whatever pattern feels right. (You can also include childhood photos or mementos as part of your collage.)

When you're finished, you can ask yourself the following questions:

- How did it feel to make this collage?

- Was I able to let go when I cut things out of the magazine? Were there things I wanted to cut out but didn't? What were they?

- What feelings are expressed in the picture? How do I feel when I look at it?

- Does my picture make sense? What connections do I see? What don't I understand?

- Is it complete? What's missing?

- What would I change, leave, or add?

- What can I learn from my picture?

When I first recovered my memories of having been sexually abused, I had one burning question: "How long? How long am I going to feel this bad? How long will I be suffering? Give me the date! When will I be fixed?"

In the beginning I held on to the erroneous idea that if I healed with more intensity, I'd get done faster. If I saw my therapist in the morning, went to a survivors conference in the afternoon, and stayed up at night reading about the long-term effects of sexual abuse, then surely I'd cross the finish line ahead of schedule. This attitude is a common one. We live in a culture that savors the fast fix. Feel pain and live with pain? Healing over time? These concepts are foreign in our "feel good" society.

Over the years, I've come to realize that healing is, in fact, a process that takes a lifetime. As survivors, we need to settle in for the long haul. It's a process that continues for the rest of our lives. Healing is not about quick pain relief. It's about the little steps. It's about learning to take care of ourselves. It encompasses both progress and backsliding. Healing is slow. It's gradual. It does not proceed in a straight line.

If you're at the beginning of the healing process and your life is filled with painful emotions, memories, and crises, the idea of healing over time may seem irrelevant. You feel terrible now, and you want to feel better. You feel desperate and you want answers. You want the pain to go away.

Unfortunately, there are no easy answers. You can't zip through this workbook and breathe a sigh of relief—"Great. Now I've dealt with that. That's over with." Healing takes time. Recovering from the effects of child sexual abuse is a painful, disorienting, and frequently confusing process, and you need inspiration, a framework that explains what the healing journey will be like, and a set of practical survival skills for healing.

In this section you will develop those skills. You will assess where you are now in the healing process, look at your support system, and develop strategies for dealing with crisis periods. You'll come up with ways to mark your progress and learn about the concepts of safety, celebration, and self-nurturing.

I strongly suggest that you work through the next five chapters before moving on to the rest of the book. Although you may want to jump to the section on memories or go to the sex chapter right away, working through the "Survival Skills" exercises will lay the groundwork for proceeding through the rest of the workbook. Strong feelings—grief, anger, fear, pain—will naturally arise as you work through this book. If you fill out these pages first, you'll have effective tools and strategies for dealing with these feelings.

CREATING SAFETY

Safety is the experience of being protected from danger and hurt. Within a safe environment, we can relax and be ourselves because we know that our well-being is secure. We feel free to take manageable risks toward growth and change. When you begin to talk honestly about your life in a safe environment, healing naturally begins to happen.

Safety is the basic right of every child, yet many of us were deprived of this right. Parents and trusted adults are supposed to protect their children from harm, yet when we were abused, these trusted adults, in many cases, *were* the harm.

Feeling safe is at the core of the healing process. You can experience moments of safety with a trusted therapist, a close friend or partner, or through sharing with another survivor. If you haven't had the benefit of safety in these circumstances yet, you can begin to explore the possibility of feeling safe with yourself.

Thinking about safety when you've known only danger, hurt, and betrayal can be terrifying. The very concept of safety may contradict all the experiences you've had thus far in life. Approach the next few pages with skepticism, if need be. Allow yourself to doubt. But try the exercises anyway. They may open up new possibilities.

The following questions can provide a starting point:

Have you ever felt safe?   _____ yes   _____ no   _____ I'm not sure

If yes, describe one time you felt safe: _____

_____

_____

_____

_____

What about that experience made you feel safe? _____

_____

_____

_____

_____

If you haven't experienced feeling safe, describe some of the experiences or beliefs that have kept you from feeling safe: *(People hurt me / I can't depend on anyone / I didn't know you could feel safe)*

_____

_____

_____

_____

_____

For me to feel safe, I would need _____

_____

_____

_____

_____

When I consider the possibility of feeling safe in the world, I _____

_____

_____

_____

_____

Things to Think About:

- Can I conceive of feeling safe? Why or why not?

- Do I deserve to feel safe? Why or why not?

THE FIVE BUILDING BLOCKS OF SAFETY

In the next few pages you will have the opportunity to create a sense of safety for yourself in a very practical way, by developing strategies for using this workbook. You'll have a chance to explore five distinct aspects of safety—creating ground rules, building a container, finding a safe spot, maintaining privacy, and establishing protective rituals. Taken as a whole, they should increase your feelings of safety in approaching the exercises in this book.

CREATE GROUND RULES

In survivor workshops I spend the first half hour going over ground rules. Ground rules are rules that everyone agrees to follow in order to make the workshop safe. I ask everyone to keep material from the workshop confidential. I tell participants that I will never be sexual with them. I give survivors permission to get up and take a break any time they want to. I tell them they can call a support person if they get scared. I put tissues around the room so people know it's okay to cry. I make sure strangers don't come into the workshop area. I reassure everyone that they'll never be forced to participate.

In workshops ground rules set a tone and establish an environment of trust and respect. They provide limits and boundaries within which healing work can be done. (For more on setting limits, see "Learning to Trust Yourself" on page 274.) They help reduce people's anxiety. When I set a ground rule in a workshop, I am saying to the survivors there, "You don't have to be looking over your shoulder every minute. By agreeing to these rules, your basic needs for protection will be taken care of."

If you're doing the exercises in this book on your own, you can set ground rules to serve the same protective function. Begin by identifying the things you think may create difficulties for you in using this book.

The following list can help you isolate issues that may be hard or scary for you. Check off any of the sentences that apply to you. Feel free to add others:

_____ I'm afraid my partner will find this and want to know what's going on.

_____ I wait until I'm totally overwhelmed before I leave emotionally charged situations.

_____ I don't notice that I'm upset until I'm in total crisis.

_____ I usually push myself further than I'm ready to go.

_____ I'm afraid this book will bring up feelings I won't be able to handle.

_____ I'm afraid of being isolated and alone when strong feelings come up.

_____ I'm afraid of going fast and not absorbing anything.

_____ I'm afraid I'll quit the minute I get uncomfortable.

_____ When things get hard, I space out and go through the motions without feeling anything.

_____ I'm afraid I'll never do anything else once I start this book.

_____ I'm scared that other people will read this and think there's something wrong with me.

_____ I know I'll criticize myself for not doing it right.

_____ I'm afraid I'll show this book to people when I don't really want to.

_____ I'm afraid I'll do something self-destructive instead of reaching out.

_____ _____

_____ _____

_____ _____

_____ _____

_____ _____

Use the issues you identified as the basis for your ground rules. If you are afraid you won't be able to stop once you start, what limits can you place on the amount of time you spend doing the exercises? If you tend to push yourself too intensely, what agreements can you make with yourself to protect you from that tendency? How can you give yourself permission to approach this work gently?

Your ground rules can include things like: "If I get too scared, I'll stop." "I'll skip over any exercises I'm not ready for. I can skip whole sections if I want to." "I don't have to share what I write with anyone unless I want to." "I'll stop after doing one exercise."

Take a few minutes to come up with some beginning ground rules for using this workbook:

• _____

_____

• _____

_____

- _____

  _____

- _____

  _____

- _____

  _____

- _____

  _____

BUILD A CONTAINER

A second way to create safety is to create boundaries around the work itself. You can choose a specific time and schedule for working on this book, and you can establish a physical place where you complete the exercises. You build a container for the work.* A container is something that has nonpermeable boundaries. A jar is a container for milk because the milk can't leak out. An envelope is a container for a letter because you can seal it and protect the letter inside. Building a container gives you some control over when and where you focus on sexual abuse. It gives you the right to say "yes" to the work and to say "no" to the work. It gives you a choice.

Think about how frequently you'd like to work on these exercises. Once you sit down, how long do you want to spend? One hour a week? Half an hour every day? One morning at the beginning of every month? If you're afraid of racing through and trying to do everything too fast, you might want to slow yourself down. If you're afraid of avoiding the work, you might want to commit to regular times.

I'd plan to do these exercises _____

_____

———————————

* Thanks to Sandra Butler for this wonderful concept.

Once you come up with a time frame, stick with it for at least a few work sessions. Set a kitchen timer or an alarm clock so you'll know when your time is over. Then stop. Knowing that you won't have to write in this book forever gives you the freedom and safety to begin. If you decide you haven't allotted enough time (or too much), you can reassess and change your time frame in between workbook sessions.

A second consideration in building a container is deciding whether you want to do these exercises alone or with other people. Do you want to fill these pages out with other members of your support group when you meet together? Do you want to keep this book at your therapist's office and only do the exercises there? Do you want to sit in a room with another survivor and write in your workbooks at the same time? Or do you want to do these exercises alone?

I plan to do these exercises   *(alone / with a friend / with my partner / in my survivors group / with my therapist)*

_____

Which of the options listed above were available to me? _____

_____

_____

Was the choice I made my first choice?   _____ yes   _____ no

Was the choice I made the most healing choice, or did it reflect an old pattern?

_____

_____

If I could work in this workbook in any setting, which would I choose? _____

_____

_____

If my first choice wasn't available, is there anything I could do to make it available? If so, what?

_____

_____

_____

     If you work on this book with your therapist or during your support group meeting, you will automatically have clear parameters around the times you do the work. You know that you won't be interrupted, that you can focus all of your attention on the task at hand, that you'll have a definite ending point. This won't happen as easily in your own home, where you're more likely to be interrupted or distracted. You will need to find ways to create limits at home as well.

     Set aside a prescribed amount of time every week when you say no to the other demands in your life. Unplug the phone. Insist that your kids and your partner don't intrude. You might want to go someplace special where you can't be reached for a couple of hours.

When I work in this workbook, I will make sure   *(I'm not interrupted / I'm not going to have to stop suddenly / that I'm still awake and alert)*

_____

_____

_____

_____

I will make sure I don't get interrupted by   *(the phone / my kids / my partner)*

_____

_____

_____

by   *(getting a babysitter / putting a "Do Not Disturb" sign on the door / unplugging the phone)*

_____

_____

_____

Setting these limits scares me because _____

_____

_____

_____

Setting these limits excites me because _____

_____

_____

_____

FIND A SAFE SPOT

Choosing a special place to work can decrease your chances of being interrupted and boost your feelings of safety. Think about the places where you feel particularly relaxed, the most calm, the least vulnerable to attack. It may be in a special corner of your house. It might be in a particular chair. It might be sitting on your back steps. You could do these exercises in your bed with a special teddy bear beside you, next to a special window, locked safely (and privately) in the bathroom, sitting in the backseat of the parked car, out in nature, or in the anonymity of a study room at the public library. The important thing is that you seek out a spot where you can be the most at ease, the most centered on yourself and the task in front of you.

The places I feel safest are: _____

_____

_____

What makes these places safe is: _____

_____

_____

The places I feel the least safe are: _____

_____

_____

What makes these places unsafe is: _____

_____

_____

The times of day I feel the safest are: _____

_____

_____

The times of day I feel the least safe are: _____

_____

_____

ESTABLISH YOUR PRIVACY

Many survivors grew up in abusive families where they had no privacy. When you were a child or adolescent, your journals may have been read. Your parents may have searched through your belongings. Even your thoughts may not have been private. Yet keeping certain things to yourself is part of establishing boundaries. That goes for this workbook as well. You get to decide why, when, and how you share the things you write.

If you're hesitating to write in this book because you don't want anyone to read what you've written, you can take steps to ensure your privacy. Consider storing the workbook in a locked file cabinet or a safe deposit box. Make a cover for it so you can take it out without everyone on the bus knowing what you're reading. Keep it in your therapist's office and work on it when you're there. Tear out sections as you finish them and mail them to a trusted friend for safekeeping. Don't show the book to other people once you've started writing in it (unless of course you want to).

What are the limits you'd like to place on sharing your work in this book with others?

I want to share my writing in this book with _____

_____

_____

I don't want to share this book with _____

_____

_____

In order to preserve my privacy, I'm going to _____

_____

_____

One word of caution on the issue of privacy: You may want to keep things in this book private because you're not used to sharing personal things. You may not have established enough trust to share so intimately. The people around you may not understand what you went through as child, or they might not respect the time you're taking to heal. Or you may simply not be ready to share your writing. You might want to come back and review your work before you reveal your thoughts and feelings to anyone else. These are all fine reasons for choosing to keep this workbook private.

But sometimes the reasons we want to keep things private have more to do with shame and keeping secrets than with maintaining appropriate boundaries. For example, you might not want anyone to know that you're a survivor because you're afraid they'll find out what a bad person you really are. You're sure they'll judge you and discover something terrible about you. You don't want to share because you were threatened to keep the abuse a secret when you were growing up. (For more on telling and fears of telling, see "Breaking Silence" on page 234.) If you're reluctant to show anyone what you're writing because you feel ashamed or afraid, gradually try to find ways to share your words. Privacy that isolates you and leaves you alone with your pain doesn't protect you; it keeps you from finding the allies you need. (For more on the difference between privacy and keeping secrets, see "A Few Choice Words on Telling the Truth" on page 244.)

Men who were sexually abused may also find it hard to share because of cultural conditioning. Growing up you were taught to keep it all in, to "tough it out," to "not be a sissy." You may not want to identify yourself as a victim; it somehow lessens your status as a "real" man. These cultural pressures can silence you and keep you in an emotional straitjacket. Although you haven't been taught to share your pain and your feelings, healing requires it. In expressing your real experience, you make room for your own healing and for the healing of other men. Take the risk. Begin to share.

Take a moment to examine your motives for privacy. Then answer the following questions:

In terms of setting boundaries and keeping things private, my goal is _____

_____

_____

_____

My reason for wanting privacy at this time is _____

_____

_____

_____

This is   _____ okay   _____ not okay   with me.

ESTABLISH A PROTECTIVE RITUAL

Protective rituals can protect your special workbook time.* (For more on creating rituals, see page 307.) You might want to play special music, light a candle, surround yourself with safe objects (a stone, a flower, a stuffed animal, a special object given to you by someone you love), or even burn some incense. You might want to sit on a special pillow or wear a certain soft piece of clothing every time you work in this book. You might want to hang a child's picture on the wall. Your ritual can be complex or basic. It might be enough for you to make yourself a cup of tea before you begin. The important thing about creating a ritual for safety is that it has personal meaning that you can use over and over again.

Whenever I sit down to write in this book, I'm going to _____

_____

_____

_____

_____

_____

_____

* The idea of any kind of ritual can be extremely threatening for survivors who were abused in a ritualistic setting. If you feel uncomfortable with the idea of ritual, skip this section and read the footnote on page 307.

I will make the time special by _____

_____

_____

_____

_____

When I'm done, I'm going to _____

_____

_____

_____

_____

If you have a hard time keeping your safe place safe, you might need some help. Make a ritual for cleansing your safe spot. Ask another survivor to help you clean out the area, to banish unwelcome influences. One survivor kept feeling that her abuser was invading her safe space. She created a totem—a scarecrow of the spirit, so to speak—which she placed in her doorway for protection.

Things to Think About:

- How do I feel when I think about setting boundaries?

- What's the difference between privacy and secrets? Between privacy and shame?

- What would it take for me to create a safe environment for working in this book? Am I closer to creating that place now than when I began? Why or why not?

REFLECTIONS: CREATING SAFETY

Safety is something many of us have never experienced. In these last few pages, you've been introduced to the idea of creating safety for yourself. You've had the opportunity to lay the groundwork for proceeding through this workbook safely. This doesn't mean that you won't have strong feelings or that you won't have moments of terror or pain, only that you will have developed some strategies for dealing with those feelings.

Here are some questions to help you assess your present feelings, goals, and needs around the issue of safety:

• What feelings did I have as I worked through this chapter?

• What am I feeling right now? What sensations am I experiencing in my body?

• How old did I feel as I worked through the chapter? How old do I feel right now?*

---

* Working on abuse-related issues can bring up strong feelings and memories from childhood. You may also experience a regression, where you go back and reexperience your life at a particular age. Regressions can be healing if you have support in coming back into your adult self. Paying attention to how old you feel can give you valuable information about your childhood experience and can let you know when you need help reestablishing yourself as an adult.

- What was hard for me in this chapter? What was confusing? What didn't I understand?

- What did I learn? What commitments have I made? What steps have I taken?

- What did I do that I'm proud of?

- What's still unsettled for me? What, if anything, do I want to come back to or follow up on?

- What do I need to do to take care of myself right now?

BUILDING YOUR
SUPPORT SYSTEM

Many survivors are severely isolated. As a child you may have been prevented from making friends outside the family, and as an adult you may still suffer from a lack of closeness with people. After a lifetime of betrayals and separation from others, it is hard to develop trusting relationships, but reaching out and asking for help is essential to healing. You already suffered the abuse alone. You don't have to heal in the same lonely isolation.

A support system is a network of people who help you make it through the scary and bewildering changes involved in healing. It's like having a cheering section, a coach, and a bat boy all rolled into one. A support system is literally that—people who provide support. They give you practical support (cooking a hot meal when you're unable to do it for yourself), intellectual support (giving you information about the nurturing and protection you should have received as a child, suggesting resources and books that might help you), emotional support (sitting with you while you cry, comforting you when you feel down, being a witness to your feelings), and spiritual support (inspiring you, giving you hope, encouraging you to see the beauty in things).

People in your support system believe you were abused and that the abuse hurt you. They believe in your capacity to heal yourself. They like and respect you, and see you as a good person who's having a rough time right now. By challenging your old ideas about yourself, support people inspire you to grow. When you're around them you should feel reassured, cared about, listened to.

People in your support system should not do any of the following: minimize your abuse, downplay your feelings, tell you to hurry up and get over it, call you names, harass you, blame you for the abuse, side with your abuser, or make you feel bad about yourself in any way. If you consistently feel depressed or full of negative thoughts after seeing a particular person, that person probably isn't giving you the support you need and deserve.

A therapist or counselor can be a very special part of your support system.* Therapists have specific training in helping people deal with emotional hurts. Many have expertise in healing from sexual abuse. In exchange for a fee (sometimes paid by insurance or waived because of financial need), therapists provide guidance, information, and consistent support. (See "Therapists and Therapy" on page 44.)

A support system is made up of individuals. If you're isolated now and can't conceive of having a whole network of support people, just try to imagine the possibility of one person believing in you and offering assistance. This may be difficult for you. The thought of even one caring person can be a big leap when you're all alone. If you don't have much support in your life today, filling out the next few exercises may be very painful for you. Seeing the blank spaces graphically in front of you can highlight your own isolation. Yet admitting that you need supportive people is the first step to filling that need.

The next few pages will give you practical tools for finding support. You will assess the quality of the relationships you currently have and look at possible ways to build a support system. You will explore the things in your life that either help or hinder your healing. The last part of the chapter deals with the issue of therapy—how you feel about it, what it can do for you, how to choose a therapist, or how to evaluate the therapy you're in.

---

* I've used the words *therapist* and *counselor* interchangeably to refer to professional helpers. Therapists and counselors range from psychiatrists (who are physicians first), to psychologists to marriage and family counselors to social workers and clergy. In many states, anyone can call himself or herself a counselor, so you may want to become familiar with the licensing requirements in your area. However, neither licensing nor academic degrees guarantee that a counselor or therapist has experience with the special needs of survivors, and you may find that social workers, pastoral counselors, or peer counselors work better with you. It's best to establish your own guidelines and standards for choosing a therapist, rather than relying solely on professional title or degree.

CREATING A SUPPORT SYSTEM

The first step in building a support system is assessing the relationships you have in your life today. Many children who grew up in abusive homes never learned to discriminate between people who hurt them and people who tried to support them (if there were any). The following exercise will help you weed out the people in your current life who aren't really allies.

Make a list of all the people you have regular interactions with. Include family members, friends, neighbors, acquaintances, co-workers, members of your religious community, people you've met through healing or recovery programs, sponsors (12-step), and counselors or other professionals. List everyone, whether you consider them supportive or not.

_____   _____

_____   _____

_____   _____

_____   _____

_____   _____

_____   _____

_____   _____

_____   _____

Put a **check mark** (✓) next to the names of people you consider to be supportive of you in general. (Does this person seem trustworthy to you? Could you ask this person to do you a favor? Could you talk over a problem with this person?) **Circle** the names of the people who know that you're a survivor and that you're working on these issues. Put a **star**

(★) next to those who directly support your healing. **Cross out** the names of people you consider unsupportive (anyone who discounts your feelings, minimizes your experience, regularly puts you down). Put a **question mark (?)** next to the names you're not sure about. Some people will have more than one mark next to their name.

Now go back and think about the people whose names are not crossed out. These are the people who support you in some way. What are the qualities that make them feel like supporters? Is it because your brother always reminds you that you're the best? Is it because your friend Barbara asks you to play Scrabble when you're really down? Is it because your neighbor invites you over for a good meal and a heart-to-heart talk just when you need it? Is it because your therapist always believes you, even when you can't believe yourself?

In the space below, copy down the names of the people you identified as supportive. Next to the name, write the quality or qualities you value in them the most   *(Jack—works out with me / Karen—listens / Natalie—holds me when I cry / Abe—loves me no matter what / Nona—sees the real person inside the problems / Dafna—makes me laugh).*

Name   **Quality**

_____   _____

_____   _____

_____   _____

_____   _____

_____   _____

_____   _____

_____   _____

_____   _____

When I look at the people (or the lack of people) in my support system, I feel

_____

_____

_____

I can see that _____

_____

_____

I wish _____

_____

_____

The following questions can help you think about ways to build your support system:

In order to build up my support system, I need to   (*join a support group / find a counselor / talk honestly to my partner about my experiences / break off my relationship with Tracy*)

_____

_____

_____

_____

_____

_____

This month, in order to build up my support system, I'm going to _____

_____

_____

This week I'm going to _____

_____

_____

Today I'm going to begin by _____

_____

_____

Once you've begun to build your support system, you will have to take an even bigger step: use it. This means actually asking for the help you need. (For more on identifying your needs and asking for help, see "Ask for Help" on page 78.)

Things to Think About:

- Were there any surprises in looking at the people in my life? What were they?

- Can I imagine someone supporting me? Why or why not?

- What's standing between me and a better support system?

HELPS AND HINDRANCES TO HEALING

People make up only a part of your support system. There are other things that reinforce your healing, or that stand in the way. Becoming aware of these assets and liabilities is an important part of building your support system.

A wide variety of things can either boost your resolve to heal or block your way. What hinders one person may be helpful to another. Key influences can be:

- Beliefs you hold about the world and about yourself

- Activities that make you feel good (or bad) about yourself

- Ways you talk to yourself

- Commitments and responsibilities

- Addictions

- Spiritual beliefs

- Inner strengths and personal attributes

In the space below, make a list of everything that helps or hinders your healing. Include things from your childhood as well as your adult life.

Things That Help

My belief in God

My love of music

My anger and determination

Learning to read

My intelligence

Working in the garden

I'm willing to work hard

My second-grade teacher, Mrs. Dennis

My daughter's innocence

The Courage to Heal

Feeling competent at work

Things That Hinder

I don't think I deserve it

My father undermines me

Feelings of family obligation

Trying to kill myself

Believing it was my fault

No money for therapy

Depression

Taking care of three kids

I still deny it sometimes

My boss's verbal abuse

Drinking too much

Things That Help

Things That Hinder

_____

_____

_____

_____

_____

_____

_____

_____

_____

_____

_____

_____

_____

_____

_____

_____

_____

_____

_____

_____

Things to Think About:

- Were there any surprises in this exercise?

- Which list was longer? What does that tell me?

- What can I do to boost the things on the helpful side? To minimize the hindrances?

One of the most important support people you can have while you're healing is a skilled counselor. A good counselor provides hope, insight, information, and consistent, loving support as you go through the healing process. By encouraging you to develop your capacity to heal yourself, effective counselors work themselves out of a job. Because they are not directly involved in your life, counselors have a unique point of view that can be a powerful catalyst for healing.

Many people are not oriented toward therapy or haven't the means or opportunity to see a therapist. That's why we wrote *The Courage to Heal,* and that's why I'm writing this book—to provide an affordable healing resource for survivors everywhere. Yet I still encourage you to consider (or reconsider) getting skilled professional help.

I can unequivocally say that I wouldn't have made it through the early stages of my own healing without my therapist. Her consistent clarity, caring, and belief in my ability to heal enabled me to keep going when I felt I just couldn't anymore. Although I eventually developed a wide variety of healing resources (other survivors, support groups, writing, reading books, drawing endlessly on my support system), my therapist was always at the core. Week after week, she heard my rage and panic and terror, witnessed my memories, and told me I would make it.

Yet before I had my incest memories, I looked down on people who went to therapy. When I was growing up, anyone who went to see a psychiatrist (the only kind of counselor I'd ever heard of) was "crazy" or, as we put it, "looney tunes." I basically held this belief—that therapy was for the weak—until desperation forced me to find a therapist myself.

There are many reasons survivors avoid therapy: not knowing how to find a therapist, not being able to pay for one, cultural, religious or personal beliefs, fear of the stigma involved, fear of facing the abuse, the lack of skilled practitioners in their area, or previous bad experiences with therapy.

Unfortunately, the latter is all too common. I've talked to many survivors who've taken the risk of going to a therapist only to have an extremely negative experience. After finally mustering the courage to broach the subject of sexual abuse, their experiences were ignored, minimized, or invalidated. Therapists have told their clients not to be angry, to forgive and forget, to consider the abusers' feelings. Worst of all, survivors have been sexually abused by their therapists. This breach of ethics is tragic and unforgivable.

If you've been sexually abused by a therapist, you have the right to be furious and to fight back (if you want to).* But try not to let it deter you from ever trying therapy again. There are wonderful, skilled counselors available, and you deserve to work with one who will empower you, not abuse you.

If you're considering (or reconsidering) therapy, complete the following:

I think therapists are _____

_____

_____

_____

People who go to therapists are _____

_____

_____

_____

If I went to therapy now, it would mean that I _____

_____

_____

_____

---

* Most counselors are responsible to a licensing board. Although professional standards of conduct vary, you can file a complaint with the appropriate licensing board if you've been sexually abused by your therapist. You may or may not receive a satisfactory response to your complaint, but speaking up for yourself can help you put a negative experience behind you. You can also contact a lawyer about the possibility of taking legal action.

I'm afraid of therapy because _____

_____

_____

_____

I'd never go to therapy because _____

_____

_____

_____

I want to go to therapy, but I can't because _____

_____

_____

_____

Bad experiences I've had in therapy so far: _____

_____

_____

_____

_____

_____

_____

Good experiences I've had in therapy so far: _____

_____

_____

_____

_____

_____

_____

_____

Right now, as far as therapy is concerned I think I want to: _____

_____

_____

My next step is _____

_____

_____

_____

FINDING A COUNSELOR

When you're looking for a counselor, it's helpful to take the attitude that you are a consumer making an informed choice about the person you're hiring to work with you. Even though you're seeking counseling to fill an emotional need, you are still paying for a service. Being a consumer gives you certain rights: the right to determine the qualities you want in your therapist, the right to choose a therapist who meets your needs, the right to be heard, believed, and treated with respect, the right to say no to any of the suggestions your therapist makes, the right to be satisfied by the services you're receiving, the right to freely discuss any problems that arise in therapy with your counselor, and the right to end a therapy relationship that isn't working for you.

Thinking in terms of rights may be hard for you when you think about seeing a therapist. Many of us are intimidated by helping professionals. It's easy to see them as the experts: We're the ones in pain; they're the ones with the answers. The fact is that you are the real authority on your life and on what you need. Although your relationship with your therapist may be tremendously significant to you, it is essential that you don't relinquish all of your power in the counseling relationship.* Remember that you are at the center of your life and your healing. A good counselor is one of the many resources you will use.

There are certain basic things that are necessary in a counselor. You should make sure your prospective counselor:

- Believes that you were abused

- Never minimizes your experience or the pain it's caused you

- Has information (or is willing to get information) about the healing process for adult survivors of child sexual abuse

- Is willing to hear and believe the worst experiences you have to talk about

- Keeps the focus on you, not on your abuser

- Doesn't push reconciliation or forgiveness

- Doesn't want to have a friendship with you outside of counseling

---

* The only exception to this is when you are endangering your own life (via suicide) or someone else's (via homicide). Then a counselor is required by law to take action to protect you or the other person. Therapists are also legally bound to report suspected child abuse. If you mention a child at risk for abuse, your therapist has a legal obligation to report your suspicions to Child Protective Services, whether you want it or not.

- Doesn't talk about his or her personal problems

- Doesn't want to have a sexual relationship with you, now or ever in the future

- Fully respects your feelings (grief, anger, rage, sadness, despair, joy)

- Doesn't force you to do anything you don't want to do

- Encourages you to build a support system outside of therapy

- Encourages your contact with other survivors of child sexual abuse

- Teaches you skills to take care of yourself

- Is willing to discuss problems that occur in the therapy relationship

There are other things you may want in a counselor. You may want to see a counselor who is available for extra sessions or emergency phone calls. You may want to choose a man or a woman, a counselor who shares your race, ethnic background, religion, or sexual preference, or who has experience with another key issue in your life (alcoholism or disability, for instance). You may want to see a therapist who is also a survivor. Money may be a major factor in your decision; you may need a counselor who has a sliding fee scale or who can see you for free at a clinic. Any of these (and other factors) can be important criteria in choosing your counselor. Try to remain flexible, however, because you may have to compromise if you can't find exactly what you want in your area.

These are the characteristics I'm looking for in a counselor: _____

_____

_____

_____

_____

_____

I'd be willing to compromise on _____

_____

_____

_____

but I won't compromise on _____

_____

_____

_____

Once you've come up with your list of wants, turn that list into questions: "How would you feel about my participation in a survivors group? Is there any circumstance in which you think sex between a therapist and a client is okay? How much work have you done with drug addiction and recovery? Could I schedule extra sessions or call you when I'm in crisis? How would you handle it if I came to you and said there was a problem in therapy?"

QUESTIONS FOR A POTENTIAL THERAPIST

- _____

_____

- _____

_____

- _____

_____

- _____

_____

- _____
  _____
- _____
  _____
- _____
  _____
- _____
  _____
- _____
  _____
- _____
  _____
- _____
  _____
- _____
  _____

Once you have your list of questions, begin looking for a therapist. This requires persistence and a little detective work. Ask friends, other survivors, or supportive family members for referrals. Ask people about their experiences in therapy. Ask for names. If you can't find names this way, call an agency that deals with child abuse, rape, or domestic violence. They will probably be able to provide referrals.

Call the therapists on your list. Many counselors will give you ten or fifteen minutes of free time on the phone. Tell them you'd like to ask them a few questions. Then ask your most important ones. Discuss fees. If you like the way the person sounds and the cost is within your range, make an initial appointment. An initial appointment does not mean you're making a commitment to an ongoing therapy relationship. You and the counselor are both checking each other out. If you're not satisfied with the first person (or even if you think you might be), try one or two others so you can compare your reactions and feelings.

At that first meeting, ask the prospective therapist your remaining questions. Observe the way you feel in the session. It's not necessary that you feel good, or even relieved. You may be more stirred up after your session than before it. Effective counseling often leaves us feeling upset, anxious, angry, or uncomfortable. But you should feel that you've been listened to, respected, understood, and cared about.

Use the space below to record the way you felt after each initial session:

1. Counselor's name: _____

   Phone number: _____

   Fee per session: _____ Insurance? _____

Did I feel respected and listened to?   _____ yes   _____ no   _____ I'm not sure

Why or why not? _____

_____

_____

_____

What did I like about the session? _____

_____

_____

_____

What didn't I like? _____

_____

_____

_____

How did I feel during and after the session (disappointed, hopeful, excited, scared)? Why?

_____

_____

_____

Could I imagine ever trusting this person? _____ yes _____ no _____ I'm not sure

Why or why not? _____

_____

_____

_____

What, if anything, do I still need to find out? _____

_____

_____

_____

Do I want to see this counselor again? _____ yes _____ no _____ I'm not sure

2. Counselor's name: _____

   Phone number: _____

   Fee per session: _____ Insurance? _____

Did I feel respected and listened to? ____ yes ____ no ____ I'm not sure

Why or why not? _____

_____

_____

_____

What did I like about the session? _____

_____

_____

_____

What didn't I like? _____

_____

_____

_____

How did I feel during and after the session (disappointed, hopeful, excited, scared)? Why?

_____

_____

_____

_____

Could I image ever trusting this person? ____ yes ____ no ____ I'm not sure

Why or why not? _____

_____

_____

_____

What, if anything, do I still need to find out? _____

_____

_____

_____

Do I want to see this counselor again? ____ yes ____ no ____ I'm not sure

3. Counselor's name: _____

   Phone number: _____

   Fee per session: _____ Insurance? _____

Did I feel respected and listened to? ____ yes ____ no ____ I'm not sure

Why or why not? _____

_____

_____

_____

What did I like about the session? _____

_____

_____

_____

What didn't I like? _____

_____

_____

_____

How did I feel during and after the session (disappointed, hopeful, excited, scared)? Why?

_____

_____

_____

Could I imagine ever trusting this person? _____ yes _____ no _____ I'm not sure

Why or why not? _____

_____

_____

_____

What, if anything, do I still need to find out? _____

_____

_____

_____

Do I want to see this counselor again? ____ yes ____ no ____ I'm not sure

Once you've interviewed several counselors, compare fees, location, availability, the way they answered your questions, the questions they asked you, and your gut feelings. Trust your instincts. Then make your decision and call for another appointment.

IF YOU'RE ALREADY IN THERAPY

If you're already seeing a counselor, you may want to periodically assess how the counseling is going. Since therapy stirs up so many painful feelings from the past, feeling good is not the best criterion for judging therapy. People often project feelings about their parents or other significant people onto their counselors (this is called transference and can be an important part of therapy), making it hard to sort out feelings in the present from old childhood feelings that are being stirred up. Instead of your changing emotions, pay attention to your gut feelings about the relationship you have with your therapist. That's a good basis for judgment.

The following assessment can help you examine your current therapy experience:

	Always	Usually	Sometimes	Never
Do I feel listened to?	_____	_____	_____	_____
Does my therapist believe what I say?	_____	_____	_____	_____
Do I get a clear feeling that my therapist likes me?	_____	_____	_____	_____
Do I think my therapist believes in my capacity to heal?	_____	_____	_____	_____
Does my therapist respect my ideas and point of view?	_____	_____	_____	_____
Do I trust my therapist?	_____	_____	_____	_____
Is my therapist respectful of my personal boundaries?	_____	_____	_____	_____
Does my therapist respond well when I'm in a crisis?	_____	_____	_____	_____
When there are problems in therapy, can we discuss them?	_____	_____	_____	_____
Does my therapist admit to making mistakes?	_____	_____	_____	_____
Does my therapist help me find my own answers?	_____	_____	_____	_____
Does my therapist encourage me to utilize other resources for healing?	_____	_____	_____	_____
Have I made any progress since I began therapy?	_____	_____	_____	_____

Things I like about my experience in therapy: _____

_____

_____

_____

_____

Things I wish were different: _____

_____

_____

_____

_____

I _____ have _____ have not   talked to my therapist about my abuse.

If not, why haven't I? _____

_____

_____

_____

_____

_____

Does my therapist know about the ways I hurt myself or put myself in danger?
(cutting myself / smoking marijuana everyday / bingeing on food and throwing up / getting drunk and driving / having unprotected sex with lots of different people / keeping a lethal dose of pills in my house)

_____ yes   _____ no   _____ somewhat   _____ I don't hurt myself

If not, what keeps me from talking about these things? _____

_____

_____

_____

_____

What secrets do I keep from my therapist?   *(I abused a child once when I was babysitting / I get sexually aroused by really sadistic fantasies / I steal things a lot / I had an orgasm when my mother abused me)*

_____

_____

_____

_____

_____

_____

_____

What would make it possible to tell my secrets? _____

_____

_____

_____

_____

Go back to your initial ranking list ("always, usually, sometimes, never"). Your answers should be mostly "always" and "usually." If you checked off "sometimes" and "never" a lot, there's a real problem with your therapy. If you checked off "sometimes" and "never" only a couple of times, talk to your counselor about those problem areas. Voice your concerns. If you don't feel satisfied or respected in that conversation, you may want to consider changing therapists.

If you haven't broached the subject of abuse with your therapist, think about doing so. Your counselor's job is to listen to you and help you work through your pain. That's possible only if you talk openly about your childhood and about what you're really experiencing today. If you're dependent on alcohol or drugs, or are doing things that threaten your safety or life, try to talk about them with your therapist. Until you begin dealing openly with these things, your progress in dealing with the abuse will be limited. And if there are other issues you haven't been able to talk to your therapist about, you should then feel safer about sharing those as time goes on.

Things to Think About:

- Where do my attitudes toward therapy come from?

- (For survivors currently in therapy.) Am I satisfied with my experience in therapy? Is there anything I want to change about it?

- (For survivors not in therapy.) Do I want to consider counseling? If so, what steps do I need to take?

REFLECTIONS: BUILDING YOUR SUPPORT SYSTEM

Developing a solid support system is a key to healing. Your support system is made up of individuals who believe in you and is bolstered by your own beliefs, strengths, and actions. If you're isolated and alone and have suffered many betrayals, it's hard to trust anyone. Begin by reaching out to one person. When you take the risk and ask for help, you will find people who support you and care about your healing.

A skilled therapist can give a special kind of support as you heal. Counselors can provide you with consistency, education, caring, and guidance. In choosing a therapist, it's important to pick someone who is both skilled and respectful of you as a person. If you're already in therapy, it's a good idea to periodically assess how your therapy relationship is going, and to make sure you're addressing the issues essential to your healing.

Here are some questions to help you assess your present feelings, goals, and needs around building your support system:

- What feelings did I have as I worked through this chapter?

- What am I feeling right now? What sensations am I experiencing in my body?

- How old did I feel as I worked through the chapter? How old do I feel right now?

- What was hard for me in this chapter? What was confusing? What didn't I understand?

- What did I learn? What commitments have I made? What steps have I taken?

- What did I do that I'm proud of?

- What's still unsettled for me? What, if anything, do I want to come back to or follow up on?

- What do I need to do to take care of myself right now?

DEALING WITH CRISIS

As someone healing from child sexual abuse, expect to feel overwhelmed some of the time. (And there may be periods when it is most of the time.) It's realistic to expect upheaval, both emotional and practical, in your life. This is not a question of if, it's a question of when. Healing stirs up old feelings of terror and powerlessness, rage and grief. It is natural that there will be times when these feelings are so strong that you will be thrown into crisis.

The first three exercises in this chapter (Phone List for Hard Times, Things I Can Do When I'm Overwhelmed, and Dealing with Suicidal Feelings) will provide you with practical coping strategies you can use in a crisis. If you fill them out, you'll have a plan to work with the next time you're feeling overwhelmed and out of control.

The second part of this chapter focuses on strategies for dealing with the emergency stage—the extended period of crisis that often marks the beginning of healing. These exercises will require more thinking and analyzing than the first three, but they will give you the opportunity to develop essential skills for dealing with long-term crisis.

WHEN I'M LOST AND SCARED

When you're feeling the worst is often the hardest time to reach out for help. When you're feeling bad, your self-esteem sinks and you say to yourself, "Who'd want to talk to me? Who'd want to help me?" Or the classic disclaimer: "It's not important. I don't want to bother anyone."

When you're in crisis, it's crucial that you reach out. (It's also important that you reach out when you're *not* in crisis, so you can develop relationships with people who can respond when you *are* in crisis.) Listing the names and numbers of the people in your support system, along with emergency phone numbers, will give you an easy reference place the next time you need to call someone. Sometimes just leaving a message for a friend or listening to a supportive voice on an answering machine can help you keep going.

Make an emergency phone list. Include names and phone numbers for your therapist, other survivors, friends, and supportive family members. Use the list of supporters you came up with on page 37 as a basis for your list. Stop now and call the operator to get phone numbers for a 24-hour crisis and suicide prevention line.

PHONE LIST FOR HARD TIMES

Name	Phone number

WHEN I START TO PANIC

Many survivors struggle with anxiety or panic attacks. Anxiety is what you experience when you're overwhelmed by your emotions, your memories, or when something in your environment reminds you of old feelings of terror or of being trapped. During an anxiety attack, you may actually be reliving what you experienced as a child. Or you may be trying like hell to push feelings and memories away.

When you're in a panic, you want to calm down but you can't, and when you can't, the panic starts to escalate. During a panic your vision can blur, your heart can start pounding, you may sweat or freeze. Frequently you feel totally out of control, certain you're going to have a heart attack or die.

If you learn to recognize the signals of impending panic, you can sometimes head off a full-blown attack. The next time you start to feel anxious, notice the things you do. Do you run around, desperate to accomplish as much as possible? Do you bury yourself in work? Wash your hands over and over again? Pick fights? Yell at strangers when you're driving? Clean compulsively? Binge on sugar? Forget to eat? Get violent? Understanding these warning signs gives you the opportunity to take care of yourself earlier.

When I'm feeling anxious, I usually _____

_____

_____

_____

Right before I have an anxiety attack, _____

_____

_____

_____

_____

Once you're in the midst of a full-blown anxiety attack, you need a plan for coping with the mounting terror. What small concrete things can you do? What won't you do? Don't hurt or kill yourself. Don't hurt anyone else. Don't do anything rash until the feelings subside. And when the panic attack is over, try to take the time to explore what caused it in the first place.

Doing the exercises in this book will bring up strong feelings. If you're not used to experiencing your feelings, and if you don't have effective support (and sometimes even if you do), you may feel overwhelmed and start to panic. Perhaps you're feeling that way right now. This page is a place to design your own personal plan for dealing with emotions that frighten you and make you feel out of control.

Make a list of things you can do to comfort yourself. What would help you calm down? If you've been working on these issues for a while, what has helped you calm down in the past? If you've never had any success in calming down, talk to other people. Ask them what they do to relax when they are extremely upset.

Include on your list simple things that satisfy as many senses as possible (I'll listen to classical music / I'll listen to a relaxation tape / I'll make a cup of warm chamomile tea / I'll put a cool washcloth on my forehead / I'll curl up in a warm, cozy blanket / I'll get my teddy bear / I'll take a hot bath / I'll ask a friend to hold me / I'll do something mundane I'm good at—like washing dishes). Include reaching out to others. Include breathing. Taking a few long, slow, deep breaths is one of the most effective ways to calm down when you're panicked.

Things to avoid on your list are alcohol, nonprescription drugs, and driving. They all are dangerous in combination with extreme stress. Drugs or alcohol might calm you temporarily, but they can also make the feelings worse. If you're taking prescription drugs for anxiety or depression, make sure you use them according to your doctor's instructions.*

---

* It's important that the doctor prescribing your medication is sensitive to the fact that you're working on abuse issues. If the doctor who prescribes medications for you is not your therapist, your doctor and your therapist should develop a working relationship so they can best serve your needs. (This does not apply to drugs prescribed for physical illnesses such as diabetes, heart disease, etc.)

THINGS I CAN DO WHEN I'M OVERWHELMED

The next time you start to feel overwhelmed, turn to this page and start by doing whatever you wrote at the top of the list. Work your way down, trying each item in turn. If you run out of things to do, start at the top again. Keep breathing. Call for help. Then breathe some more. The feelings will pass.

- _____
- _____
- _____
- _____
- _____
- _____
- _____
- _____
- _____
- _____
- _____
- _____
- _____
- _____
- _____

DEALING WITH SUICIDAL FEELINGS

Most survivors have suicidal feelings at some point in the healing process, usually in the emergency stage. If they didn't feel suicidal before they started to heal (many survivors have been suicidal their whole lives), the intensity of the healing process may cause them to contemplate suicide for the first time.

There's only one thing to say about suicide: Don't do it. Get support. Get help. Reach out. It's normal to have suicidal feelings as you deal with childhood feelings of terror and pain. When you experience the depths of your shame, it's likely that you will think about killing yourself. But having suicidal feelings is very different from acting on them. Acknowledge the feelings, *but don't kill yourself.* The abusers have stolen enough from us already. Don't let them have you.

Look back at the list you just made on the facing page. If you start to feel suicidal, this list can help you. It can also be beneficial to come up with a no-suicide contract with your therapist, your partner, or a friend. In a no-suicide contract, you agree not to kill yourself for a set period of time (a week, a night, until your next therapy session), and you agree to call your support person the next time you feel the urge to kill yourself. If you're feeling suicidal and you're thinking of going out for a drive on

MY SUICIDE PREVENTION PLAN

When I am feeling suicidal, I will _____

_____

_____

_____

_____

I will not _____

_____

_____

_____

_____

the freeway, if you want to cut or burn yourself or to take an overdose of drugs, if you're starting to feel that you can't trust yourself, you agree to call your therapist, group leader, partner, or other support person immediately, before you take any action that could jeopardize your life. A no-suicide contract can also include reasons why you should live. Write them out yourself. If you can't think of any, have your support people write down several reasons (You're not bad / You deserve to live / You did nothing wrong / I love you).

If you are concerned that you can't control your suicidal feelings, take the time now to create a plan for keeping yourself alive. Make sure there are people in your support system who know how desperate you're

I will call _____ at _____
             (name)   *(phone number)*

If I can't get through, I will call _____
                                      (name)

at _____ as my backup.
   (phone number)

The phone number for suicide prevention is _____

I deserve to live because (If you can't think of any reasons to write down, ask someone who cares about you to fill in these lines)

_____

_____

_____

_____

_____

feeling. If you're in a group, tell the members of your group that you're thinking about suicide. If you've already made preparations to kill yourself (bought a gun, gotten a lethal dose of pills), tell your therapist or someone else trained to work with suicide, so they can help you. If there's no one in your support system who has experience in dealing with suicide, call the operator and get the number for suicide prevention. Then call the number. The people who answer the phone there are trained to listen, to understand, and to help you find other ways of coping with extreme distress. A call to them can save your life.

If you're actively suicidal now, take the time to write out a plan for keeping yourself alive.

THE EMERGENCY STAGE

When you first remember the abuse or begin to delve into the feelings connected with it, you often experience a period of ongoing crisis. In *The Courage to Heal* we called this period of crisis the emergency stage. You're obsessed with sexual abuse and find it impossible to talk or think about anything else. Unfamiliar sensations and emotions bombard you, and you wonder if living is really worth it.

The emergency stage is a critical time for healing. Although it is often the most overwhelming part of the healing process, it can also be one of the most fruitful, although many survivors don't realize the strides they've made until much later: You are forced to reach out for help. You come to terms with the fact that you were abused. Memories are shaken loose. You make a commitment to see the healing process through.

The emergency stage is frightening and overpowering, but it does not last forever. With skilled support, it is possible to get through the healing crises of the emergency stage to a more stable place. In addition to the strategies you've just developed, you'll need additional tools for

If there are people on this list of supporters who don't yet know that you are a survivor of sexual abuse, you might consider telling them. If they already support you in other ways and you've been afraid to tell them, work on the exercises in "Breaking Silence" on page 234. When people have already demonstrated that they care about you, there's a good chance they'd be supportive of your healing as well. Enlisting the help and understanding of the people on this list is one good way to build your support system.

If they knew, I think the following people might be supportive:

_____   _____

_____   _____

_____   _____

_____   _____

I'm going to consider telling:

_____   _____

_____   _____

_____   _____

_____   _____

If you've been fairly isolated and are just starting to reach out, the last few pages may have been very difficult for you. You may not have had anyone to put on your list of supporters. Or you may have just had one or two names. Looking at the empty page forces you to acknowledge how far you have to go in building a real support system. If you're feeling isolated, start by taking one small step. Reach out to one person. Adding one name to a blank list can radically change your experience.

Complete the following sentences as honestly as you can:

coping with a crisis that lasts over a long period of time. The rest of this chapter will teach you to shift your expectations of yourself, reach out to others for help, and find inspiration and reassurance to help you keep going.

SIMPLIFY YOUR LIFE

When you enter the emergency stage, you lose the ability to maintain your life as you've known it. Your day-to-day life becomes filled with crises. You may find yourself emotionally and physically exhausted, consumed by nightmares and memories. Preoccupied with counseling and other healing activities, your attention is distracted from everyday concerns. As a result you may find yourself unable to work, meet family obligations, or function in any way.

If you're in the emergency stage, it's important to recognize that your life is temporarily changed. You are no longer as capable or competent as you were before all this started. Don't expect yourself to be able to handle things. Don't expect yourself to keep to your normal schedule, to have as much energy, or to be as productive. Don't expect to give much attention to your intimate relationships. When you're in the emergency stage, you're running on empty, and until you accept it, you will continue to fight yourself. You can't do the things you need to do to take care of yourself until you recognize the fact that you're in a crisis.

This can be particularly difficult for men who are traditionally expected to be strong, to be the rock, to provide for their families. For a man to fail as a breadwinner or to need time off from being the provider can be devastating to his self-esteem. Yet the expectation that men will always function, no matter what, is unfair and oppressive. If you are healing from child sexual abuse you need and deserve, if at all possible, to share or relinquish some of your responsibilities. You deserve the time and space to heal, no matter what your obligations.

Make a list of things you're responsible for in your life. Include everything you can think of, breaking each item down as much as possible. If you're a parent, list all of the things you're responsible for (making breakfast / getting the kids off to school / cutting Toby's hair and telling him bedtime stories / helping Ruby with her math homework). If you're in a relationship, list the things you need to do to keep the relationship going (talk to my partner / initiate communication). If you have to earn money, how much do you have to earn? What are your responsibilities at work?

THINGS I'M RESPONSIBLE FOR

Financial: _____

_____

_____

_____

_____

Work: _____

_____

_____

_____

_____

Home management: _____

_____

_____

_____

_____

Parenting: _____

_____

_____

_____

Intimate relationship / partner: _____

_____

_____

_____

_____

_____

Myself: _____

_____

_____

_____

_____

Family obligations: _____

_____

_____

_____

_____

Friends: _____

_____

_____

_____

_____

Community: _____

_____

_____

_____

_____

Many abused children have an overblown sense of responsibility, believing they have to do everything themselves or the world will cave in. Taking responsibility for everything is a way to gain a sense of control. Staying in control was an important way of coping when you were growing up, but it may be keeping you isolated today.

Look over your list of responsibilities and then complete the following statements:

If I don't honor all of my commitments, _____

_____

_____

If I don't do everything I'm supposed to, _____

_____

_____

_____

_____

_____

_____

My sense of responsibility ties into my experience as a child in the following ways:

_____

_____

_____

_____

Now go back to your list of responsibilities. Look them over carefully, and then answer the following questions: Which things are absolutely essential? Which can be put aside for a while? Is there anything you can let go of entirely? Rank the items on your list on a scale of 1 to 3. Put a 1 next to things that are absolutely necessary. Put a 2 next to things that you'd like to continue but which aren't essential. And put a 3 next to things that you can let go of more easily.

Things to Think About:

- Were most of the things on my list essential or nonessential? What does that tell me about my sense of responsibility? About my backup support system?

- What kind of judgments or criticism will I face if I stop doing the things marked 2 and 3 on my list? How would I judge myself?

ASK FOR HELP

In the last chapter you gained skills in creating a support system. Yet support systems are effective only when we use them. We must learn to ask for help when we need it and to accept help when it is offered. This is harder than it sounds. Those of us who grew up in abusive families frequently believe we have to do everything ourselves. Many of us (particularly girls) were expected to sacrifice ourselves and take care of everyone else. Others (mostly boys) were raised to be self-sufficient, to not need anyone's help. As a result, you may feel that you don't deserve assistance and support, or that you can't ask for help until you're in a dire emergency. Or you may be afraid to ask for help because it means giving up control, depending on someone else, admitting "weakness," or risking rejection.

Complete the following sentences:

When I consider asking for help, I feel _____

_____

_____

If I ask for help, I'm sure that _____

_____

_____

The only situations in which I would consider asking for help are: _____

_____

_____

One thing that may keep you from reaching out is the nature of the hurt you're experiencing. It is harder to ask for help for emotional injuries, particularly ones that stem from old hurts. You may be able to imagine asking for help if you were the victim of a natural disaster (like a flood or an earthquake), struck down by a physical illness (you need emergency surgery), or in an accident (your hand gets caught in a piece of machinery). It's much harder to imagine asking for help when you're struggling with the effects of having been raped when you were six.

If you can't imagine asking for help, ask yourself if you'd be willing to provide practical assistance to a friend in your position. How much support do you think you would offer? Then reassess whether you could ask someone to do the same for you.

Now go back to the list of responsibilities you began on page 74. Put a **star (★)** next to things someone else could do for you. Write the name of a potential helping person next to the star.

Once you've identified ways that other people can help you, you have to take the big step and actually ask for it. Although there are times when you'll be turned down, support can also come from unexpected quarters. Frequently people in our lives are confused about what we're going through. They feel our pain. They see our suffering. They feel powerless and wish there were something they could do to help. In asking for assistance, we not only help ourselves, we give the people who care about us an opportunity to do something concrete.

In the spaces below, list three situations in which you can ask for help. Specify whom you're going to ask, and what for:

1. I'm going to ask _____ to _____

_____ for me.

If I get the help I ask for, _____

_____

_____

If my request is turned down, _____

_____

_____

_____

2. I'm going to ask _____ to _____

_____ for me.

If I get the help I ask for, _____

_____

_____

If my request is turned down, _____

_____

_____

3. I'm going to ask _____ to _____

_____ for me.

If I get the help I ask for, _____

_____

_____

If my request is turned down, _____

_____

_____

Once you've asked, pay attention to the reaction you get. You may
be turned down. You may get the offer of help you need. Your request
might be treated respectfully or it might be criticized. Without judgment,
take note of the responses. If you consistently get negative responses,
you may be asking the wrong person (someone who doesn't care or isn't
interested in helping you) or asking in the wrong way (not being direct

and clear, not being specific enough, asking for too much at once). Consider getting feedback from the person you're asking for help; it might help you improve your style of asking the next time.

Take a few minutes to report on what happened each of the three times you asked for help.

1. When I asked for help, _____

_____

_____

_____

Next time, I'll _____

_____

_____

2. When I asked for help, _____

_____

_____

_____

Next time, I'll _____

_____

_____

3. When I asked for help, _____

_____

_____

Next time, I'll _____

_____

_____

Things to Think About:

- Did my experience of asking for help change from the first time to the third time? If so, how?

- If my request for help was honored, how did it affect me? If I was turned down, how did it affect me?

CREATE A LIGHT AT THE END OF THE TUNNEL

One of the best resources for getting through the emergency stage is the example of someone who's already gone through it. Role models can give us hope and inspire us to keep going when things seem most bleak. In a powerful film about abuse, *Orphans,* a gangster (played by Albert Finney) befriends two abused and abandoned brothers who live alone in a condemned house in New Jersey. The older brother is violent and psychotic. The younger is agoraphobic, withdrawn and terrified of life. The older brother kidnaps Finney while he's drunk in a bar. He intends to steal the older man's money, but instead finds his own life transformed by Finney's love and his firm guiding hand. In a powerful scene, Finney raises his arm to the side and coaxes the younger brother to come up and place his body within the curve of his arm, so he can give his shoulder a little squeeze. "All you need," Finney tells the boy, "is a little encouragement." Later he teaches the boy that it's okay to breathe the air outside, and he gives the boy a map so he'll feel safe when he goes out in the world. Over and over, as the younger boy goes through a total transformation, he goes to Finney for another squeeze. "I just need a little encouragement," he says as he sidles up for a comforting hug around the shoulders.

To make it through the emergency stage, you need more than a little encouragement. You need a lot of encouragement. You need to find people who can inspire you and give you hope.

Find a survivor who's further along in the healing process than you are. It could be a friend, a partner, an acquaintance, a 12-step sponsor, someone in your support group, a person referred to you by your therapist or by anyone else you respect. Ask that person to write you a reassuring letter in the space below or to mail you a letter that you can tape onto this page. (Yes, this is another opportunity to ask for help.) Ask them to specify the fact that they've been where you are and that they've gotten through it. Ask them to tell you why it's worth it to heal. Ask them to encourage you—creatively. Have them date the letter.

A LETTER OF ENCOURAGEMENT

Dear _____,
     (your name here)

Read this letter over—frequently. Then when you're having a good day, complete the list below, "Things That Give Me Hope." Turn back to it on the bad days. (For more on hope and the role it plays in healing, see page 189.)

THINGS THAT GIVE ME HOPE

- _____
- _____
- _____
- _____
- _____
- _____
- _____
- _____
- _____

Things to Think About:

- How could I make the best use of the letter and list I just developed?

- Have I ever had a role model or mentor in my life? How could I find one now?

REFLECTIONS: DEALING WITH CRISIS

Crisis is part of the healing process. When you dig through the pain of your childhood and struggle to reclaim your life, you experience uncertainty, fear, and turmoil. Crisis is part of the change process. It is necessary if you want to realize new opportunities.

While you may not be able to eliminate crisis, you can learn to deal with it more effectively. This chapter has given you some concrete tools to use the next time you start to feel overwhelmed by feelings and memories. You've identified people you can call in a crisis, things you can do to calm yourself down, and ways to cope with suicidal feelings.

The emergency stage is an ongoing period of crisis that frequently accompanies new memories and feelings. If you're in the emergency stage, cut out everything that isn't absolutely essential in your life. Lean on other people a little more. Ask for help until you find it. Find reassurance from people who've already been through it. You need to hear that healing is possible, that what you're going through is worth it.

Here are some questions to help you assess your present feelings, goals, and needs in dealing with crisis:

- What feelings did I have as I worked through this chapter?

- What am I feeling right now? What sensations am I experiencing in my body?

- How old did I feel as I worked through the chapter? How old do I feel right now?

- What was hard for me in this chapter? What was confusing? What didn't I understand?

- What did I learn? What commitments have I made? What steps have I taken?

- What did I do that I'm proud of?

- What's still unsettled for me? What, if anything, do I want to come back to or follow up on?

- What do I need to do to take care of myself right now?

NURTURING
YOURSELF

Many times when I talk to survivors about nurturing themselves, they roll their eyes and give me a tired look, as if to say, "We'll bear with you. We know you're from California." Nurturing yourself is seen as some New-Age practice. Or as something self-indulgent (and therefore wrong) that we only do under duress (like a major illness). In reality, learning to love and take care of yourself is at the very core of the healing process.

When survivors want to know how far along they are in the healing process, I ask them what they're doing to take care of themselves before I ask anything else. I don't ask if they have memories. I don't ask if they're angry. I don't ask if they've confronted their abuser. I ask, "Are you gentle and forgiving with yourself when you make a mistake? Are you able to take breaks? Are you able to do things you enjoy? Are you on your own side or are you still fighting yourself every step along the way? Do you give yourself credit for your accomplishments? Are you proud of yourself?"

When you're able to say yes to those questions, you're far along in the healing process. However, if you're in the emergency stage, you may not be able to answer yes to a single question. Many of us have been too busy running, surviving, and just getting by to consider the possibility of nurturing ourselves. But even if you're just starting out, I encourage you to take as many small steps toward self-care as you possibly can. It's the beginning of loving yourself.

When you were abused, you didn't receive the kind of love, nurturing, and positive reinforcement that build solid self-esteem (good feelings about yourself) and lay the foundation for a healthy adult life. Since you didn't get these things as a child, you need to learn to give that love and to care to yourself now. In the beginning others (a therapist, a partner, a close friend) can do it for you, but ultimately you have to learn to do it for yourself.

This can be particularly hard for male survivors. Women are conditioned to be the nurturers and caregivers in our society. The whole concept of being tender or gentle with anyone—particularly yourself—is foreign to most men. Yet nurturing is necessary to healing yourself—even if it seems unfamiliar or "feminine."

One place to begin is by taking a gentle attitude toward the very process of healing. You don't have to abuse yourself (overstimulate yourself with material about sexual abuse, repeatedly put yourself in overwhelming situations because "it's good for you," never take breaks) in order to heal. Accept where you are and then take one small step forward, not ten. Stressing yourself doesn't promote healing; it impedes it.

Try to break away from the old victim's adage "If it feels intense, something must be happening." Having grown up in a chaotic situation, you may continue to create crises in your adult life because it's familiar to you. You know how to respond to a crisis. You don't know that there's an alternative. And there's no doubt that parts of the healing process are cathartic and full of drama. But you also need quiet time for integration, for gathering your strength. You have to give yourself time to rest, to digest the small and sometimes tumultuous changes of healing.

It's just as important that you learn to eat well, to have fun, to have "average" noncrisis moments, as it is to grapple with memories, to feel pain and express outrage. You need to give yourself some time to relax and assimilate the changes in your life, to pace yourself along the way.

LEARNING TO NURTURE YOURSELF

Nurturing is one of the primary ways we show love to ourselves and to others. It is a learned behavior; we are taught about nurturing through our primary caretakers. If you weren't loved, encouraged, and comforted as a child, or if you were raised as a typical boy, the concept of nurturing may be foreign to you. If you were never shown gentleness or tenderness, or were abused "in the name of love," you may be confused about what it means to nurture yourself. Many abused children comfort themselves by doing things that also have self-destructive aspects. Cutting yourself may have been the only way you knew to nurture yourself. Although it provided comfort at the moment, it also hurt you.

Even if you understand what it means to nurture yourself, the idea of doing so might upset you. You may feel resentful that someone else isn't doing it for you. You might feel sad and angry that you weren't taken care of as a child. Feelings of guilt and shame may keep you from feeling that you deserve to be cared for, by yourself or anyone else.

When I think about nurturing myself, I feel _____

_____

_____

_____

_____

If you believe you deserve nurturing only when you're extremely upset, you're like the majority of survivors who feel they have to be totally falling apart before they slow down and take care of themselves. But taking care of yourself should not be confined to times of crisis. Nurturing and taking care of your needs should become a daily habit, like brushing your teeth or eating balanced meals. It should become part of the fabric of life, not something special to be pulled out in emergencies.

Even if you don't do much to take care of yourself now, you started out trying to comfort yourself when you were a child. Although you may have done things that had hurtful aspects, you did find ways to make yourself feel better. Some of those ways may still be helpful to you today.

When I was a child, I nurtured myself by: _____

_____

_____

_____

_____

Put a **star (★)** next to anything you'd still like to use to nurture yourself.

If you have no idea how to begin taking care of yourself, ask other people how they nurture themselves. Ask several people you respect about the things they do to take care of themselves. Record their responses below:

1. Name: _____ takes care of her / himself by _____

_____

_____

_____

_____

_____

_____

2. Name: _____ takes care of her / himself by _____

_____

_____

_____

_____

_____

_____

3. Name: _____ ___ takes care of her / himself by _____

_____   _____

_____

_____

_____

_____

_____

_____   _____

4. Name: _____ takes care of her / himself by _____

_____

_____

_____

_____

_____

_____

_____

Put a **star** (★) next to ideas you might like to try.

WAYS TO NURTURE MYSELF

- _____
- _____
- _____
- _____
- _____
- _____
- _____
- _____
- _____
- _____
- _____
- _____
- _____
- _____
- _____
- _____
- _____

Turn back to this page frequently. Make it a particularly well-worn page.

Make a list of ways you can nurture yourself. Start with the things you starred in the last two exercises, and add anything else that you can think of that would make you feel more relaxed, calm, or centered. (I'll go roller skating / I'll make myself some polenta with cheese / I'll write a letter to a friend I haven't seen in a while / I'll go out and walk in nature / I'll take myself out to a movie). Some of the simpler things may overlap with ideas you wrote down on your list for dealing with panic. Others may be brand new and require more planning and forethought. All of them should be things you can do on a regular basis.

Things to Think About:

- What are my attitudes about nurturing myself? How are they changing?

- How would my life change if I nurtured myself?

- Am I willing to start taking care of myself today? If so, how?

REFLECTIONS: NURTURING YOURSELF

Many of us received little or no nurturing when we were young. You may even have a hard time conceiving of the idea. But learning to take care of yourself is at the very core of healing. It's a way to demonstrate love and respect for yourself.

Nurturing is not just for crisis times; it's important in our daily lives. By combining the strategies you knew as a child with newer, less practiced ones, you can develop a plan for taking care of yourself in a consistent, loving way.

Here are some questions to help you assess your present feelings, goals, and needs around the issue of nurturing yourself:

- What feelings did I have as I worked through this chapter?

- What am I feeling right now? What sensations am I experiencing in my body?

- How old did I feel as I worked through the chapter? How old do I feel right now?

- What was hard for me in this chapter? What was confusing? What didn't I understand?

- What did I learn? What commitments have I made? What steps have I taken?

- What did I do that I'm proud of?

- What's still unsettled for me? What, if anything, do I want to come back to or follow up on?

- What do I need to do to take care of myself right now?

MARKING THE WAY

It's easy to feel you're not getting anywhere when you're faced with the enormity of sexual abuse. When you begin to see the impact abuse has had on your life, the path before you can seem endless and unattainable.

Even survivors who have been healing for a long time go through periods in which they say, "I'm not getting anywhere. I've been doing this for three years already, and here I am having new memories again. I'm back at the beginning." Although this may feel true at the time, the fact is you're dealing with the abuse at a different level.

When I first remembered my abuse, a new memory (and they were coming all the time) would devastate me for several months. I was in a constant state of crisis for well over a year. Then I had a break—a year with no new memories. I was struggling with other things, but I didn't have to deal with memories. But as soon as I entered my next intimate relationship, there they were. New memories started breaking loose all over the place. I was devastated, certain I was back to zero. It wasn't until that crisis was over that I could look back and see that things really had been different the second time around. My feelings of depression and panic hadn't lasted as long. I knew how to take care of myself. I had places to go for help and was capable of reaching out. I bounced back faster.

I haven't had a new memory for well over a year now (although I expect I will again). The last time I remembered something new, it felt terrible while it was happening, but it was all over in an hour. I looked at the memory, felt it, assimilated it, accepted it, and was done with it. It didn't disrupt the whole rhythm of my life.

As you move up the spiral of healing, you deal with the abuse differently. Your perspective shifts and so do your responses. These gains can be subtle at first. In the grips of an immediate crisis, it's hard to differentiate between today's pain and the pain you experienced the last time around.

The truth is that survivors do heal. They get their lives back. It's just that in the thick of things, that progress can be hard to see. That's why regularly assessing where you are along the way is so important. It allows you to gain perspective, to see that you are, in fact, making progress.

This chapter will provide you with some basic tools for charting the way. Using the technique of freewriting, you will assess where you are now in the healing process. You will learn to acknowledge and appreciate your accomplishments by celebrating the small steps you take along the way.

MARKING THE WAY: A WRITING EXERCISE

Creating a written record is an effective way to track your progress through the healing process. Writing is tangible. You can come back to it and compare thoughts and feelings you had six months or a year ago with the way you feel today.

If you've been healing for a while, this exercise will give you a chance to see the changes you've already been through. Use it to refocus on the areas you still need to work on. Repeat this exercise periodically. It will give you a concrete way to measure your progress.

If you're just beginning to look at these issues and have only read through the first section of this book, the writing you're about to do will probably focus on painful, unresolved feelings, rather than on ways you've grown. That's okay. Highlighting problem areas that need attention will help you decide which part of the workbook you want to use next. The following section, "Taking Stock," will continue this assessment process.

Ask yourself these questions: How long have I been actively dealing with the abuse? Am I in a crisis or am I focusing more on a particular problem area? What aspects of healing have I mostly resolved? What's left for me to do? What issue am I the most concerned with right now? Then set an alarm or timer for twenty minutes. Reread the guidelines for freewriting on page 11. Write about where you are in dealing with abuse at this point in your life.

WHAT HAVE I ALREADY ACCOMPLISHED?

Survivors have a tendency to look at how much there is to be done instead of at what they've already accomplished. For instance, a survivor sets a personal goal—to get out of an abusive relationship, to stop binge-ing and throwing up, to pay attention to feelings. The survivor works like hell to attain the goal. Then as soon as the goal is accomplished the survivor says one of two things: "Oh, it wasn't so hard. Anybody could have done it." Or "What's next?" We minimize our accomplishments.

It is important to give yourself credit for all of your successes, no matter how small. If you wait to get to the end of the healing process, until you're "finished," before you recognize your progress, you'll wait forever. Each small step is a building block, an accomplishment in and of itself, and by acknowledging each step along the way you make room for further growth.

Make a list of things you've accomplished in your life so far. Include historical things (I got away from my father / I went to college even though I spent my childhood being told I was stupid / I chose a non-abusive partner). Include things you've accomplished as an adult, before or after you consciously began to deal with sexual abuse (I quit shooting drugs / I didn't kill myself / I made some phone calls to a therapist / I went to a survivors workshop / I told my best friend that my uncle abused me). Your accomplishments can be large or small, finished or still in progress. Even if the only healing thing you've ever done is to buy this book, you can write "I picked up this book. I took it to the counter and paid for it. And then I started reading."

List your accomplishments with pride (and feel free to add more later).

Things to Think About:

- Do I see myself as someone who can accomplish things?

- Was I able to come up with a list of accomplishments? What, if anything, surprised me about the list?

- Do I tend to minimize my accomplishments as insignificant? If so, what would help me appreciate them more?

CELEBRATING YOUR ACCOMPLISHMENTS

It's great to note successes, but it's also important to actually stop and celebrate. In doing so, you inspire yourself and you inspire others, and you give yourself a well-deserved breather.

Take a few moments to think about various ways you might celebrate your accomplishments. You could throw a party. Go out to dinner. Brag to a friend. Get a massage. Try skywriting. (Be creative.)

In one workshop, survivors got together in groups of four and made lists of ways to celebrate. One group came back and proudly read their list: "Dance naked on the beach. Fly a kite. Go shopping. Eat dessert. Spend time with kids. Don't call Mom." Everyone in the room cracked up.

MY ACCOMPLISHMENTS

- _____
- _____
- _____
- _____
- _____
- _____
- _____
- _____
- _____
- _____
- _____
- _____
- _____
- _____
- _____
- _____
- _____
- _____

IDEAS FOR CELEBRATIONS

- _____
- _____
- _____
- _____
- _____
- _____
- _____
- _____
- _____
- _____
- _____
- _____
- _____
- _____
- _____
- _____
- _____
- _____

Make a list of possible ways to celebrate. Every time you accomplish something (no matter how small), try one of them. Add to your list regularly.

Things to Think About:

- What could I celebrate right now?

- What, if anything, is standing in my way?

REFLECTIONS: MARKING THE WAY

The process of healing from child sexual abuse is a gradual one. It's easy to feel frustrated by the ups and downs of the process, and by the time it takes. Keeping a record of the stages you go through can help you recognize the progress you're making over time. Writing and other forms of creative expression are excellent ways to gain this perspective.

Survivors often neglect to take the time to acknowledge their successes. Celebrating and paying attention to accomplishments inspires you and paves the way to future healing.

Here are some questions to help you assess your present feelings, goals, and needs around marking the way:

- **What feelings did I have as I worked through this chapter?**

- What am I feeling right now? What sensations am I experiencing in my body?

- How old did I feel as I worked through the chapter? How old do I feel right now?

- What was hard for me in this chapter? What was confusing? What didn't I understand?

- What did I learn? What commitments have I made? What steps have I taken?

- What did I do that I'm proud of?

- What's still unsettled for me? What, if anything, do I want to come back to or follow up on?

- What do I need to do to take care of myself right now?

PART TWO
TAKING STOCK

The next three chapters will help you recognize the ways abuse has shaped and molded your life. In "Where Did I Come From?" you'll have a chance to look at your past and name the abuse you suffered. In "The Effects" you'll learn that many of the issues you struggle with in your daily life are a direct result of being sexually abused as a child. In "Coping" you'll identify the strategies you used to survive the abuse, and look at the negative and positive aspects of each one in your life today. This is the first step in replacing self-destructive coping patterns with healthier ones.

These chapters will not be easy. In naming the abuse, you'll come face to face with childhood experiences that were filled with fear, shame, and terror. Looking squarely at the damage requires that you make a painful, honest assessment of the toll abuse has had on your life. You may find it hard to feel hopeful as you look at the depth and extent of your pain, yet it is only when you face the parts of your life that trouble you that you can make lasting changes. As you uncover the source of your struggles, you will discover that you're not crazy or alone. Things will start to make sense. You'll start fighting back.

WHERE DID
I COME FROM?

Many survivors have shut their childhood memories away in a closed and lonely room. You may never yet have talked to anyone about what you experienced growing up. You may have blocked the memories out entirely (for more on amnesia see "Remembering," page 204). Maybe no one ever asked, or maybe you were sure no one would ever believe you. Or perhaps you didn't think it mattered.

If you've picked up this book, you've been doing some thinking about things that happened to you when you were young. You may still have your doubts: you may be unsure the abuse really happened, uncertain whether your form of abuse counted, or wondering if this book will talk about your particular experience.

Many survivors come to workshops wondering if they're really qualified to attend. They say things like "It only happened once," or "It was just my brother," or "It wasn't actually intercourse," or "It was my mother. That doesn't count, does it?" If your boundaries were violated as a child, even once, your experience counts.

The following checklists are ways for you to recognize and name your experience. Although it won't be easy, checking off the items that pertain to you will help you feel that your experience matters. (Even if you were not sexually abused but grew up in a different kind of dysfunctional home, you will find a place where you fit in.)

WHEN I WAS GROWING UP

There are common characteristics that exist in families where abuse takes place. You may not have experienced all of them, but you probably experienced several. If you were abused outside your home, fewer of these statements will apply to you.

Check the statements that apply to your childhood. Add any others that pertain to you:

_____ I felt ashamed of my family. There were things I couldn't talk about.

_____ There were always a lot of secrets in my household.

_____ I was threatened not to talk about the things that went on.

_____ Along with the bad things, there was a lot of good in my family.

_____ I had a good situation at home; the abuse took place on the outside.

_____ At least one of my parents took drugs or drank a lot.

_____ There was never enough money for necessities.

_____ Someone in my family was considered "crazy" or "mentally ill."

_____ I was often humiliated and put down.

_____ I never felt respected as an individual.

_____ A lot of my basic needs weren't taken care of.

_____ I was taking care of other people in my family from an early age.

_____ Sometimes I felt like the parent.

_____ I felt isolated in my family.

_____ I wasn't allowed to have relationships with other kids my age.

_____ Things were chaotic and unpredictable in my household.

_____ There were a lot of broken promises.

_____ I was beaten as a child. There was a lot of violence in my family.

_____ I wasn't abused myself, but I witnessed lots of terrible things.

_____ I was always scared something terrible was going to happen.

_____ I was removed from my home and placed in foster care or sent to live with other relatives.

_____ I never had any privacy concerning my body or bodily functions.

_____ People made inappropriate, intrusive comments to me about sex.

_____ I was fondled or touched sexually by someone who had more power than I did.

_____ I was made to touch another person (other people) sexually.

_____ I was sexually abused, but it only happened once.

_____ I was forced to perform oral sex.

_____ I was raped.

_____ I was forced to watch people have sex.

_____ I was forced to undergo unnecessary medical procedures.

_____ I was goaded or shamed into sex.

_____ I was told I was only good for sex.

_____ People took sexual pictures or movies of me.

_____ I was sold for sex or given away to others.

_____ I was forced into child pornography or prostitution.

_____ I was brainwashed or forced to take drugs.

_____ I was sexually abused and/or tortured in a group ritual.

_____ I was forced to do violent or sexual things to other victims.

_____ I'm not sure if I was abused, but when I hear about sexual abuse and its effects, it all sounds creepy and familiar.

_____ I don't remember my childhood, but I have this terrible feeling that something really bad happened to me.

_____ _____

_____

_____ _____

_____

_____ _____

_____

NAME THE ABUSER

In the Courage to Heal workshops, I always put several sheets of newsprint on the wall and write in big letters at the top: "Name the Abuser." Throughout the day survivors go up to the wall and write the names of their abusers in bold magic marker. Sometimes they are shaking, terrified, and crying; sometimes they need a friend to walk them over to the wall; but it is always an empowering experience to write down the name of the abuser. Some survivors write a single name. Others write many. One woman asked if it was okay if she took the space to write sixteen names. I said, "Of course."

Check off the people who abused you. If you're ready, write out their names in the space provided.

_____ I was abused by my father.

_____ I was abused by my stepfather.

_____ I was abused by my grandfather.

_____ I was abused by my uncle.

_____ I was abused by my mother.

_____ I was abused by my stepmother.

_____ I was abused by my grandmother.

_____ I was abused by my aunt.

_____ I was abused by my brother.

_____ I was abused by my sister.

_____ I was abused by my cousin.

_____ I was abused in a foster family.

_____ I was abused by a teacher.

_____ I was abused by a minister or religious leader.

_____ I was abused by a camp counselor or scout leader.

_____ I was abused by a doctor or other medical person.

_____ I was abused by a neighbor.

_____ I was abused by a friend of the family.

_____ I was abused by other kids at school.

_____ I was abused by a stranger.

_____ I was abused by a counselor or other person who was supposed to help me.

_____ Lots of different people abused me.

_____ I know I was abused, but I don't know who did it.

_____ I was also abused by _____

_____ I was also abused by _____

_____ I was also abused by _____

_____ I was also abused by _____

_____ (If you're not sure) I think I might have been abused by _____

_____

_____

_____

_____ Then as an adult, I was abused by _____

_____

_____

_____

Naming the abuser(s) is a powerful act. It can feel empowering and exciting, or it can be terrifying. Breathe deeply as you take a few moments to notice how you're feeling. Are you feeling exhilarated and free? Panicky and frightened? Numb and uncertain? Or a combination of all three?

NAME THE ABUSER

(fill in the actual name or names)

If you are scared right now, you're having a natural reaction to naming the abuser. In breaking silence, you're shattering a taboo of secrecy that has kept you under control. (For more on the difficulties of telling see "Breaking Silence," page 234.) Remember, you don't have to show this page to anyone until you're ready. If you're feeling overwhelmed, go back to the list you made on page 68.

REFLECTIONS: WHERE DID I COME FROM?

Healing requires going back and facing your childhood pain. Naming what happened to you is crucial. It enables you to claim the fact that you were hurt, and it ends the lonely silence that has surrounded so much of your experience. Even though it empowers you, writing down the truth can be terrifying. It's important that you take care of yourself and reach out for help if you feel shaky.

Here are some questions to help you assess your present feelings, goals, and needs around naming the abuse:

• What feelings did I have as I worked through these checklists?

• What am I feeling right now? What sensations am I experiencing in my body?

• How old did I feel as I worked through the lists? How old do I feel right now?

• What was hard for me in completing the lists? What was confusing? What didn't I understand?

- What did I learn? What commitments have I made? What steps have I taken?

- What did I do that I'm proud of?

- What's still unsettled for me? What, if anything, do I want to come back to or follow up on?

- What do I need to do to take care of myself right now?

THE EFFECTS: HOW DID IT CHANGE MY LIFE?

In the Courage to Heal workshops, I often begin by asking survivors to look at the long-term effects of abuse in their lives. As soon as I bring up the topic, a heaviness descends over the room. As we tally the long list of effects, I see three primary reactions: recognition, despair, and anger.

Survivors are frequently unaware of the connections between sexual abuse and current problems. As I write the many and varied effects on a big sheet of paper, survivors around the room nod their heads, saying things like "Oh, me too. Me too. I didn't know that was connected. Oh, so that's why I space out and disappear!" They're experiencing recognition—the realization that the difficulties they face are in fact a direct result of abuse.

With recognition comes relief. You realize that many problems in your life are the natural result of an abusive childhood, not some bizarre quirk you invented on your own. You see that the problems you face are shared by other survivors, and your sense of shame and isolation decreases. Your burden feels a little lighter.

But as the litany of effects mounts up, the second response is often despair. The assessment process is one of naming losses. You may be devastated when you see all the ways abuse has affected and limited you. You may feel hopeless and think, "How can I ever overcome the weight of all this damage?"

The third common response is anger. As you realize that your adult life has been ravaged because of someone else's selfish acts, you become furious at what was done to you. You think, "How could this have been done to me? I hate my abuser. I want revenge."

In this chapter you will assess the way sexual abuse has affected your life, identifying the effects in seven different areas. Some of these specific problem areas may be familiar to you; others will make you think about the abuse in a new way. At the end of the assessment, you'll list your strengths. The third exercise, an art activity, allows you to experience the effects on a more emotional level. Finally you'll look at the role abuse has played in your life in comparison with other influences.

The next exercises may be very upsetting to you. Many of us have minimized the effects of the abuse as well as the abuse itself. As a result, these are particularly hard exercises to do alone. Do them with other survivors, or share your thoughts and feelings with someone once you're through.

ASSESSING THE DAMAGE

The statements listed below are typical of the experiences and feelings of survivors of child sexual abuse. Since abuse affects people in different ways, some of the statements will apply to you and others won't. Looking at your answers can show you the areas of your life that have been most strongly influenced by the abuse.

If you've been working on these issues for some time, you can use this assessment to identify the progress you've made. Statements you would have identified with in the past may seem irrelevant to you today. A sentence you would have ranked "usually" a year or two ago may now get a "rarely" rating. If you've been healing for a while, try to focus on the areas in which you've made gains. Let yourself feel proud of the ways your answers have changed. Then go back through your answers and take a look at the areas that still need healing and attention.

Read each sentence and indicate how frequently you have that experience or feel that way:

Self-Esteem	*Always*	*Usually*	*Sometimes*	*Rarely*	*Never*
I feel dirty, like there's something wrong with me.	_____	_____	_____	_____	_____
Sometimes I think I'm crazy.	_____	_____	_____	_____	_____
I feel ashamed.	_____	_____	_____	_____	_____

Self-Esteem	Always	Usually	Sometimes	Rarely	Never
I'm different from other people.	_____	_____	_____	_____	_____
I feel powerless.	_____	_____	_____	_____	_____
If people really knew me, they'd leave.	_____	_____	_____	_____	_____
I want to die.	_____	_____	_____	_____	_____
I want to kill myself.	_____	_____	_____	_____	_____
I hate myself.	_____	_____	_____	_____	_____
I have a hard time taking care of myself.	_____	_____	_____	_____	_____
I don't deserve to be happy.	_____	_____	_____	_____	_____
I don't trust my intuition or my feelings.	_____	_____	_____	_____	_____
I'm often confused.	_____	_____	_____	_____	_____
I don't know how to set goals and follow through on them.	_____	_____	_____	_____	_____
I'm scared of success.	_____	_____	_____	_____	_____
I'm a failure. I don't feel capable of doing a good job.	_____	_____	_____	_____	_____
I use work to make up for empty feelings inside.	_____	_____	_____	_____	_____
I'm a perfectionist.	_____	_____	_____	_____	_____
I've made up a lot of stories about my life.	_____	_____	_____	_____	_____

Self-Esteem	Always	Usually	Sometimes	Rarely	Never
I've done a lot of shoplifting.	_____	_____	_____	_____	_____

My Feelings

	Always	Usually	Sometimes	Rarely	Never
I don't think feelings are very important.	_____	_____	_____	_____	_____
I usually don't know what I'm feeling.	_____	_____	_____	_____	_____
I can't tell one feeling from another.	_____	_____	_____	_____	_____
I only experience one or two emotions.	_____	_____	_____	_____	_____
I have a hard time expressing my feelings.	_____	_____	_____	_____	_____
I have a hard time crying freely.	_____	_____	_____	_____	_____
I cry all the time.	_____	_____	_____	_____	_____
I get uncomfortable when I feel too happy.	_____	_____	_____	_____	_____
I get nervous when things are relaxed and calm.	_____	_____	_____	_____	_____
I feel enraged a lot of the time.	_____	_____	_____	_____	_____
I'm rarely angry. Anger scares me.	_____	_____	_____	_____	_____
I get depressed a lot.	_____	_____	_____	_____	_____
I have a lot of nightmares.	_____	_____	_____	_____	_____
I have panic attacks.	_____	_____	_____	_____	_____

My Feelings

	Always	Usually	Sometimes	Rarely	Never
If I really let myself go, my feelings would be out of control.	_____	_____	_____	_____	_____
I've been violent.	_____	_____	_____	_____	_____
I haven't been violent yet, but I'm worried I might be.	_____	_____	_____	_____	_____

My Body

	Always	Usually	Sometimes	Rarely	Never
I'm not "in my body" a lot of the time.	_____	_____	_____	_____	_____
I frequently space out.	_____	_____	_____	_____	_____
My body often feels numb.	_____	_____	_____	_____	_____
I feel as if my body is separate from the rest of me.	_____	_____	_____	_____	_____
I don't pay too much attention to my body's signals (hunger, tiredness, pain).	_____	_____	_____	_____	_____
I think my body is ugly.	_____	_____	_____	_____	_____
I hide my body.	_____	_____	_____	_____	_____
I'm dyslexic. I had learning disabilities when I was growing up.	_____	_____	_____	_____	_____
I use drugs or alcohol more than I think I should.	_____	_____	_____	_____	_____
I often eat compulsively.	_____	_____	_____	_____	_____
I keep myself from eating, or eat and throw up.	_____	_____	_____	_____	_____

My Body

	Always	Usually	Sometimes	Rarely	Never
I hurt myself on purpose (cut, burn, or injure myself).	_____	_____	_____	_____	_____
I have illnesses I think are related to my abuse.	_____	_____	_____	_____	_____
I've worked out to make my body strong so I wouldn't feel like a victim.	_____	_____	_____	_____	_____
I've had flashbacks of the abuse during surgery or other medical procedures.	_____	_____	_____	_____	_____
I'm scared to go to the dentist. I hate the feeling of things in my mouth.	_____	_____	_____	_____	_____
(For women) I'm scared to go to the gynecologist.	_____	_____	_____	_____	_____

Intimacy

	Always	Usually	Sometimes	Rarely	Never
I often feel alienated from other people, as if I'm from another planet.	_____	_____	_____	_____	_____
Most of my relationships just don't work.	_____	_____	_____	_____	_____
I don't have many friends.	_____	_____	_____	_____	_____
I'm okay with my friends, but I just can't work things out with a lover.	_____	_____	_____	_____	_____
I think I'm really meant to be alone.	_____	_____	_____	_____	_____
I'm not sure I really deserve to be loved.	_____	_____	_____	_____	_____

Intimacy	Always	Usually	Sometimes	Rarely	Never
I don't know what love is.	_____	_____	_____	_____	_____
I find it hard to trust people.	_____	_____	_____	_____	_____
I think people are going to leave me.	_____	_____	_____	_____	_____
I test people a lot.	_____	_____	_____	_____	_____
It's hard for me to be nurtured or to nurture someone else.	_____	_____	_____	_____	_____
I'm clingy with people I'm close to. I'm afraid to be alone.	_____	_____	_____	_____	_____
I'm scared of making a commitment. When people get too close, I panic.	_____	_____	_____	_____	_____
I have a hard time saying no.	_____	_____	_____	_____	_____
People take advantage of me in relationships.	_____	_____	_____	_____	_____
I get involved with people who are inappropriate or inaccessible.	_____	_____	_____	_____	_____
I've had relationships with people who remind me of my abuser.	_____	_____	_____	_____	_____
I'm struggling a lot with my partner.	_____	_____	_____	_____	_____
Sometimes I think my partner is my abuser.	_____	_____	_____	_____	_____
Sexual abuse is really creating problems in my relationship.	_____	_____	_____	_____	_____

Sexuality

	Always	Usually	Sometimes	Rarely	Never
I avoid sex. Deep down, I wish I never had to deal with sex again.	———	———	———	———	———
I'm celibate. I haven't had sex in years.	———	———	———	———	———
I really think sex is disgusting.	———	———	———	———	———
I don't feel sexual desire. I think there's something basically wrong with it.	———	———	———	———	———
Sex isn't pleasurable for me. I usually have sex to make the other person happy.	———	———	———	———	———
I try to use sex to meet most of my needs.	———	———	———	———	———
It really feels like I'm "oversexed."	———	———	———	———	———
Sex and aggression are really connected for me.	———	———	———	———	———
I find it hard to be close in nonsexual ways. It just isn't satisfying.	———	———	———	———	———
I frequently go after sex I really don't want.	———	———	———	———	———
Sex is the thing I'm best at.	———	———	———	———	———
I've sold myself for sex.	———	———	———	———	———
I've had sex with people who don't respect me.	———	———	———	———	———

Sexuality	Always	Usually	Sometimes	Rarely	Never
I've been sexually abused as an adult.	———	———	———	———	———
I need to control everything about sex.	———	———	———	———	———
I have a hard time staying present when I make love. I'm numb a lot during lovemaking.	———	———	———	———	———
When I am sexual, I have terrifying, scary feelings I don't understand.	———	———	———	———	———
I often have flashbacks of my abuse when making love.	———	———	———	———	———
I get sexually aroused when I read or talk about sexual abuse.	———	———	———	———	———
Violent, sadistic fantasies turn me on.	———	———	———	———	———
I'm ashamed of my sexuality.	———	———	———	———	———
I've sexually abused others.	———	———	———	———	———

Children and Parenting

	Always	Usually	Sometimes	Rarely	Never
I feel awkward and uncomfortable around children.	———	———	———	———	———
I have a hard time being affectionate with kids.	———	———	———	———	———
I have a hard time setting boundaries with kids.	———	———	———	———	———

Children and Parenting

	Always	Usually	Sometimes	Rarely	Never
I have a hard time balancing children's needs with my own.	_____	_____	_____	_____	_____
(For parents) I feel inadequate as a parent.	_____	_____	_____	_____	_____
I have trouble protecting children I take care of.	_____	_____	_____	_____	_____
I tend to be overprotective.	_____	_____	_____	_____	_____
I've successfully protected children.	_____	_____	_____	_____	_____
I'm scared I'll be abusive.	_____	_____	_____	_____	_____
I have abused children.	_____	_____	_____	_____	_____
My kids have been abused (by someone else).	_____	_____	_____	_____	_____

My Family of Origin

	Always	Usually	Sometimes	Rarely	Never
I have strained relationships with my family.	_____	_____	_____	_____	_____
Members of my family have rejected me (or vice versa).	_____	_____	_____	_____	_____
I have a hard time setting limits with my family.	_____	_____	_____	_____	_____
People in my family invalidate my feelings and experiences.	_____	_____	_____	_____	_____
I feel crazy when I'm around my family.	_____	_____	_____	_____	_____
I can't be honest with the people in my family.	_____	_____	_____	_____	_____

My Family of Origin	Always	Usually	Sometimes	Rarely	Never
Sexual abuse is still a secret in my family.	_____	_____	_____	_____	_____
There's still incest in my family.	_____	_____	_____	_____	_____
I'm waiting for the people in my family to come around and support me.	_____	_____	_____	_____	_____

If many of the statements on this list were familiar to you, you may feel overwhelmed right now. But the purpose of this assessment is not to overwhelm you; it's to show you that there's a reason why you experience the things you do. It's to point out the areas that need healing.

Although this workbook doesn't specifically address all the areas covered in the assessment, it is possible to heal each of the long-term effects mentioned.* It is possible to dramatically alter your life so that your answers two years from now will bear little resemblance to your answers today.

When I look over my responses, I feel _____

_____

_____

I've been most strongly affected in the area(s) of _____

_____

_____

_____

——————————

* *The Courage to Heal* offers specific information and resources on all of the topics covered in this assessment. You can also talk to your therapist or other support person about additional resources to help you deal with issues raised by the assessment.

I was least affected in the area(s) of _____

_____

_____

_____

The hardest statements for me to acknowledge were:

- _____

_____

- _____

_____

- _____

_____

- _____

_____

- _____

_____

I feel the most hopeful about making changes in _____

_____

_____

_____

I've already made major strides in the following areas: _____

_____

_____

_____

_____

I feel the most hopeless about changing _____

_____

_____

_____

_____

I was surprised by _____

_____

_____

_____

_____

I learned _____

_____

_____

_____

_____

┌───┐

Things to Think About:

- How did my answers compare to what I expected?

- How does this assessment affect the direction I want to take in my healing?

└───┘

IDENTIFYING MY STRENGTHS

When you look at the negative effects of abuse in your life, it's hard to imagine that you could have developed strengths at the same time. But we all developed strengths in spite of our abuse, or perhaps *to* spite it. I don't mean to say, *in any way*, that there's a good side to the abuse or that you should "look on the bright side."

In a recent interview I was asked to discuss the success of *The Courage to Heal* and the seminars I'd been leading. At one point the interviewer asked if I was glad the abuse had happened, not because of the pain, but because of the opportunities it had brought me. We had been laughing and fooling around, but when she asked that question I grew serious. "Absolutely not," I told her with a vehemence that surprised me. "I would give it all up for the abuse not to have happened. I could have been motivated to write a book because of a positive influence, because I was moved by a piece of music or because I had a profound experience of love. I wrote *The Courage to Heal* because I was in terrible, unbearable pain. I don't care what comes from this. I'll never be glad it happened."

Recognizing your strengths does not mean you have to minimize your abuse or discount the negative effect it's had on your life. Rather, it's a way to feel good about yourself despite what happened to you. It's a way to recognize the abilities and qualities that enable you to heal.

On the list below, check off the statements that apply to you. Add any other strengths you can think of.

_____   I'm stubborn. I won't give up.

_____ I'm determined. When I set my mind to something, I persist.

_____ I won't let anyone abuse me anymore.

_____ I have empathy for other people in pain.

_____ I understand human suffering.

_____ If I lived through the abuse, I can live through anything.

_____ I don't have many illusions about the world. I see things as they are.

_____ I'm self-sufficient. I can take care of myself.

_____ I'm courageous.

_____ I'm perceptive and can figure out what's really going on.

_____ I know how to handle a crisis.

_____ I survived.

_____ I'm calm and patient.

_____

_____

_____

_____

_____

_____

_____

If you weren't able to identify many (or any) strengths, you're not alone. Sometimes, when you're inundated with negative effects and feeling bad about yourself, it's hard to recognize your strengths. But they are there. Otherwise you wouldn't have survived. If you had a hard time with this exercise, come back and try it again once you've worked through more of this book. Or ask people close to you about the strengths they see in you.

ACTIVITY: PICTURING THE EFFECTS

Sometimes it's hard to express the way we feel in words. It can be easier with another medium, like art or dance. On a separate sheet of paper, draw a picture of the ways the abuse has hurt you. Use crayons, colored pencils, paints, or charcoal.

If you prefer, make a collage (see page 13). Leaf through magazines, circulars, newspapers, and advertisements and cut out pictures and words that reflect the ways you've been negatively affected by the abuse. When you're through, make a second collage. Let it depict the strengths you've developed as a result of your abuse. These can include things like courage, perseverance, self-sufficiency, and determination. Let the collage express your pride at surviving against the odds.

PUTTING THE ABUSE IN PERSPECTIVE

Once survivors begin to look at the long-term effects of abuse, they often maintain that everything they experience is a direct result of having been sexually abused. Although it's tempting to think this way, it usually isn't accurate. Although sexual abuse has long-lasting, severe effects, it is still only one of many factors that shaped you. For some survivors it is by far the most pervasive influence. For others, growing up in a racist society, being adopted, living in poverty, or being the first child of five had equal or greater impact. In assessing its effects in your life, it's important to put the abuse in perspective with the other forces that shaped you.

Make a list of factors that most strongly influenced your development as a child. Include both positive and negative influences (my grandmother's love / growing up poor / learning to read / my football coach / my father's alcoholism / growing up Puerto Rican in a black neighborhood / being a twin / my love of music / Miss Johnson, my fifth-grade teacher). Some items may have both positive and negative aspects. Sandwich them in the middle.

Positive Influences   **Negative Influences**

_____   _____

_____   _____

_____   _____

_____   _____

_____   _____

_____   _____

_____   _____

_____   _____

_____   _____

_____   _____

_____   _____

Look over the items on your list. Consider their influence on your life today. Then rank each item in order of importance on a scale of 1 to 3. The things that influenced you the most get a 1. The things that were the second most important influences get a 2, and so on. (You can give the same number value to more than one item.) When everything has a number, complete the following sentences.

The biggest factor(s) affecting my development was (were) _____

_____

_____

_____

_____

The positive influences that enabled me to survive were _____

_____

_____

_____

_____

A good influence I forgot about was _____

_____

_____

_____

Compared to the other influences, sexual abuse _____

_____

_____

_____

I was surprised _____

_____

_____

_____

I learned _____

_____

_____

_____

This is an exercise you might want to try again later on. As you continue to heal, the influence of sexual abuse on your present life will decrease. A year or two from now, you will probably evaluate things differently.

Things to Think About:

- Was it harder for me to come up with positive or negative influences? Why?

- Do I think my answers to this exercise will change over time? If so, how?

REFLECTIONS: THE EFFECTS OF ABUSE

In order to heal, you must first look at the ways abuse has influenced and shaped your life. This painful process can provide a context for your experience and give you valuable information about the areas you need to work on.

As you assess the long-term effects, it's crucial to remember that it is possible to reverse much of the damage. The strengths you've developed as a survivor are enabling you to make substantial, long-lasting changes in your life. As you continue to make changes, the negative effects of abuse will naturally diminish.

Sexual abuse does not happen in isolation. It happens in a context. It's helpful to look at the ways abuse connects with the other influences in your life. By doing so, you will gain a realistic perspective of the forces that have shaped you.

Here are some questions to help you assess your feelings, goals, and needs as you look at the long-term effects of abuse in your life:

- What feelings did I have as I worked through this chapter?

- What am I feeling right now? What sensations am I experiencing in my body?

- How old did I feel as I worked through the chapter? How old do I feel right now?

- What was hard for me in this chapter? What was confusing? What didn't I understand?

- What did I learn? What commitments have I made? What steps have I taken?

- What did I do that I'm proud of?

- What's still unsettled for me? What, if anything, do I want to come back to or follow up on?

- What do I need to do to take care of myself right now?

COPING: HOW DID I SURVIVE?

There's an old expression, "Whatever gets you through the night." Implicit in the phrase is permission to do anything that enables you to make it through until the morning, whether it be sex with strangers or two Seconals and a Bloody Mary. We all have strategies for getting by, compensating for the hurts we've suffered, dealing with discomfort and pain. We usually don't think about these coping mechanisms consciously, but we come back to them again and again: We drink to numb our feelings, minimize the bad things, maintain control over everything in our lives.

Everyone uses coping mechanisms. They're helpful, necessary survival tools. If we faced everything all of the time with no defenses, we'd be overstimulated and overwhelmed. We need coping mechanisms to pace ourselves, to provide essential boundaries.

The problem is that many coping mechanisms have self-destructive aspects. They become entrenched patterns that we turn to whenever we feel discomfort. We become addicted to gambling or drugs, run away when anyone gets too close, or consistently ignore important problems that need to be dealt with. In doing so, we keep ourselves isolated, damage our health, and block out important information, awareness, and feelings.

This chapter will help you identify the coping mechanisms you use, look at the reasons you use them, examine their positive and negative aspects, and develop strategies for change.

IDENTIFYING COPING MECHANISMS

No two survivors use exactly the same set of coping mechanisms. The list below reflects many of the common ones. (Lots of other people use these as well.) **Circle** the ones that apply to you.

denial	creating new personalities	hiding behind a partner
rationalizing	forgetting	sleeping excessively
creating chaos	leaving your body	not sleeping
repeating abuse	staying in control	humor
fantasizing	gambling	dogmatic beliefs
perfectionism	minimizing	running away
self-mutilation	staying busy	suicide attempts
compulsive eating	alcoholism	drug addiction
compulsive exercising	anorexia / bulimia	compulsive sex
shoplifting	workaholism	avoiding sex
abusing others	gambling	spacing out
avoiding intimacy	taking care of others	staying super-alert

When I look at the coping mechanisms I identified, I feel _____

_____

_____

_____

I realize _____

_____

_____

_____

Coping mechanisms I've used that weren't mentioned are: _____

_____

_____

_____

Things to Think About:

- Are there coping mechanisms I used as a child that I don't use anymore? What new coping mechanisms have I developed as an adult?

- How have my coping mechanisms changed over the years?

- Which coping mechanisms do I feel ashamed about? Which, if any, feel okay to me? What's the difference between those in the first category and those in the second?

FORGIVING YOURSELF

Many survivors have lost decades to self-destructive coping patterns. You may have spent years addicted to drugs or alcohol, living on the streets, being involved in abusive relationships, or doing things to yourself or others that you still can't talk about. But the most important thing is that you survived. You used whatever resources you had to make it through your childhood, so you could grow up and become an adult with the oppportunity and free will to heal. Quite literally, many survivors would have died if it weren't for their coping mechanisms.

As survivors we should be proud of our resourcefulness in staying alive, yet many of us feel terribly ashamed instead. The truth is, as a traumatized, isolated, and frightened young person, you did whatever you had to do to survive the abuse. And once you grew up, you continued the same patterns of behavior because they worked for you (at least somewhat), because they'd become habits, because you still didn't have other options (who was there to teach them to you?).

The important thing is that you've grown up since then. You have the ability to reexamine your life. You can stop doing things you're ashamed of and begin the painstaking work of changing your behavior. But you have to start by forgiving yourself for the things you've done in order to cope. Feeling ashamed and terrible about yourself can keep you trapped and powerless, unable to mobilize your energy to make the necessary changes in your life.

If, however, your coping behaviors included things that hurt other people (hitting your children with misdirected rage, abusing a younger child when you were growing up), forgiving yourself is not enough. When you hurt someone else, you need to take responsibility for the hurt, grieve over the fact that you've injured another human being, ensure that the behavior won't be repeated, and make any amends that are possible, before you forgive yourself.*

The following exercises will help you look at the coping mechanisms you feel ashamed of.

List any coping behaviors you feel particularly bad about. Include things from childhood or adult life—one-time incidents (The time I tortured my cat / When I was eight, I stole the grocery money from my grandmother) or long-term patterns (I've been eating compulsively since I was eight / I get verbally abusive when I'm angry).

- _____

- _____

- _____

- _____

- _____

---

* Although it is beyond the scope of this workbook to assist you in coming to terms with your own abusive or hurtful behavior, it is essential that you seek professional help if you are currently hurting others or worrying that you might. You may also need counseling to help you deal with the repercussions of hurts you've caused in the past.

- _____

- _____

- _____

Now transfer the items from this list to the "coping mechanism" blanks below. Then ask yourself, "What are the reasons I can forgive myself for doing this?"

Since you are currently feeling bad about these things, it's unlikely that you will fully (or even partially) believe the reasons you write down. That's fine for a start. Make this an intellectual exercise. Be analytical. Why might you be able to forgive yourself? What could possibly justify such behavior?

If you feel so ashamed that you can't conceive of ever forgiving yourself, imagine another survivor, either a child or a grown-up, doing the same things. Ask yourself what might have forced them to choose that particular behavior. See if you can feel any compassion for them. If you're still stuck, ask your counselor, a fellow survivor, or a friend who wasn't abused for reasons you might be able to forgive yourself. Put their answers in the space below. Then move slowly toward believing them.

If your coping mechanisms include ways you've hurt others, change the exercise. Instead of asking yourself "How can I forgive myself?" ask instead "What do I need to do before I can forgive myself?" This will give you room to explore your responsibility and need to make amends.

Coping mechanism: *Promiscuity*

I can forgive myself for doing this because:

- *My father's abuse taught me that my only value was sexual.*

- *No one ever told me that I could say no.*

- *Being sexual was the only way I knew to feel cared about. And I needed to feel cared about in order to survive.*

Coping mechanism: _____

I can forgive myself for doing this because:

- _____

_____

- _____

_____

- _____

_____

- _____

_____

Coping mechanism: _____

I can forgive myself for doing this because:

- _____

_____

- _____

_____

- _____

_____

- _____

_____

Coping mechanism: _____

I can forgive myself for doing this because:

- _____

  _____

- _____

  _____

- _____

  _____

- _____

  _____

Coping mechanism: _____

I can forgive myself for doing this because:

- _____

  _____

- _____

  _____

- _____

  _____

Coping mechanism: _____

I can forgive myself for doing this because:

- _____

_____

- _____

_____

- _____

_____

- _____

_____

Coping mechanism: _____

I can forgive myself for doing this because:

- _____

_____

- _____

_____

- _____

_____

- _____

_____

THE PROS AND CONS OF COPING BEHAVIORS

When I first started working through the sexual abuse, I was certain that healing required me to identify and obliterate every coping mechanism I'd ever used to survive. Had I denied the abuse? Well, now I would completely and totally face everything. I'd forgotten what happened to me? The new me would be absolutely vigilant—nothing would slip my attention.

I divided everything I did into two categories: good and bad. Anything connected to my old (abused) self was bad and needed to be overhauled. If I had used it in the past, it was contaminated. Anything connected to my new life—my post-healing world—was good. And the good list was very, very short.

Fortunately for me, black-and-white thinking was one of the coping mechanisms on the "bad" list. I had to look at it. I had to examine it. And when I did, I realized my life needed some gray, some middle ground. Could it be that there was something good in my coping mechanisms? Was there anything still useful to me about denial? Were there times when it was helpful to split off from my body? Could the independence and autonomy I'd developed to such a high degree serve me well?

When I do workshops for survivors, I frequently wear a small pink button that says, "Queen of Denial." When asked why I wear the button, I get the chance to launch into one of my favorite subjects. I say, "There are two kinds of denial, capital 'D' denial and small 'd' denial. Capital 'D' denial is the kind families often have: 'This never happened. You're crazy. You're making it up.' Small 'd' denial is the kind we use when we're fully committed to healing but just need a break. We need to go home, turn on the TV, pick up a copy of *People* magazine, and say for just a few minutes, 'Maybe nothing happened.' We know we were abused. We're going back to therapy tomorrow. We know we're going to work on it. We're just pretending it didn't happen for a little while so we can get some rest. Small 'd' denial gives you a chance to catch your breath, a chance to absorb the truth slowly. It's a tricky distinction—particularly when we first start dealing with the abuse—but it's an important one to make."

When I was working on *The Courage to Heal,* I was very concerned about how my family would respond to the publication of the book. I was terrified at the thought of putting my name and photograph on the cover, and yet all along I knew I was going to do it. From the beginning, I knew that I would go public with my story. But the implications of that decision were so terrifying that I periodically had to pretend I still had a choice, that I hadn't committed myself already. That's small "d" denial. It doesn't stop us from moving forward. It's not a brick wall. It's a thin, gauzy curtain that allows us to move at a pace we can handle. It's an important part of taking care of ourselves.

Like denial, many coping mechanisms have their useful side. Others have hurtful aspects that make them less worthwhile today. To develop healthier ways of coping, you will have to begin by sorting through the coping skills you use today to see which ones work for you and which ones don't. Once you do this, you can target certain behaviors for change.

In the space below, copy down the list of coping mechanisms you circled on page 145. If you thought of any that weren't included on that list, add them below.

_____ _____

_____ _____

_____ _____

_____ _____

_____ _____

_____ _____

_____   _____

_____   _____

_____   _____

_____   _____

_____   _____

Go back and put a **star (★)** next to four coping mechanisms you'd most like to focus on for the rest of this chapter. List them below, describing the healthy and damaging aspects of each.

Coping mechanism: *Fantasy*

Ways this coping mechanism can still be useful to me: *I have a wonderfully vivid imagination. I'm great at entertaining children. I've written successful short stories. I'm very creative. I don't get bored easily.*

Ways this coping mechanism is damaging to me: *Sometimes I use fantasy as a way to avoid dealing with issues I have to face in my life. I pretend that things are really okay when they're not. Sometimes I enjoy my fantasies so much that I lose my motivation to set real goals and accomplish them.*

Coping mechanism: _____

Ways this coping mechanism can still be useful to me: _____

_____

_____

_____

_____

Ways this coping mechanism is damaging to me: _____

_____

_____

_____

_____

Coping mechanism: _____

Ways this coping mechanism can still be useful to me: _____

_____

_____

_____

_____

Ways this coping mechanism is damaging to me: _____

_____

_____

_____

_____

Coping mechanism: _____

Ways this coping mechanism can still be useful to me: _____

_____

_____

_____

_____

Ways this coping mechanism is damaging to me: _____

_____

_____

_____

_____

Coping mechanism: _____

Ways this coping mechanism can still be useful to me: _____

_____

_____

_____

_____

Ways this coping mechanism is damaging to me: _____

_____

_____

_____

DEVELOPING HEALTHIER WAYS OF COPING

All coping mechanisms have an inherent logic and serve an important function. Underlying each coping mechanism is a need. If you discard a coping mechanism without finding another way to understand and meet the underlying need, the change won't last. Therefore you have to identify the need before you can effectively replace a self-destructive coping pattern with a healthier one. Drinking, for instance, can protect you from feeling the pain you experienced as a child. When you quit drinking, painful feelings and memories start to surface. And if you don't develop a new way to deal with those feelings, the pull to start drinking again will be irresistible.

It is not enough to go "cold turkey" on your coping mechanisms. Approach these changes slowly, with love for yourself and respect for your needs, so you can make changes that will last.

In the spaces below, write down the names of the four coping mechanisms you chose in the last exercise (page 154). Then answer the questions "What needs am I meeting with this behavior?" and "How else can I meet these underlying needs?" If you can't come up with any ideas on your own, ask a couple of the people in your support system for suggestions.

Coping mechanism: *Running myself ragged and getting sick all the time.*

The needs I'm meeting with this behavior are: *When I get sick, I get nurturing, I feel justified asking for help, and I finally get to set limits and say no. Getting sick is the only way I know to quit overworking and take a break. I get sympathy for being sick that I never get for emotional hurts.*

Healthier ways to meet these needs would be to: *Admit when I'm overwhelmed and need a break, instead of pushing to the point of exhaustion. Build up a support system that allows emotional hurts to count. Find new ways to get nurturing. Start saying no before I get sick. Pay attention to the warning signs before I burn out entirely. Stop trying to do everything myself. Ask for the help I need.*

Coping mechanism: _____

The needs I'm meeting with this behavior are: _____

_____

_____

_____

_____

_____

_____

Healthier ways to meet these needs would be to: _____

_____

_____

_____

_____

_____

_____

Coping mechanism: _____

The needs I'm meeting with this behavior are: _____

_____

_____

_____

_____

_____

Healthier ways to meet these needs would be to: _____

_____

_____

_____

_____

_____

Coping mechanism: _____

The needs I'm meeting with this behavior are: _____

_____

_____

_____

_____

_____

Healthier ways to meet these needs would be to: _____

_____

_____

_____

_____

_____

Coping mechanism: _____

The needs I'm meeting with this behavior are: _____

_____

_____

_____

_____

_____

Healthier ways to meet these needs would be to: _____

_____

_____

_____

_____

_____

REFLECTIONS: COPING

Coping mechanisms are a normal, natural part of life. They enable us to handle the stresses and challenges of daily living. As a survivor you had to develop extraordinary coping strategies. Fostering an attitude of pride, rather than shame, about your survival skills can give you the strength to make lasting changes.

To change a particular coping pattern, you have to assess its positive and negative aspects, recognize the underlying need it meets, and then gradually find healthier ways to meet those needs.

Here are some questions to help you assess your present feelings, goals, and needs around the ways you cope:

- What feelings did I have as I worked through this chapter?

- What am I feeling right now? What sensations am I experiencing in my body?

- How old did I feel as I worked through the chapter? How old do I feel right now?

- What was hard for me in this chapter? What was confusing? What didn't I understand?

- What did I learn? What commitments have I made? What steps have I taken?

- What did I do that I'm proud of?

- What's still unsettled for me? What, if anything, do I want to come back to or follow up on?

- What do I need to do to take care of myself right now?

PART THREE
ASPECTS OF HEALING

In the first five chapters of this workbook, you were introduced to many of the basic skills necessary to healing: taking care of yourself, building a support system, reaching out for help, creating safety, coping with crisis, and acknowledging the healing you've already accomplished. You will continue to develop and refine these tools as you move through the rest of the book. They will provide you with a core of knowledge that will help you handle the feelings and issues that are raised as you work through the exercises in this section.

"Taking Stock" gave you the chance to name your abuse, assess the ways it has affected you, and examine the coping skills you developed. You got a clear (though probably painful) picture of the areas that need healing in your life, and you were introduced to the basics of making changes.

"Aspects of Healing" moves a step further by delving into the stages of the healing process. You will not necessarily experience these stages in the order they're presented here, but you will probably grapple with all of them repeatedly. Whether you're just beginning to work on these issues or have been working with them for a long time, you will discover new information and challenges as you work through these pages. This section will also provide practical exercises for exploring your feelings, boosting self-esteem, and dealing with your family.

"The Decision to Heal" looks at the reasons healing is scary, talks about courage, introduces the concept of willingness, and encourages you to develop new hopes and goals. "Remembering" gives you information that will help you deal with memories of abuse—or the lack of memories. "Believing It Happened" further examines the phenomenon of denial and emphasizes the need to believe and trust yourself. "Breaking Silence" gives guidelines for talking about your abuse with supportive people. "Understanding That It Wasn't Your Fault" delves into the core issues of shame and self-blame, and introduces you to the concept of the child within. "Learning to Trust Yourself" introduces basic skills for boosting self-esteem—learning to say no, discovering the inner voice, and rooting out negative internalized messages. The next two chapters,

"Grieving and Mourning" and "Anger," teach you about your most basic emotions—how to recognize them, learn from them, and use them effectively in your life. "Confrontations" and "Dealing with Your Family Now" give step-by-step guidance in confronting abusers, disclosing abuse to family members, and assessing the positive and negative aspects of family relationships. And finally, "Resolution and Moving On" gives you a chance to assess your progress, set new goals for yourself, and celebrate your accomplishments.

Survivors who have worked through the exercises in this section have been profoundly moved and challenged. They've grappled with painful, sometimes terrifying emotions, faced new memories and hard truths. They've made tremendous gains and set new resolutions for themselves. But these changes have taken time. These pages are not to be rushed through. If you spend several weeks, or longer, on one chapter, that's fine. If you want to skip around, to work through the sections that interest you most, feel free to leave the rest for another time. These pages are for you. Use them in the way that suits you best.

THE DECISION
TO HEAL

The "decision to heal" refers to the decision to face your fears and to change your life. The moment you say "I am a survivor and I want the pain to go away," you begin shaping your commitment to heal. Yet the decision to heal is not a decision you make once; it is one you have to make over and over again. Each stage of the healing process presents new challenges, risks, fears, and opportunities; each requires that you renew your commitment. Every time you pay attention to your emotional needs and make healing activities a priority, you strengthen your commitment to the healing process.

The decision to heal is one of the scariest and most empowering decisions you'll ever make. This book is called *The Courage to Heal Workbook* because it takes courage to say yes to your own healing. It takes courage to face the unknown, claim your right to heal, get the help you need, and deal with the pain involved.

If the prospect of making a commitment to the healing process scares you, you're not alone. You're having a sane, valid response to a situation which is truly frightening. It is terrifying to face the unknown, to give up coping patterns that are familiar, to relive painful memories and feelings from the past. There's good reason for your fear. The crucial thing is not whether you're afraid (you're bound to be), but whether you learn to act anyway.

This chapter will explore some of the key issues that emerge when you make the commitment to heal. You will examine the nature of your fears and develop resources to work with them. You will be asked to identify the things you stand to gain—and lose—as you realize your commitment to heal. You'll learn about the concept of willingness and explore the role courage plays in your life. And you'll be asked to dream again—to consider what your life might be like if the trauma of sexual abuse were behind you. The chapter includes a mask-making project that can help you create a personal healing symbol.

PREPARING FOR CHANGE

Although healing ultimately brings a better life, it also threatens to permanently alter life as you've known it. Your relationships, your position in the world, even your sense of identity may change. Coping patterns that have served you for a lifetime will be called into question. When you make the commitment to heal, you risk losing much of what is familiar. As a result, one part of you may want to heal while another resists change.

As you contemplate your commitment to the healing process, it's a good idea to look at the changes you may face. Take the next few minutes to think about parts of your life that may change as you heal. Then fill out the following; starting with whatever areas seem most important to you.

If I stick with my commitment to heal, the following things will probably change:

Inside myself (feelings, attitudes, beliefs, self-image):

- _____
- _____
- _____
- _____
- _____
- _____
- _____

In my work:

- _____
- _____
- _____
- _____
- _____

In my lifestyle (habits, patterns, leisure-time activities, types of friends):

- _____
- _____
- _____
- _____
- _____
- _____

With my partner:

- _____
- _____
- _____
- _____
- _____
- _____

With my children:

- _____
- _____
- _____
- _____
- _____

With my family:

- _____
- _____
- _____
- _____
- _____

In my other relationships:

- _____
- _____
- _____
- _____
- _____

Other things that might change:

- _____

- _____

- _____

- _____

- _____

Look over the lists you just made. Put a **check mark** (√) next to those things that you *want* to change. Put **two checks** (√√) next to those things you're not sure you want to change. **Circle** those things that you would consider losses.

The fact that there are losses may be surprising to you. Many of us think only about the things we stand to gain from healing. We don't stop to acknowledge the things we'll have to give up. Yet every time we let go of something familiar, even if it's unhealthy or painful, there is a loss. Looking at the things you stand to lose can help you understand your fears and develop a more patient attitude toward yourself. The following exercise will help you name those losses.

Quickly, without thinking too much about what you're going to write, fill in the following sentence as many times as you can:

If I healed, I'd have to give up   *people feeling sorry for me / blaming my parents for all my problems / not applying myself at work / always being the strong one.*

If I healed, I'd have to give up _____

_____

If I healed, I'd have to give up _____

_____

If I healed, I'd have to give up _____

_____

If I healed, I'd have to give up _____

_____

If I healed, I'd have to give up _____

_____

If I healed, I'd have to give up _____

_____

If I healed, I'd have to give up _____

_____

If I healed, I'd have to give up _____

_____

Look back over your answers, and then complete the following:

What surprised me about my responses? _____

_____

_____

_____

What am I the most afraid to give up? Why? _____

_____

_____

_____

What seemed easiest to give up? Why? _____

_____

_____

_____

What specific fears are holding me back at this time? _____

_____

_____

_____

How are my fears affecting my commitment to the healing process? _____

_____

_____

_____

FACING AN UNCERTAIN FUTURE

In "Coping" (page 144), you learned that every behavior pattern satisfies a need, and that in order to free yourself from a destructive pattern you have to find a healthier way to meet that need. A frightening limbo exists when you give up an old behavior and haven't yet replaced it with a new one. That in-between time is terrifying. You have to face the unknown, step out onto shaky ground, and repeatedly choose paths you've never taken before. If I allow myself to feel vulnerable, won't the people around me think I'm weak? If I leave my abusive partner, will anyone ever love me again?

None of us are experts at dealing with change, yet our whole society is undergoing rapid shifts and transitions. Learning to deal successfully with change is essential for everyone, not just survivors of child sexual abuse. Those of us who have survived abuse, in fact, often have a head start in developing these skills. When we were growing up, we had to face fear, deal with uncertainty and stress, and adapt to changing conditions.

All of us have developed strategies for dealing with uncertainty and change, whether we're consciously aware of them or not. Some of these strategies may work for us; others have elements we may want to change. The following questions will help you assess the ways you currently deal with periods of limbo:

When I face uncertainty, I feel _____

_____

_____

When I don't know what to do, I _____

_____

_____

When I face the unknown, I expect _____

_____

_____

When I face the unknown, I usually cope with it by _____

_____

_____

When I face the unknown, I wish that I could _____

_____

_____

_____

The time I was most successful in handling the unknown was when _____

_____

_____

_____

_____

In that circumstance, I _____

_____

_____

_____

_____

I felt successful in that situation because I _____

_____

_____

_____

_____

I was able to respond that way because _____

_____

_____

_____

_____

To duplicate that success today, I'd have to _____

_____

_____

_____

_____

Things to Think About:

- What did I learn about the ways I deal with fear and uncertainty? What, if anything, would I like to do differently?

- Am I satisfied with my strategies for integrating change in my life? Why or why not? What, if anything, would I like to do differently?

- How does the way I handle fear and uncertainty influence my feelings about the healing process?

WILLINGNESS

The decision to heal is a moment-by-moment choice. You take one small step forward, you commit to one particular action, and then you take a second step. By saying yes in the moment, to the immediate task at hand, you gradually build your commitment to heal: "Yes, I'll go to therapy today." "This morning I will call a friend."

If you see yourself at the center of your own healing process, able to make decisions and choices about what happens to you, it's easier to make the commitment to heal. Knowing that you're in control, that you won't be forced to do anything against your will, is crucial to feeling safe as you heal. When you are certain that your "no" will be respected, you gain the freedom to say "yes." Willingness is that yes.

JoAnn Loulan, a noted sex therapist and author, introduced the concept of willingness when she created a new model for female sexual response.* Loulan exploded the myth that you have to be physically aroused to have sex. She said you could choose to have sex for many reasons: because you want to be close to your partner, because you want to work through sexual issues, because you think you'll enjoy it once you start. According to Loulan, you don't have to be physically aroused to begin sexual activity—you simply have to be willing to begin.

We wrote about the concept of willingness in *The Courage to Heal* because it seemed so important for survivors struggling with sexual issues. More recently I've realized that it can help survivors in other arenas as well. This is true for men as well as women.

Willingness is the key to making informed choices as you heal. If you're in the early stages of the healing process, you may be too inundated with memories and feelings to pace your healing in any way. But when the emergency stage ends and you emerge from that initial period of crisis, you'll be able to take breaks. You'll be able to think of other things. You'll start making choices about healing.

Ultimately you'll be able to say to yourself, "Am I willing to go one step further in trusting this person? Am I willing to be condemned and blamed if I confront my family? Am I willing to do one more exercise in this workbook? Am I willing to schedule one thing a day just for fun, for pleasure, just for me? Am I willing to take *this* risk at *this* time? Am I willing to heal?"

The concept of willingness flies in the face of abuse. In fact it is the opposite of abuse. When you were abused, you were powerless to make any kind of real choice. Now you can make choices. Reliving painful feelings and taking terrifying risks are part of the healing process. But willingness lets you ask yourself, "Is this the right time? Am I willing to go through this now? Do I want to open up this memory and see what's there, or do I want to shut down? Do I want to fall back on my old ways of coping, or am I willing to try something new?"

Willingness is not a static thing. It's a decision made in the moment, by checking in with yourself and paying attention to what you really feel. Over and over again, many times a day, you can ask yourself, "Am I willing . . . ?" Sometimes the answer will be yes. Other times it will be no.

---

* JoAnn Loulan, *Lesbian Sex*. San Francisco: Spinster's / Aunt Lute, 1984.

One day you may be willing to be vulnerable, even though it terrifies you, and the next day you may not. That's okay. You get to pace yourself, to trust your inner judgment. You get to say yes and you get to say no. (For more on setting limits and making choices, see "Create Ground Rules" on page 22 and "Learning to Say No" on page 290.)

Take a few minutes to think about what you've just read. Then complete the following sentences:

I think that willingness is _____

_____

_____

_____

_____

I am willing to _____

_____

_____

_____

_____

I am not willing to _____

_____

_____

_____

_____

ABOUT COURAGE

I love working with survivors because I'm inspired by their courage. Yet many survivors insist they're not courageous: "If I were courageous, I would have been able to stop the abuse." "If I were courageous, I wouldn't have doubts and uncertainties." "If I were courageous, I wouldn't be scared."

This is more likely to be true for women than for men. In our culture, men are encouraged and expected to be courageous. Women are more conditioned to be hesitant and frightened, to wait for rescue from a courageous man. Both of these roles are limiting—in one you deny your courage; in the other, you deny your fear.

Recently I attended a workshop on courage with Lauren Crux, a wise therapist from Santa Cruz, California. She got right to the heart of the matter. "Most people have got it mixed up. You don't start with courage and then face fear. You become courageous *because* you face your fear."

My experience of healing is that I have to face one void after another. I identify a pattern I want to change. I start to change it. Suddenly everything known and familiar drops away, and I'm totally terrified. I am standing at the edge of the known world, and there's no guarantee of a safety net if I jump off the cliff. I don't know what's on the other side. I'm certain I can't move because the fear is so great, but I reach out for the reassurance of the people who love and support me, and I jump anyway. I've done this over and over again. In doing so, I've gained courage.

Our concept of courage is apt to come from comic books, mythology, cultural conditioning, and folk tales. Paul Bunyan and Abraham Lincoln are the kinds of heroes we learned about in school. As a result, you may find it hard to recognize the kind of everyday courage it takes to heal.

Take a few minutes to explore your current attitudes about courage. Begin by completing the following:

Courage is _____

_____

_____

_____

My personal heroes and heroines are: _____

_____

_____

_____

I find these people courageous because they _____

_____

_____

_____

My concepts of courage have come from _____

_____

_____

_____

Am I satisfied with my concept of courage? ____ yes ____ no ____ I don't know

Does it leave room for me to be courageous? ____ yes ____ no

Why or why not? _____

_____

_____

_____

What would it take for me to have the same kind of courage as my heroes?

_____

_____

_____

_____

All of us have had moments of courage. This is true for everyone, but it is particularly true of abuse survivors. The fact that you were abused and managed to survive is in and of itself a tremendous act of courage. You could have given up and died, and you didn't. You decided to live. That was an act of defiance and courage.

Think about times you've been courageous. Then complete the following:

When I was a growing up, I was courageous when I _____

_____

_____

_____

_____

As an adult, I showed courage when I _____

_____

_____

_____

_____

I am courageous now because I _____

_____

_____

_____

_____

I don't see myself as courageous because _____

_____

_____

_____

_____

(If you don't see yourself as courageous) In order to become courageous, I'd have to _____

_____

_____

_____

_____

_____

Once I had courage, I would _____

_____

_____

_____

_____

Things to Think About:

• Was there a particular time in my life when I gained or lost courage? What happened?

• What kind of courage does it take to heal from child sexual abuse? Do I have that kind of courage? If not, how can I get it?

ACTIVITY: DESIGNING A WARRIOR MASK

When facing fear and uncertainty, it helps to develop a warrior spirit. A warrior faces the unknown and moves proudly and confidently into it. Warriors feel fear and act anyway. A warrior has pride, discipline, perseverance, and courage. One of the things that helps warriors feel courageous is a personal totem, or symbol, that reminds them of their own strength. A warrior mask is a powerful totem.

The following directions will teach you how to make your own warrior mask. The process involves covering your face with strips of wet gauze, which harden into a mask that you then remove. The mask is a permanent impression of your features. Once it has hardened, it can be decorated and painted. You can hang it on the wall or even wear it sometimes, as a reminder of your own courageous spirit.

A WORD OF WARNING

While for some survivors the process of mask-making can be empowering and fun, for others it can be a frightening experience. The physical sensation of the mask hardening and the awareness of your eyes, nose, or mouth being covered can make you feel claustrophobic. If you've ever been traumatized by having your face covered or if you tend toward claustrophobia, this isn't the activity for you. If you decide it's too scary or that you don't feel safe about doing it, that's okay. Don't push yourself. If you're not sure you want to do it, talk it over in therapy or with a friend. You can practice first on your hand (in a non-hairy place), so you know what the tightening feels like. If you decide to try it, *don't do it alone*. And make sure you read through the directions carefully, using the safety guidelines below.

SAFETY GUIDELINES

There are some things you can do to increase your sense of safety during the mask-making process. First of all, talk about the sensations you feel as the gauze is being applied or as it tightens. Have your partner talk to you and reassure you the whole time the strips are being laid down, saying things like, "Now I'm going to put a strip over your eyes. Now I'm going to work on your mouth. Now I'm going to get some water. I'll be right back." Your partner should remind you regularly to breathe deeply. You might want someone to hold your hand, or for your partner to touch you reassuringly on the shoulders or back of the head. (Tell your partner what you think you'd like ahead of time.) Keep your pad and pen accessible so you can write messages once your mouth is covered: "It's getting tight." "I have to cough." "It feels funny." "Turn up the music." "This is weird. I'm scared." If you continue to feel uncomfortable, allow yourself to stop. Remember, your partner can peel off the unfinished mask at any point. (Develop a hand signal for stopping that you can use once your mouth is covered, in case you want out and can't talk).

MAKING THE MASK

To make your mask, you'll need to get a roll of the specially treated gauze that's used to make casts for broken bones. Use plaster casting material rather than fiberglass. You should be able to locate a roll through a doctor, nurse, or hospital supply company. You'll also need a bowl of warm water, Vaseline, scissors, tempera paints, a smock or old clothes, a large towel, and someone to help you. This is a project you should undertake with a friend, another survivor, or with your survivors group.

Before you begin: Lay sheets of newspaper or a dropcloth on the floor. Set a comfortable chair on top of it, but choose an old chair that can get wet and be wiped off. If you want, pick out some music you'd like to listen to as the mask hardens. Or find a book or story you'd like your partner to read to you. Think about what you need in order to stay grounded and relaxed while the mask is hardening (30 to 45 minutes). It helps to have something to concentrate on besides the strange sensations on your face. (Remember, you won't be able to see or talk during that period of time.)

If there's a part of your face that you think will be harder to have covered, tell your partner so he or she can work on that part last. (If you don't want your mouth covered entirely, you can make your mask around it; the mask will have an open mouth.)

What you do: Put on a sweatshirt or other old garment. (Plaster will be dripping all over both of you.) Take off any earrings or other jewelry. If you wear contact lenses, remove them. Pull your hair back so it is off your face. You might want to put it in a tight shower cap, a bathing cap, or a bandanna. Plaster sticks to hair, so it's important that your hair is totally hidden. (Men with beards or moustaches should make shortened masks that don't cover facial hair.) Sit in the chair, keeping a towel in your lap for wiping the drips that will run down your face or onto your neck. Have your pad and pen ready next to you so you can reach them easily. Then spread a thick coating of Vaseline all over your face. Pay special attention to your eyebrows and eyelashes; make sure they're fully coated. (Do this with your eyes closed.) Make sure your nose is clear and that you can breathe comfortably while your mouth is closed. (If your nose or sinuses are clogged, do this another day.)

What your partner does: Set up a bowl of warm water next to the chair. Cut the roll of gauze into strips no more than half an inch wide. Most of them should be equal to the width of your face, from ear to ear. Allow room for the swell of your nose and the roundness of your cheeks. You'll also want some strips that are thinner (quarter of an inch wide) and shorter for the fine-featured areas of your face. Keep the scissors available for cutting additional strips as needed.

Have your partner wet each strip, squeeze it out slightly, and lay it across your face, starting with your forehead and working down to your chin. Start with a single area and work until there's a thickness of four or five strips. Overlap them slightly as they're laid down. Strips can be laid horizontally or vertically, following the contours of your face. Strips should be pressed close to the bones and hollows of your face, particularly around the eyebrows, nose, cheeks and mouth. You can help in this by periodically using your fingertips to press the cast in firmly around your eye sockets and nose. This adds to the definition of the mask, and it's generally more comfortable to press around your eyes yourself than to have your partner do it. When your partner gets to your nose, leave the nostrils clear for breathing. Continue adding strips, one layer at a time, until they reach the bottom of the chin (don't do the area underneath the chin). This casting process usually takes thirty to forty-five minutes.

Once the initial casting is complete, you can move if you want to be more comfortable (lie on a couch or the floor, or recline in some way). You will not be able to talk or see while the mask is hardening. Your partner should stay with you, reading to you, holding your hand, or otherwise entertaining you and keeping your interest directed outward. As the mask hardens, it will tighten and feel itchy, and you'll want to move your facial muscles around. Try not to in the beginning. Eventually, moving your face inside the mask will loosen the hardening plaster from your skin. This will tell you that the mask is hard enough to pull off (it usually takes half an hour). On the outside, it should sound hard when tapped with a finger. Remember that it all wasn't cast at the same time, so the plaster on your forehead or around your nose may be ready before the area around your chin. When the mask is no longer wet to the touch (it will still feel somewhat tacky) and when you can pull on the edges without their caving in, it's time to remove the mask. You can do it alone, or you can have your partner do it with you. Pull on either side to loosen the mask from your face. Go slowly to see if there are any places where it is sticking. If it is stuck, peeling it off can hurt—like pulling off adhesive tape or a bandage. Once the mask is off, wash your face and eyes immediately with warm water and a washcloth to remove the Vaseline and any remnants of plaster. Set the mask down in a safe place and allow it to harden completely overnight. When it is dry, paint the mask. You can decorate it with ribbons, feathers, shells, or pieces of hair. Be creative. Express your own warrior spirit.

EXPANDING YOUR CAPACITY FOR HOPE

In order to make the commitment to heal, you have to believe that healing is possible. You need to believe that there is "a light at the end of the tunnel," that others have made it before you, and that you too can succeed. You need to have hope. Hope is a powerful motivator and a great antidote to fear. Unfortunately, most survivors find it difficult to hope.

When you were growing up, your hopes were smashed again and again. You thought, "If only I get straight A's, then Dad won't be so angry all the time." "If only I clean up the blood on the floor and take care of all my brothers and sisters, then I'll turn into a good girl and Poppa will stop touching me funny." Or "My coach doesn't really mean it. If I just do better at practices, he'll stop." As a child daring to hope, you were crushed when things didn't change. Hope seemed like a cruel sham. Out of a need for sheer survival, you set hope aside.

Think about the times your hopes were crushed while you were growing up. Then complete the following:

1. When I was growing up, I hoped that _____

_____

_____

_____

What happened instead? _____

_____

_____

_____

When my hopes were shattered, I _____

_____

_____

_____

2. When I was growing up, I hoped that_____

_____

_____

_____

What happened instead? _____

_____

_____

_____

When my hopes were shattered, I _____

_____

_____

_____

3. When I was growing up, I hoped that _____

_____

_____

_____

What happened instead? _____

_____

_____

_____

When my hopes were shattered, I _____

_____

_____

_____

PUTTING HOPE ASIDE: A WRITING EXERCISE

Many children keep hoping things will change, even when they're in a hopeless situation. Children hope for change until it is crushed out of them. Think about your childhood. Was there a time when you set hope aside? Try to remember that time. What led up to it? How did you feel? How were things different afterward?

Reread the guidelines for freewriting on page 11. Then set a timer or an alarm clock for twenty minutes, and write about the loss of hope in your childhood.

When you're done writing, take a few minutes to complete the following:

What feelings came up for me as I wrote? _____

_____

_____

_____

How do I feel when I read over my writing now? _____

_____

_____

_____

Was life easier or harder for me after I stopped hoping? Why? _____

_____

_____

_____

What's changed in my life since the incident I wrote about? _____

_____

_____

_____

_____

Are my circumstances different enough that it might be worth trying to hope again? Why or why not?

_____

_____

_____

_____

MY HOPES TODAY

Even though you may have set aside hope when you were young, consider feeling hopeful today. You are an adult now. Things are not the same as they were when you were growing up. What would happen if you allowed yourself to hope again? What's the best thing that could happen? The worst? How might hope be different today?

When I think about hope, I feel _____

_____

_____

If I had hope, the worst thing that could happen would be _____

_____

_____

_____

If I had hope, the best thing that could happen would be _____

_____

_____

_____

_____

If you were to allow yourself to hope, what would you hope for? Make a list. Don't censor as you go. Include everything.

- _____

- _____

- _____

- _____

- _____

- _____

- _____

- _____

- _____

- _____

- _____

- _____

- _____

- _____

- _____

- _____

- _____
- _____
- _____
- _____

There are two kinds of hopes—realistic hopes and unrealistic hopes. Realistic hopes are based on knowledge. You know that other survivors have made it through the emergency stage of healing, so you believe that you can too. You know that you've been able to trust your counselor in small ways, so you hope that you can trust him or her with bigger things. You know that you and your lover are getting closer all the time, so you hope that you will get even more intimate.

Unrealistic hopes are based on fantasy. There is little likelihood that they will come to pass. You hope to win the lottery. You hope that your abuser will apologize and take full responsibility for hurting you. You hope that you can go to one weekend workshop and be healed. You quit drinking and then hope that you can have "just one more" beer.

Look over your list of hopes. **Circle** the items on your list that are realistic. **Cross out** those that are based on fantasy. Then answer the following questions:

Was I able to write down a list of hopes? _____ yes _____ no _____ not yet

How did it feel to commit my hopes to paper? _____

_____

_____

_____

Were most of my hopes realistic or unrealistic? _____

What does that tell me? _____

_____

_____

_____

_____

If I could hope for one thing that I knew would come true, what would it be?

_____

_____

_____

_____

What small thing could I hope for right now? _____

_____

_____

_____

_____

MAKING HOPES COME TRUE

Many of us were raised to believe that once you hope for something, you just sit back and wait for it to magically happen. Hope doesn't work that way. You have to do something to realize your dreams. Hope motivates you, enables you to take risks, and gives you the impetus to heal, but it doesn't do the work for you.

Go back to your list of hopes on page 197. Copy down the realistic ones in the spaces below. Then write down at least one thing you can do to realize each hope. In doing so, you will be transforming your hopes into goals. You will be shaping your commitment to heal.

Hope / Goal #1 _____

What I can do to make it happen: _____

_____

_____

_____

_____

Hope / Goal #2 _____

What I can do to make it happen: _____

_____

_____

_____

_____

Hope / Goal #3 _____

What I can do to make it happen: _____

_____

_____

_____

_____

Hope / Goal #4 _____

What I can do to make it happen: _____

_____

_____

_____

_____

Hope / Goal #5 _____

What I can do to make it happen: _____

_____

_____

_____

_____

Hope / Goal #6 _____

What I can do to make it happen: _____

_____

_____

_____

_____

REFLECTIONS: THE DECISION TO HEAL

The decision to heal is one you will have to make over and over again as you navigate the frightening, unpredictable, and empowering process of healing. This chapter has introduced you to five key elements in making and renewing that commitment: willingness, accepting change, recognizing your courage, daring to hope, and working to meet your goals.

Here are some questions to help you assess your present feelings, goals, and needs around making the commitment to heal:

- What feelings did I have as I worked through this chapter?

- What am I feeling right now? What sensations am I experiencing in my body?

- How old did I feel as I worked through the chapter? How old do I feel right now?

- What was hard for me in this chapter? What was confusing? What didn't I understand?

- What did I learn? What commitments have I made? What steps have I taken?

- What did I do that I'm proud of?

- What's still unsettled for me? What, if anything, do I want to come back to or follow up on?

- What do I need to do to take care of myself right now?

REMEMBERING

One of the most effective coping mechanisms available to children who have been abused is to block out the memories, to forget the abuse. Some survivors have always remembered what happened to them, but many adults have completely forgotten the experience. Then, twenty, thirty, or forty years later, something happens and they suddenly start to remember. You wake up one day and say, "I was sexually abused." You begin seeing images of your stepfather in your room at night, or you have vivid dreams of your brother on top of you. When you've forgotten the abuse for years, it's easy to discount these memories—Where are they coming from? What do they mean? When will they stop?—or even to question your own sanity. But blocking out abuse, and then remembering it, is a survival skill that makes sense.

When you were young, you couldn't afford to remember what was happening to you. As an eight-year-old, you couldn't sit across the table from your stepfather over Cheerios first thing in the morning if you remembered what happened the night before. *You forgot in order to live through it.*

Once repressed, memories can reemerge at any time. Life transitions—childbirth, a commitment to an intimate relationship, the death of a parent, retirement, menopause, aging, divorce, losses of any kind—frequently trigger early memories of sexual abuse. So does sobriety. When you quit drinking or using drugs, the first thing to emerge can be memories of abuse. Medical treatment—a trip to the dentist, an exam by the gynecologist or urologist, surgery or other intrusive medical procedures—can also jar buried images and feelings. Adult experiences of victimization—a robbery, an assault, a rape—often stir up memories of earlier abuse. Parents sometimes remember their own abuse when their child is abused, or when that child reaches the age they were when the abuse first took place. Survivors remember while making love, exercising, or getting massages. Or when they see a show on TV, hear a friend's story, or read a book like this one.

If you've always remembered the abuse, the memories you recover may have more to do with feelings than with specific events. Frequently survivors can rattle off the details of their abuse like items on a grocery list, but they are disconnected from the way the abuse really felt. In those instances, remembering involves reconnecting with those feelings.

Remembering is an ongoing process of discovery. It involves going back and excavating the early years of your life—piecing together and reinterpreting things you already know, starting to connect feelings with images you've always had, experiencing unfamiliar body sensations. At times you may experience flashbacks in which you relive aspects of the abuse or reexperience the feelings you had at the time—terror, extreme physical pain, tremendous isolation. These experiences can be disruptive and terrifying. You may respond with shock, horror, or disbelief. You may feel panicky and suicidal, or relieved to finally know the truth about your life.

The exercises in this chapter are designed to help you learn more about your childhood. Whether you have clear memories, sketchy memories, or just a funny feeling, this chapter will help you come to terms with what you do and don't remember. You'll be given information about the process of remembering, asked to broaden your idea of what a memory is, and given the opportunity to reexamine your experience from a new perspective. And finally you'll be encouraged to develop a sense of respect for your own internal process—what you remember, how you remember, if and when you remember.

Working through the exercises in this chapter is likely to stir up new memories and feelings. Although they are a natural part of the healing process, these feelings and memories can be overwhelming. Before you go any further, take a few minutes to review the lists you made in the Survival Skills section of this workbook. (If you haven't filled out those pages, go back and fill them out now before you go on with this chapter.) Remind yourself that there are people you can call, ways to make yourself safe, options if you start to panic. Your list of "Things I Can Do When I'm Overwhelmed" (page 68) can give you step-by-step guidance if you start to have new memories or flashbacks.

WHAT IS A MEMORY?

Many survivors call me to ask permission to come to workshops because they're afraid they don't qualify. They don't have clear memories of their abuse, only an icky feeling or intuition. Bells ring when they read about abuse or talk to other survivors, but they don't have visual pictures of what took place. They despair of ever healing because they don't know exactly what happened.

Whenever I get these kinds of calls, I reassure the survivor. I say, "Yes, come. Many adults don't remember what happened to them. Come anyway. You deserve to heal whether you have clear memories or not. In fact, you can heal from the effects of abuse even if you never remember."

Survivors are sometimes so distressed by their lack of memories that I wish I could offer them videocassettes marked "your sexual abuse" that could be slipped into the VCR and played from beginning to end, showing them clearly what happened to them. Then they would have proof. There would be no more doubts.

Yet there is a lot more to memory than crisp snapshots, movie images, or Kodak slides of incidents: your stepfather reaching for a belt, your brother pulling down your pants, the minister's penis. Visual memory is just one kind of memory. You may never get visual pictures of your abuse because you never saw anything. Your face was pushed down into the upholstery. The abuse took place in the dark, so there was nothing to see. You were so scared you closed your eyes. There are no pictures to remember.

In our vision-oriented culture, it's hard to validate other forms of memory, but the fact is we store memories with all of our senses. Smells, sounds, tastes, and textures can all evoke powerful memories. So can physical touch. Memories are stored in the body, and often, when we are touched in a particular way, memories come pouring back.

The process of remembering is like putting a jigsaw puzzle together. When you expand your concept of memory, you find that your memories expand too: You were happy and cheerful in fifth grade, but by the time sixth grade rolled around, you were depressed and suicidal. That's a memory—something happened to you that summer. Whenever your partner touches you in a particular way, your body goes numb and you start to panic. You feel as if you're on the ceiling, looking down. You feel like a scared child. Those are memories. You get violently nauseated whenever you smell bourbon on someone's breath. You have an anxiety attack whenever you go back to your hometown. You hate it when your father tries to hug you. You have nightmares and can't sleep without a light on. You check under the bed every night to make sure a monster or a rapist isn't there. When you get a massage, you start sobbing uncontrollably.

These are all memories. They aren't snapshots. They aren't movies. They won't stand up in court, but they count. And when you start to piece them together, you end up with a substantial body of evidence that will help you believe the abuse really happened. If you start with what you do know and go from there, you frequently will find the validation you seek.

PIECING TOGETHER THE PUZZLE

You can use the guidelines below to help you piece together your memories. By writing down the clues you already have, you will gain valuable information and make new connections.

Read through the examples that follow and then begin to fill in the pieces of memory that you have, at your own pace. Be as complete as possible, but go slowly. Don't expect to fill out these lists in one sitting. Reflecting on just one or two clues may be enough. As you remember other incidents or feelings, you can always come back and add to what you've written.

Respond to as many of the categories listed below as possible.

• Pieces of memory:

I remember knowing more about sex than the other kids. When anyone wanted to know about "doing it," they came and asked me.

I remember hiding in the basement while my uncle beat my cousin with a belt.

_____

_____

_____

_____

_____

_____

_____

_____

_____

- Acknowledged family history:

  Everyone in the family always laughed and said that Jim and I were kissing cousins.
  I was taken to the doctor for a vaginal infection when I was eight.
  My grandfather used to inspect all the girls' breasts when they reached puberty.

_____

_____

_____

_____

_____

_____

_____

- Sensory clues:

  I detest the smell of Chanel No. 5.
  Whenever I hear someone opening my door at night, I freeze.
  Whenever I see an ambulance or hear a siren, I get shaky all over.

_____

_____

_____

_____

_____

_____

_____

_____

_____

- Body memories:
  I often feel like I'm not in my body.
  When I get aroused, I feel immediately disgusted.
  When I have an orgasm, I always start sobbing.
  When I make love, I can't stand my partner's weight on top of me.

_____

_____

_____

_____

_____

_____

_____

_____

_____

- Creepy feelings:

  When I see a father and his son walking down the street, I'm sure he's abusing that kid. Every time I read about incest, waves of nausea wash over me.

_____

_____

_____

_____

_____

_____

_____

_____

- Gaps in your memory:

  I don't remember anything between the ages of eight and fifteen. I don't remember ever being a child.

_____

_____

_____

_____

_____

_____

_____

_____

_____

Whenever you add new items to these lists, take a few minutes to answer the following questions:

Were there things I didn't consider memories that I can now recognize as memories? What were they?

_____

_____

_____

_____

What patterns, if any, emerged in the things I wrote down? _____

_____

_____

_____

_____

Did one memory lead to others? _____ If so, where did the associations lead?

_____

_____

_____

_____

_____

When put together, do the pieces of memory give me more of an idea about what happened to me?   _____ yes   _____ no   _____ I'm not sure

If yes, what have I learned? _____

_____

_____

_____

_____

How do I feel about this new information? _____

_____

_____

_____

_____

Is there someone I could share these memories with? If so, who? _____

_____

_____

IF YOU DON'T REMEMBER

There are many reasons survivors experience amnesia. The severity and duration of the abuse, the age at which it happened, the conditions surrounding the abuse, and the way the abuse was handled can all influence your ability to remember. Depending on these and other factors, you may or may not ever have clear memories of what happened to you.

If you don't remember clearly and want to, this can be extremely frustrating. It's natural to want undeniable facts. Survivors who don't remember are often jealous of those who do. Yet the reverse can also be true. In one workshop, several survivors were lamenting about not having memories. Finally, after they had spoken up several times, another survivor burst out in anger: "You should be glad you don't remember! I'm having flashbacks all the time. My life feels out of control. I hate it. I think you're the lucky ones."

The bottom line is that you can't control what you do or don't remember. You can try exercises like the ones below, and they may give you additional clues or pieces of information, but they won't necessarily give you the kind of "proof" you seek. Try them anyway, and bear in mind the most important fact—that you can heal whether you remember clearly or not.

WHAT AM I AFRAID OF?

One factor that can influence remembering is readiness. If you don't have support in your life, aren't ready to handle the information, or are already overwhelmed, not remembering may be a way you protect yourself.

Our defenses perform an important function. Instead of tearing them down, it's wise to respect them and learn to work with them. By taking a look at the reasons you're afraid to remember, you may learn what you're protecting yourself from.

Fill in the following sentences without thinking about what you're going to write. Write the first thing that comes into your mind, even if it doesn't make sense. Don't censor yourself.

If I remember the abuse,	*I'll die.*
If I remember the abuse,	*my Dad will come and get me.*
If I remember the abuse,	*I'll end up in the hospital.*
If I remember the abuse,	*I'll kill myself.*
If I remember the abuse,	*I'll lose my family.*
If I remember the abuse,	*it will mean my Mom was bad.*

If I remember the abuse, _____

_____

_____

_____

If I remember the abuse, _____

_____

_____

_____

If I remember the abuse, _____

_____

_____

_____

If I remember the abuse, _____

_____

_____

_____

If I remember the abuse, _____

_____

_____

_____

Things to Think About:

- What am I protecting myself from? What am I afraid of?

- Which of my fears are realistic?

- Can I make peace with the fact that I may never clearly remember the abuse? Why or why not?

ACTIVITY: PICTURING WHAT I DON'T KNOW

You can sometimes get information if you take a more indirect approach. Reread the directions for making a collage on page 13. Make a collage of "things you don't know yet." As you start to leaf through the magazines, ask yourself, "What can't I remember? What can't I talk about?" Without thinking or questioning your decisions, cut out words, phrases, or pictures. Don't try to figure out why you're selecting particular things. Don't worry about what it means. Don't question whether your choices make sense. Suspend your judgment. Let your unconscious mind make the choices. Keep asking yourself, "What can't I remember? What can't I talk about?" Cut things out until you feel finished. Then arrange the things you've cut out on a large piece of paper. Glue them down in whatever pattern feels right. Then go back and answer the questions on page 13.

WHAT HAPPENED TO YOU: A WRITING EXERCISE

This powerful exercise was developed by Ellen Bass in the I Never Told Anyone workshops. We put it in *The Courage to Heal* and have gotten such positive feedback about it that I've decided to include it here. If you've already done the exercise, consider doing it a second time. Often new feelings and memories emerge each time you try it.

Many survivors have found it very difficult to tell people that they were sexually abused. When they do tell, it is often in very generalized terms: "I was molested by my brother." "I was raped when I was ten." Rarely do you share the details, partly because it's hard to tell even the general facts and partly because you want to spare the listeners. You don't want to impose.

But the tight statement "My stepfather abused me" is not the way you live with abuse, not the way you deal with flashbacks. That's not indicative of the creepy feelings you get when something triggers your memory. What you remember is the way the light fell on the stairway, the pajamas you were wearing, the smell of liquor on his breath, the feel of the gravel between your shoulder blades when you were thrown down, the terrifying chuckle, the sound of the TV downstairs. When you write, include as many of these sensory details as you can.

If your abuse covers too much time and too many abusers to write it all in half an hour, just write what you can. Don't worry about which experience to start with. Begin with what feels most accessible or what you feel you most need to deal with. This is an exercise you can do over and over again.

If you don't remember what happened to you, write about what you do remember. Or write about whatever you can remember that comes closest to sexual abuse—the first time you felt ashamed or humiliated, for instance. Re-create the context in which the abuse happened, even if you don't remember the specifics of the abuse yet. Describe where you lived as a child. What was going on in your family, in your neighborhood, in your life? Start with what you have. When you utilize that fully, you usually get more.

If you come to things that feel too difficult to say, too painful or humiliating, try to write them anyway. You don't have to share them with anyone if you don't want to, but in order to heal you must be honest with yourself. If there's something you feel you absolutely can't write, then at least write that there's something you can't or won't write. That way you leave a marker for yourself, you acknowledge that there's a difficult place.

If you go off on tangents, don't pull yourself back too abruptly. Sometimes what may look irrelevant leads us to something more essential. Although you want to stay with the subject, do so with loose reins.

There is no one right way to do this exercise. Your writing may be linear, telling your story in chronological order. It may be a wash of feelings and sensations. Or it may be vague, weaving together scattered bits and pieces. As with all the writing exercises, try not to judge or censor. Don't feel that you should conform to any standard and don't compare your writing with others. This is an opportunity to uncover and heal, not to perform or to meet anyone's expectations—not even your own.*

Reread the guidelines for freewriting on page 11. Then set a timer or alarm clock for twenty minutes, and write about your experience being sexually abused as a child.

---

* From *The Courage to Heal: A Guide for Women Survivors of Child Sexual Abuse.* New York: Harper and Row, 1988. Thanks to Ellen Bass for the use of this exercise.

REFLECTIONS: REMEMBERING

Many children block out memories of being sexually abused. Those memories can stay repressed for years. For many adult survivors, one of the most painful, terrifying parts of the healing process is remembering the feelings, sensations, and experiences they had when they were being abused.

Remembering is like assembling a puzzle; images, recollections, and sense and body memories are pieced together to create a picture of the past. Not all survivors will remember in the same way, but all survivors can recover from the long-term effects of abuse. Even if your memories are vague or unclear, you can still heal.

The process of recovering memories can be overwhelming. It's crucial that you don't relive the memories in isolation. You need to reach out and talk to someone who will listen, hear the worst, and believe you. You need to take care of yourself, and to have others take care of you. You are engaged in agonizing, essential work. You deserve support.

Here are some questions to help you assess your present feelings, goals, and needs around the issue of remembering:

- What feelings did I have as I worked through this chapter?

- What am I feeling right now? What sensations am I experiencing in my body?

- How old did I feel as I worked through the chapter? How old do I feel right now?

- What was hard for me in this chapter? What was confusing? What didn't I understand?

- What did I learn? What commitments have I made? What steps have I taken?

- What did I do that I'm proud of?

- What's still unsettled for me? What, if anything, do I want to come back to or follow up on?

- What do I need to do to take care of myself right now?

BELIEVING IT HAPPENED

It is often difficult for survivors to maintain the belief that they were abused. One day you may be certain that you were abused, and the next you may find yourself doubting whether it really happened or questioning whether your experience counts as abuse. This process of doubt and reaffirmation, doubt and reaffirmation, is a natural part of the healing process. If you have doubts, it doesn't mean you weren't abused. It just means you're not yet ready to live with the consistent knowledge that you were abused. Sometimes this process can take years. This seems paradoxical, but there are many reasons survivors struggle to believe the abuse really took place.

To begin with, you may desperately want the abuse to go away. You don't want it to have happened. You don't want to believe that the people who were supposed to care for you could have hurt you so badly. You don't want to deal with the repercussions in adulthood. Or maybe you're just not ready.

If you don't have many memories, you may take that as proof that the abuse didn't really happen. If you do have memories, you may be convinced they're not "the right kind." (See "Remembering," page 204.)

Like many survivors, you may have trouble trusting your own feelings and perceptions. When children are abused, their sense of reality is manipulated. The picture your abuser presented to the world may have been totally at odds with your experience. How could your wonderful, devoted doctor father have tortured you with enemas in the night? How could your mother, a respected civic leader, have forced you to masturbate her?

Your abuser may have brainwashed you or told you directly that you were a liar: "You have a wild imagination. You're crazy. No one would ever believe anything you say." Or you may have experienced torture and atrocities that are difficult to believe. That doesn't mean they didn't happen. It just means we have to stop being naive. We have to broaden our perception of evil.

Not all survivors doubt their abuse. Sometimes the evidence and memories are so clear, there's no room for doubt. (You took your abuser to court. You have siblings who remember. You never forgot anything that happened to you. The abuse was never denied in your family.)

If you already believe that it happened, the next step for you may be believing that it mattered—that the abuse had an impact on your life and that you deserve to do something about it. If you don't think the abuse really affected you, try working through the opening exercises in this chapter, substituting the words, "If I believed it mattered" for "If I believed it happened." If, on the other hand, you consistently believe you were abused and know that it affected you, you might want to skip the exercises in this chapter.

I believe that I was abused _____% of the time. The rest of the time, I _____

_____

_____

_____

_____

I have no doubts about my abuse because _____

_____

_____

_____

_____

I ____ do ____ don't   think the abuse really mattered (counted) because:

_____

_____

_____

I DON'T WANT TO BELIEVE IT

If you're having trouble believing that the abuse really happened, you probably have good reasons. In the preceding chapter you looked at your reasons for not remembering. This time, take a few minutes to examine the reasons you don't want to believe the abuse took place. (It's okay if some of the reasons overlap.)

I don't want to believe it because   *my father really loved me.*
I don't want to believe it because   *I'd want to kill my uncle.*
I don't want to believe it because   *it's just too horrible. Adults don't torture children.*

I don't want to believe it because _____

_____

_____

I don't want to believe it because _____

_____

_____

I don't want to believe it because _____

_____

_____

I don't want to believe it because _____

_____

_____

_____

You may not want to believe the abuse because you think it will inevitably lead to certain actions and conclusions. You might have to shift your relationship with your abuser, make a deeper commitment to heal, or give up your fantasies about your lovely childhood.

If I believed that it happened, I would have to _____

_____

_____

If I believed that it happened, I would have to _____

_____

_____

If I believed that it happened, I would have to _____

_____

_____

If I believed that it happened, I would have to _____

_____

_____

RESEARCH YOUR CHILDHOOD

A little detective work can sometimes help you confirm that the abuse took place. Ultimately the only "proof" you need is your own memories and perceptions, but along the way it can be fruitful and reassuring to research childhood sources of information still available to you. Survivors have talked to relatives, friends of the family, neighbors, and acquaintances and gleaned valuable information and validation. Siblings have been able to corroborate stories and bits of memory. Aunts and uncles have revealed family secrets that have been covered up for years. Neighbors have reported things they saw and heard. Tracing school and medical or psychiatric records has, in some cases, provided tangible evidence.

You may not have access to any information of this kind. You may have cut ties with everyone from your past and have no interest in rekindling them. You may have grown up in another country or in a place you never want to see again. Everyone from your childhood may be dead. You may feel too afraid or ashamed to broach the subject. You might attempt to contact people from your past, only to find no one who's willing to cooperate. Or the abuse may have been covered up so effectively that no one saw or heard anything. In these instances, you will have to rely on your own perceptions and experiences to form the basis of your belief.

Whether or not you choose to do this kind of research is up to you. You may not want to invest the energy. You may not think it's worth it. You may feel confident without doing it. Or you may feel it's essential because there's currently a child at risk for abuse.

I _____ am _____ am not   interested in researching my childhood because

_____

_____

_____

This kind of information-gathering can be particularly effective if you are doing it in conjunction with other survivors. If you are in a support group, for instance, and several of you agree to do this kind of research, you can compare notes and encourage each other.

If you do decide to go back into your past and investigate, do so carefully. Protect yourself. Talking to family members or other people from your past can be explosive. When you tell them about your abuse, you won't be able to control their reactions. If you're considering approaching people from your past, work through the exercises in "Breaking Silence" (page 234) and "Confrontations" (page 340) first, so you'll have a clearer idea of what to expect.

Then ask yourself what steps you can take. Whom can you talk to? Is there anyone who might give you unbiased information about who you were as a child? About your abuser? Are there any records you could trace? Is there anyone in the family who might offer information, either directly or indirectly?

The following questions can help you come up with an information-gathering plan:

What do I hope to find out? _____

_____

_____

_____

Whom will I have to contact? _____

_____

_____

_____

What's my goal in contacting this person? _____

_____

_____

_____

How will I make contact? _____

_____

_____

_____

How much information do I want to reveal about myself and my real purpose?

_____

_____

_____

_____

Once I've established contact, what are the questions I want to ask?

● _____

- _____
- _____
- _____
- _____
- _____
- _____
- _____
- _____
- _____

Once you've developed your plan, keep a file to document your progress. Take notes on phone calls or other contacts. Keep track of whom you've talked to and why. Keep copies of any correspondence. Write down the things you learn. Note things you have to follow up on.

Things to Think About:

- What will I do if I get the information I'm looking for? What if I don't come up with anything?

- Am I ready to have my perceptions validated? Why or why not?

- What do I stand to gain or lose in this process?

REFLECTIONS: BELIEVING IT HAPPENED

It is often hard to maintain the belief that you were sexually abused when you were growing up. It is perfectly normal for your conviction to waver during the early stages of the healing process. Over time, the knowledge that you were abused will solidify and become steadier.

In the meantime, there are a few things you can do to reassure yourself along the way. You can validate and accept your reasons for not remembering, research things that happened in your childhood, and take another look at the way abuse has shaped your life.

Ultimately there is nothing you can do to force yourself to believe that you were abused. If you are still wavering in your belief, try to be patient and gentle with yourself. Give yourself time.

Here are some questions to help you assess your present feelings, goals, and needs around the issue of believing it happened:

• What feelings did I have as I worked through this chapter?

• What am I feeling right now? What sensations am I experiencing in my body?

• How old did I feel as I worked through the chapter? How old do I feel right now?

- What was hard for me in this chapter? What was confusing? What didn't I understand?

- What did I learn? What commitments have I made? What steps have I taken?

- What did I do that I'm proud of?

- What's still unsettled for me? What, if anything, do I want to come back to or follow up on?

- What do I need to do to take care of myself right now?

BREAKING SILENCE

One of the most damaging aspects of abuse is the silence that so often surrounds it. Most children endure terrible atrocities without ever being able to tell anyone. Secrecy increases feelings of shame in the victim and allows the abuse to continue unchecked. For most abused children, isolation and silence are a way of life.

Part of healing is breaking through that isolation and telling the truth about your life. But talking about abuse can be terrifying. When you talk about the abuse, you are breaking the twisted pact of secrecy you were forced to uphold as a frightened child. You are telling on your abuser. You are trusting someone enough to share your real life story and risking a human response to your pain. Every time you tell, it's harder to pretend the abuse didn't take place.

Talking about your abuse is essential. You don't have to tell everyone. Nor should you tell indiscriminately. But you need at least one other person who can be a witness to your pain and to your healing. Hopefully there will be many. But as a start, consider the possibility of telling one other person what your life has really been like.

This chapter will provide guidelines for talking about your abuse with supportive people. (See "Simple Telling or Confrontation?" on page 236 for help in deciding if the person you want to tell is likely to support you.) You will identify the reasons you want to tell and look at the ways silence was encouraged or enforced when you were growing up. If you told someone about the abuse when you were young, you'll have a chance to explore the ways that experience affected you. Finally, you'll learn about the difference between privacy and lying, and be given practical guidelines for telling.

WHY TELL?

There are many benefits to talking about your abuse, although it can be hard to identify them when you're feeling scared about doing so. Listed below are some common reasons survivors find it empowering to tell. Check off the ones that apply to you. Add any others you can think of:

_____ Telling will help me overcome feelings of shame.

_____ I'll find out that I'm no longer alone or different.

_____ I'll experience someone else's compassion and love.

_____ I'll stop following the abuser's rules.

_____ I'll expose the offender.

_____ Once I tell, I can get help and support.

_____ I'll move through my denial.

_____ I'll get more in touch with my feelings.

_____ When I'm more honest, my relationships will become more intimate.

_____ People around me will get information and be less confused about what I'm going through.

_____ I'll establish myself as a person in the present dealing with the abuse I suffered as a child.

_____ I'll help end child sexual abuse by breaking the silence in which it thrives.

_____ I'll be a model for other survivors.

_____ I'll be a model for the kids in my family who are still being abused.

_____ I can stop abuse that's still going on.

_____ I'll feel relieved.

_____ _____

_____ _____

_____ _____

Things to Think About:

- How can I benefit from talking about the abuse?

- Was there anything that scared me in the list of potential positive outcomes? Why?

- Has my resolution to tell shifted because of this exercise? If so, how?

SIMPLE TELLING OR CONFRONTATION?

There are two kinds of people you can tell about your abuse—those who have a supportive or neutral response, and those who respond with hostility. The people who are likely to respond favorably to your disclosure require "simple telling," the kind that's described in this chapter. When you're talking to someone who may attack or undermine you, however, you're dealing with a confrontation, and that takes a different kind of planning and strategy (see "Confrontations," page 340).

People you've met as an adult, or even strangers, are more likely to be supportive than are family members when faced with the information that you were sexually abused. Family members, the abuser, or anyone who has a vested interest in or a relationship with the abuser is likely to be extremely upset when you bring up the abuse. If you're considering talking to a person who may respond with anger, challenges, or disbelief, that disclosure may turn into confrontation. The following exercise can help you distinguish between the two.

Make a list of people you're considering talking to about your abuse:

_____   _____

_____   _____

_____   _____

_____   _____

_____   _____

_____   _____

_____   _____

_____   _____

_____   _____

Think about each person whose name you just wrote down. Using the following questions as a guide, decide whether they require "simple telling" or a "confrontation."

- What is my relationship to this person?

- Does this person have a relationship with the abuser?

- Does this person have any stake in believing or not believing me?

- What, if anything, does this person have to protect?

- Has this person been supportive in listening to me talk about personal things before?

- Have we discussed feelings before?

- Do I trust this person?

- Do I think this person will believe me?

- Do I expect this person to become a supporter?

Go back to your list. Next to each name, place **"ST"** for "simple telling," or **"C"** for "confrontation." If you give someone an **"ST,"** it means you have no reason to expect a hostile or negative response when you talk about your abuse. The person in question has no vested interest in the abuser. You've already established open communication. In your experience so far, the person has your best interests at heart.

If you give someone a **"C,"** it means you have reason to anticipate a negative or hostile response. The person has reasons to protect the abuser. He or she doesn't deal well with feelings or hasn't supported you in talking about other personal things. Often **"C"** people are directly connected to your family of origin or childhood.

If you're not sure, or if you think you might get a mixed reaction, put a **question mark (?)** next to the name.

Look over the classifications you came up with, and then answer the following questions:

Who will be the easiest to talk to? _____

_____

Why? _____

_____

_____

_____

Who will be hardest to talk to? _____

_____

Why? _____

_____

_____

_____

What's the best place for me to start? Whom should I consider telling first?

_____

Why? _____

_____

_____

_____

_____

The rest of this chapter will deal with strategies for talking to the **"ST"** people on your list, people who are basically neutral or supportive —partners, friends, other survivors, counselors. If you're considering confronting someone who's a **"C"** on your list—your abuser or another potentially hostile person—turn to the chapter on confrontations (page 340) for help.

Things to Think About:

- Did my classifications surprise me? If so, why?

- Could I distinguish between the people who require a confrontation and those who don't? What tipped me off? What did I look for?

- Whom do I want to tell first? Will my disclosure entail simple telling or a confrontation? What does that tell me about how I need to prepare?

CHILDHOOD LESSONS: SILENCE

When you consider talking about your abuse, one of the first feelings that's likely to come up is fear. To work with this fear, start by tracing its roots. By understanding how you were silenced as a child, and why it's scary to tell now, you can take steps to go slowly and protect yourself.

Abused children are kept silent in many ways. You may have been blackmailed into not telling with things you wanted or needed—love, food, special attention, clothes, gifts, or as I was, simply with a piece of candy or a stick of gum. If you kept quiet, you may have been allowed to go out with friends or do things other kids weren't allowed to do—drink alcohol, take drugs, smoke cigarettes, stay up late.

Your role in your household may have been to keep things together. You knew that if you told, your family's stability would be jeopardized. You had to comply and be silent in order to fill your role as peacekeeper.

Your abuser may have threatened you directly: "If you tell, I'll kill you." "If you tell, your father and I will get divorced." "If you tell, they'll take you away and put you in a jail with all the other kids who aren't wanted." "If you tell, I'll abuse Sara too. If you don't, I'll leave her alone." "If you tell, I won't love you anymore." Or the threats may have been unspoken. Just the fact that your abuser was unpredictable, violent, larger and more powerful than you, created a menacing atmosphere. Your abuser may have tortured or killed your pets, implying that he or she could do the same to you if you didn't cooperate and keep silent.

In some instances, particularly in cases of ritual abuse, children are drugged and brainwashed, forced to watch or participate in abuse or murder. The clear and undeniable lesson is that any slip can and will result in death. In the case of ritual murders, children are made coconspirators, so that telling on the abusers also means telling on themselves. (This is absolutely not true. Children manipulated in ritual abuse are not responsible for actions they're forced to perform. They are victims trying to survive.)

Whether direct or indirect, these kinds of threats and manipulation were used to control you and protect the abuser. They added secrecy and silence to an already growing horror. By ensuring your isolation, they kept you from getting the help and assistance you deserved. They allowed the abuser to continue to use you for selfish, self-gratifying ends.

Naming the ways you were manipulated into silence is the first step in freeing yourself to talk about the abuse today:

When I was being abused, my abuser told me that _____

_____

_____

_____

_____ if I told.

My silence was bought with: _____

_____

_____

_____

_____

I witnessed the following things that made me scared to tell: _____

_____

_____

_____

_____

I felt I had to protect _____

_____

_____ Therefore, I couldn't tell.

If I had told, then people would have known that I _____

_____

_____

_____

Directly or indirectly, the message I got about telling was _____

_____

_____

_____

_____

Things to Think About:

- How was I manipulated into silence as a child?

- Who was protected by my silence as a child? Who is protected by my silence now?

IF YOU TOLD

Not all children keep their abuse a secret. Many do tell someone that they're being abused. If you are an adult today and you told when you were a child, chances are that you did not receive a sympathetic, helpful response. Instead of being believed and protected, you were probably ridiculed, ignored, blamed, or further abused. Even if you were believed, the abuse may have been minimized or justified. You received the message that you weren't worthy of protection.*

---

* This is beginning to change. As children are being taught to differentiate between good touching and bad touching, and to tell someone about bad touching, more and more children are getting sympathetic, protective responses when they disclose abuse. Children who tell and are treated with respect, acknowledgment, and appropriate action will have a chance to heal as children and won't need this workbook in the years to come. However, many children telling today are continuing to have negative experiences—testifying in an insensitive court atmosphere, being made to repeat a story again and again, going to the trouble of telling only to have the abuser vindicated, punished insufficiently, or granted custody. These further violations of the child add new layers of abuse to the original violation, and teach the child that talking openly about the abuse is futile and self-destructive.

If you did tell and you were believed, your disclosure may have been handled poorly. You may have been asked to repeat your story over and over. You may have been cast out of the house while the rest of your family stayed together. Your parents may have gotten a divorce and you may have been blamed for subsequent financial struggles. In cases where telling is mishandled, the aftermath of a disclosure can sometimes be more traumatic than the abuse itself.

If you disclosed the abuse when you were a child or an adolescent, the responses you received (or failed to receive) gave you powerful messages about telling. Those messages set a precedent for your fears and feelings about talking about your abuse now.

If you told as a child, take a few minutes to write about what happened.

When I told, _____

_____

_____

_____

_____

_____

_____

_____

_____

_____

_____

_____

_____

_____

_____

_____

_____

Things to Think About:

- (If you told as a child) How did the responses affect me? What decisions or assumptions did I make as a result?

- How is the response I received still affecting me?

- If I tell again today, will the same thing happen? Why or why not?

A FEW CHOICE WORDS ON TELLING THE TRUTH

The rest of this chapter will give some practical guidelines for talking about your abuse. You will have the opportunity to make choices about whom you want to talk to, to plan what you want to say and when you want to say it. You will be asked if there are things you don't want to talk about. Are there people you don't want to tell? That you're not ready to tell? Are there times you want to share only part of your story?

I went through this dilemma when I was first researching *The Cour-*

age to Heal. I'd go to a party and people would ask me what I did for a living. I'd say I was a writer. They'd ask, "Are you published?" And I'd say, "Yes." (I always answered in monosyllables.) Then they'd ask, "What do you write?" And I'd say, "Nonfiction." And then if they were very persistent, they'd ask, "What kind of nonfiction?" That was the point of no return. I'd take a deep breath and say, "Well, actually, I'm writing a book for women about healing from child sexual abuse." At that point, one of three things would happen: they'd either get a panicked look in their eyes and get away from me as fast as possible, they'd go numb and a blank look would come over their face, or they'd start to tell me their own story or the story of someone they knew. It was predictable.

In the beginning I enjoyed talking about being a survivor. It was empowering. I felt proud of what I was doing and I wanted to educate people about sexual abuse. I knew that if I talked about my abuse, it would give other people the permission to talk about theirs. But after a while I got sick of being a professional incest survivor. I wanted to dance and flirt and eat and talk about superficial things when I was at parties. I knew it was time for a change in strategy. I took to making up stories about what I did.

At first I said I was an electrician. But I quickly learned that women electricians were fascinating. I'd find myself confronted with questions I couldn't possibly answer about wiring or DC currents. Finally I came up with the magic solution. When someone at a party asked me what I did for a living, I looked at them and said I was a housewife. Given the status of women in our society, most people never asked a follow-up question. They changed the topic or talked about themselves. It was the perfect way to keep sexual abuse out of my conversations.

Not telling is a tricky concept for survivors, who are often concerned with telling the whole truth. As children, most of us lived with the lies and distortions of our abusers ("Your parents will kick you out if you tell them what we do together" "I'm doing this because I love you"). As a result, many survivors take to the truth with a vengeance: "I have to tell the absolute truth about everything all the time." The problem with this stance is that it doesn't protect you. When you feel compelled to tell everyone everything, you leave yourself vulnerable and overexposed. You give people more information about you than they deserve. You fail to protect your privacy. Choosing to omit a certain piece of information because you don't trust someone enough, because you want to test the waters, because you consider it private, or simply because you don't want to share it is not the same as lying.

The concept of lying is confusing for survivors. Many of us made up stories in order to survive. We were accused of lying, but we were not lying. We used stories to protect us. Many of us still do this. We reveal only as much information as we can safely risk at a given time.

Real lies hurt people. They are used to manipulate, control, and isolate people, to maintain power, to shirk responsibility. Not telling everyone everything about your abuse does none of these things. Rather, it protects you. It allows you to gauge the appropriateness of your sharing. It allows intimacy and closeness to grow slowly. It maintains your privacy, enables you to set boundaries, and gives you the opportunity to make choices. (If you don't want to tell because you're ashamed of yourself or of what happened to you, that's a different issue. See "Establish Your Privacy," page 29, for more about the relationship between shame and privacy.)

When I was growing up, lies were _____

_____

_____

_____

_____

When I was growing up, telling the truth was _____

_____

_____

_____

_____

If I tell the truth, _____

_____

_____

_____

_____

If I don't tell the truth, _____

_____

_____

_____

_____

Things to Think About:

- Did I make up stories as a child? Do I still make up stories? How does making up stories protect me? How does it get in my way?

- What does it mean to tell a lie? To tell the truth? What does it mean to be an honest person?

- How do I feel when I consider withholding information about my abuse? What's the difference between maintaining privacy and lying?

GUIDELINES FOR TELLING

You can create more safety in talking about your abuse if you think through the interaction ahead of time. You can choose the best time (when your partner isn't running out the door) and the best circumstances (when things are relaxed, when you've established that you want to talk about something personal). You can also ask for the response you want (a hug, not to be touched, verbal responses, silence) and set limits on whom, if anyone, the other person repeats your story to.

Complete the following each time you consider talking to someone:

I'm thinking about telling _____

I want to talk about _____

_____

_____

_____

_____

_____

I don't want to talk about _____

_____

_____

_____

_____

_____

I expect _____

_____

_____

_____

_____

_____

I'm going to do it (when) _____

_____

I'm going to do it (where) _____

_____

I'm going to set it up ahead of time by _____

_____

_____

_____

_____

The response I'd like is _____

_____

_____

_____

_____

I'm going to ask for _____

_____

_____

_____

_____

It's okay for _____ to tell _____

_____

but it's not okay for them to tell _____

_____

_____

When you are first telling, you will probably care a great deal about how people react when you talk about the abuse. That's why it's important to choose carefully in the beginning. You want to pick people whose responses you can predict fairly accurately so you build up some successes. Once you've had more practice and have a few positive experiences under your belt, you may want to branch out and tell people whose responses are more uncertain. You may, in fact, go through a period where the response you get isn't the important thing—telling is. Many survivors go through a stage when they tell everyone they meet. When healing from sexual abuse is all-consuming, often there's little else you can talk about. Accept it. Talk freely. Over time, your need to disclose will change.

No matter how careful you are in choosing people to tell, you will probably have a mix of satisfying and disappointing experiences. You can't control everyone's reactions. People respond to stories of sexual abuse with their own attitudes, experiences, and history. They bring a set of assumptions and biases to the interaction that have nothing to do with you. If they were abused and are denying it, your revelation may threaten them and make them angry. If they've forgotten their own abuse, they may go blank when you talk to them. Or they may challenge or minimize your experience. This doesn't have to do with you or with your right to tell; it has to do with the other person.

There is some weeding out that always happens when you begin to share the truth of who you are. You may be disappointed or angered by some of the rude or insensitive responses you get. You'll also be surprised by the people who respond more favorably than you expected.

Taking some time to assess the results of a particular disclosure can help you regroup and prepare for the next time you talk about your abuse:

When I told _____ , _____

_____

_____

_____

_____

I wish _____

_____

_____

_____

The things that worked were _____

_____

_____

_____

The things that didn't work were _____

_____

_____

_____

_____

_____

I was surprised when _____

_____

_____

_____

_____

I don't feel finished. I still want to _____

_____

_____

_____

_____

If I had it to do over again, I'd _____

_____

_____

_____

_____

_____

I learned _____

_____

_____

_____

_____

_____

Next time, I'll _____

_____

_____

_____

_____

I'm proud that I _____

_____

_____

_____

_____

Things to Think About:

- How does it feel to plan my disclosures? To ask for what I want when I tell?

- How has my experience of telling changed over time?

REFLECTIONS: BREAKING SILENCE

Sexual abuse takes place in an atmosphere of secrecy. Part of healing is breaking that secrecy and telling the truth about your life. Talking about abuse is an essential part of reducing shame, believing in yourself, ending isolation, and gaining allies. In the beginning, however, it can be terrifying to talk about the abuse. Growing up, you may have been trained and threatened into silence, or met with hostile responses when you did tell. Despite these negative experiences, it is still important to tell today.

As an adult survivor, you can make choices about telling. By putting thought into whom you tell and how you tell them, you can create safe settings to talk about the abuse. Although you can't control other people's reaction to your story, you can take concrete steps to make your experience of telling a more positive one.

Here are some questions to help you assess your present feelings, goals, and needs around the issue of breaking silence.

- What feelings did I have as I worked through this chapter?

- What am I feeling right now? What sensations am I experiencing in my body?

- How old did I feel as I worked through the chapter? How old do I feel right now?

- What was hard for me in this chapter? What was confusing? What didn't I understand?

- What did I learn? What commitments have I made? What steps have I taken?

- What did I do that I'm proud of?

- What's still unsettled for me? What, if anything, do I want to come back to or follow up on?

- What do I need to do to take care of myself right now?

UNDERSTANDING THAT IT WASN'T YOUR FAULT

Every survivor I've ever met has battled with shame, with the awful sense that there was something wrong with them deep down inside that caused the abuse. Although this belief is universally held, it is universally false. I have talked with thousands of survivors and I have never yet met one who was to blame for being sexually abused.

There are many reasons why children (and later, adult survivors) hold themselves responsible. The abuser may have told you it was your fault. Other adults may have reinforced that idea. If you told, you may have been punished or blamed. Your religion may have talked about sin, hell, and damnation. If the abuse took place in your family, it was less painful to take on the blame than to accept the reality of your situation —that the adults who were supposed to love and protect you were trying to hurt you. If you believed that the abuse was your fault, at least you could maintain the illusion that there was something you could do to stop it.

There are certain circumstances that make survivors feel even more responsible for the abuse. If your body responded to the stimulation, if you experienced sexual pleasure or enjoyed the closeness that came with the abuse, you may take these things as proof that it really was your fault. If you didn't say no, sought out the attention, were abused by a sibling who was just a little older than you, or you were older yourself, you may feel particular shame. And if you're a man, you have to deal with the added myths that boys aren't victims, and that you were "lucky" to be initiated into sex at a young age.

But even if you experienced all of this, it doesn't mean the abuse was your fault. It is never justified for a more powerful person to take advantage of a young person's vulnerability, naiveté, curiosity, or need for attention. Sexual abuse is never the responsibility of the child. It is always the responsibility of the adult.

The exercises in this chapter are designed to help you understand why the abuse wasn't your fault. You'll identify the reasons why you feel responsible for the abuse and look for information that discredits those reasons. You'll be sent on a field trip to observe children or teenagers who are the age you were when the abuse began, and you'll have the chance to research your own childhood for evidence of your vulnerability and innocence. An art project will help you get in touch with the child who still lives inside of you, and the final writing exercise will ask you to reach out to an abused child who is feeling responsible and ashamed today.

LETTING GO OF SHAME

Before you can let go of shame, you have to recognize it, name it, and hold it out in the light of day. When you keep shame a secret, it gains power over you. Yet you may feel too ashamed to tell anyone why you think the abuse was your fault. Or maybe you've never taken the time to actually look at the reasons. But admitting shame is a first step in deflating its power.

The following exercise is in two parts. The first asks you to identify the reasons you blame yourself for the abuse; the second asks you to gather information to negate those reasons. Filling out the answers in the first section can bring up intense feelings of shame and self-hate. It's important that you counter those feelings by filling out the more positive affirmations in the second section. Try to complete both parts at once.

IDENTIFYING HIDDEN SHAME

Fill in the following sentences. Don't hesitate or censor your answers. Write down the first thing that comes into your mind. (Feel free to use any of the examples that pertain to you).

A. It was really my fault because *I kept going back for more. I'm the one who asked for a backrub.*

B. It was really my fault because   *I had an orgasm. I must have wanted it.*
C. It was really my fault because   *I never said no.*
D. It was really my fault because   *it was only my brother. And he was only a year older than me.*
E. (For women) It was really my fault because   *my father said I was a slut. He told me I wanted it.*
F. (For men) It was really my fault because   *I had an erection. It must have felt good to me.*

1. It was really my fault because _____

_____

_____

2. It was really my fault because _____

_____

_____

3. It was really my fault because _____

_____

_____

4. It was really my fault because _____

_____

_____

5. It was really my fault because _____

_____

_____

6. It was really my fault because _____

REPLACING SHAME WITH REALITY

A good support person will readily tell you that the sexual abuse wasn't your fault. A great support person will tell you *why* it wasn't your fault. If you start with an intellectual understanding of why you weren't to blame, that understanding often begins to infiltrate and replace the false beliefs you carry. Your sense of shame is gradually alleviated and you begin to realize, in your deepest self, that you really weren't to blame.

Go back through "the reasons it was my fault" you just came up with. For each reason, write down a corresponding rebuttal (see the examples below). If you can't think of anything to write, talk to other survivors. Read *The Courage to Heal.* Read other books about healing from child sexual abuse. Ask your therapist to explain it to you. If you don't have a therapist, what do you think a good counselor would tell you? This is a research project. It's your job to come up with facts and information that contradict your reasons for blaming yourself.

When you've done your research, write the reasons down. Even if you don't believe them at first, write them down anyway. Putting the truth down on paper is the first step in replacing a false belief with a true one.

A. It wasn't my fault because   *children need attention and affection to survive. Sex with my grandfather was the only touching that was available to me. That's why I went back for more.*

B. It wasn't my fault because   *my body responded. My body did what it was supposed to do. It wasn't my fault.*

C. It wasn't my fault because   *I was never taught to say no. No one in my family ever taught me that it was okay to set boundaries or say no.*

D. It wasn't my fault because   *my brother was older and stronger than me. He had a lot more power in the family. I looked up to him and wanted to do anything to please him. When you're a young twelve and your big brother is thirteen, one year is a big age difference.*

E. (For women) It wasn't my fault because   *my dad was wrong. I was an innocent child. He called me a slut to justify his own sick behavior.*

F. (For men) It wasn't my fault because   *penises are supposed to respond to touch. I had an erection because my abuser stimulated me sexually, not because I wanted to be abused.*

1. It wasn't my fault because _____

_____

_____

_____

2. It wasn't my fault because _____

_____

_____

_____

3. It wasn't my fault because _____

_____

_____

_____

4. It wasn't my fault because _____

_____

_____

_____

5. It wasn't my fault because _____

_____

_____

_____

6. It wasn't my fault because _____

_____

_____

_____

Things to Think About:

- Which was harder for me, the first part of this exercise or the second? Why?

- Which response brought up the most shame in the first part? Which answer was hardest to counter?

- Do I believe the things I wrote down in the second part of this exercise? If not, what would help me to do so?

OBSERVING CHILDREN

Many survivors believe they're to blame because they think they should have done something to stop the abuse. This is because most survivors are grossly out of touch with how vulnerable children are. They have an unrealistic picture of children's ability to protect themselves. The best way to gain an accurate view is to observe children.

Go to a place where you can watch children who are the age you were (or think you might have been) when the abuse began. If you were a baby, go to a nursery. If you were a four-year-old, go to a preschool. If you were nine years old, watch a bunch of fourth-graders at recess. And if you were a teenager, go to a shopping mall. If you have kids of your own, step back and watch them with an observer's eye. Take notes on your observations.

As you watch, look carefully. Physically, how big are the kids? What do their voices sound like? How do they communicate? What are they talking about? What are they interested in? If they're older kids, look for the vulnerability underneath their apparent maturity. How do they interact with their peers? With other adults? Do you think these kids want to have sex with adults? Can you see that they might be easily manipulated? If you found out that one of them was being abused, would you think he or she deserved it?

Write your observations in the pages that follow.

- What did I think kids were like before I did my observations?

- Were my expectations realistic? If not, why not? How did my observations change my perspective?

- Did this exercise influence my own feelings of shame and responsibility in any way? If so, how?

EVIDENCE OF CHILDHOOD

Recognizing the vulnerability of today's children is an important step in overcoming shame. But you also have to recognize that you were just as vulnerable, if not more so, when you were a child. Children today are being taught to say no and to tell someone if they're being abused.* Few of us were told more than a vague "Don't take candy from strangers" when we were children. Yet many of us still feel responsible.

One of the problems is that many adult survivors fail to recognize the fact that they really were children when the abuse took place. You conceive of childhood as a time when you were a miniature version of your adult self. You believe you had the same resources and skills then that you do today.

---

* Child sexual abuse prevention work is essential, but saying no and telling won't stop every perpetrator. It's a mistake to think that children are universally safe because of several hours of prevention training in school. Although some children have stopped perpetrators with the skills they've learned, others have been abused anyway. Even a very determined child has little power when confronted with a manipulative adult. Teaching children personal safety skills does not guarantee their safety. While empowering children is important, it is imperative that we don't place the responsibility for stopping abuse on the shoulders of our children. As adults in a sick society, it's *our* responsibility to protect children.

There are many ways to remind yourself how young you really were when the abuse took place. Mementos from childhood can help. If you have childhood photographs, look at them. Show them to someone else. Talk about what you see. Look at how young you were, how physically small. Note the expression on your face. Look at the clothing you wore.

In a recent professional training, I mentioned using photographs as a way to help survivors get in touch with their childhood. A therapist added that she asks her clients to try to find samples of writing they did when they were children. The spindly, shaky writing, the child's thought process, the simple language, serve as excellent reminders of how young you really were.

Not all survivors have access to these kinds of records. Everything connected with your childhood may have been destroyed. You may have no contact with the people who have these things, and you may not want to. But if you do have the access and the inclination, such records can provide valuable insight into the fact that you really were a child, and that the abuse wasn't your fault. (Before you look for materials from your past, reread "Research Your Childhood" on page 228 for ideas, suggestions, and cautions.)

Take a few minutes to write down any ideas you have for locating writings or drawings from your childhood. Are there mementos you have or can locate? Is there anything tangible that can remind you that you were a child? That you were not an adult, but rather a vulnerable target for abuse? Note anything you might be able to look for.

POSSIBLE REMINDERS OF CHILDHOOD

_____

_____

_____

_____

_____

_____

_____

Things to Think About:

- Do I want to go back and look for childhood mementos? Why or why not?

- (If you've decided to look for things) What do I hope to gain through this process? Are my expectations realistic? What's my next step?

THE CHILD WITHIN

No matter how grown-up and adult we are, we each have an inner child (or many inner children) hidden under the layers of sophistication, maturity, and protection. The inner child is the part of us that is still connected to the longings and pain of childhood. When you go back and reexperience your abuse, get in touch with your vulnerability and softness, feel your childhood anger, fear, and grief, you are in touch with your inner child.

Yet survivors often hate, ignore, or fear the child within. You may scoff at the idea that a child lives inside you. Or you may be angry, believing the child got you into this trouble to begin with. You don't want to feel vulnerable, to reexperience childhood feelings of abandonment and pain. The last thing you want to develop is tender feelings for this troublesome brat. But the child within does not deserve your anger and judgment. Instead, that child needs your love, respect, and consistent caring. Until you become allies and learn to respect and care for the inner child, you will be leaving a part of yourself behind.

ACTIVITY: PICTURING THE CHILD WITHIN

Make a collage that represents both the adult and the child in you. Find a shoebox. Reread the directions for making a collage on page 13. Get out your collage materials. Start by thinking about your life as an adult. Cut out words and pictures that remind you of all the diverse aspects of your adult self. Paste them on the outside of the box. This is what people see when they meet you now. Then think about the child inside you, the child you once were. Cut out words and pictures that reveal the feelings and thoughts of that child. Paste them on the inside of the box. These represent the more tender, vulnerable parts of you.

You do not have to show the inside of your shoebox to anyone, but at least you'll know what's inside.

Things to Think About:

- How do you feel about the idea of the child within?

- What kind of relationship do you have with the child within now?

- How would you like this relationship to change in the future?

LETTER TO AN ABUSED CHILD: A WRITING EXERCISE

This is a very helpful exercise if you are still blaming yourself for the abuse or if you are hating the child within. Imagine a child who is the age you were when you were first abused (or think you were first abused). In your mind's eye, look at the way that child is dressed. How is his hair cut? What does she look like? Give the child a name. Now imagine that he or she is being abused, just as you were.

Reread the guidelines for freewriting on page 11. Then set a timer or alarm clock for twenty minutes, and write a letter to that child, explaining why the abuser is at fault. Tell her not to blame herself. Let him know that he is innocent. You are the one link that child has to hope and self-love. As you pick up your pen, think of yourself as a lifeline. Take the next twenty minutes to write.

REFLECTIONS: UNDERSTANDING THAT IT WASN'T YOUR FAULT

Knowing it wasn't your fault, deeply accepting your innocence and worth, is crucial to the healing process. There are many reasons survivors blame themselves for the abuse they suffered as children, and none of them are justified. Abuse is always the abuser's fault.

Letting go of shame and self-blame is a gradual process. Spending time with children, getting in touch with your own childhood, and developing a healing relationship with the child within are three things that can help overcome the myth that you were somehow responsible.

Here are some questions to help you assess your present feelings, goals, and needs around the issue of understanding it wasn't your fault:

- **What feelings did I have as I worked through this chapter?**

- **What am I feeling right now? What sensations am I experiencing in my body?**

- How old did I feel as I worked through the chapter? How old do I feel right now?

- What was hard for me in this chapter? What was confusing? What didn't I understand?

- What did I learn? What commitments have I made? What steps have I taken?

- What did I do that I'm proud of?

- What's still unsettled for me? What, if anything, do I want to come back to or follow up on?

- What do I need to do to take care of myself right now?

LEARNING TO TRUST YOURSELF

Many adult survivors have trouble believing their perceptions, senses, and feelings. You may doubt your intuitions and fail to trust your own instincts. You may not be connected to the inner gauge that tells you how you feel about what's going on around you. This lack of self-awareness is a direct result of child sexual abuse.

Children are naturally trusting. Their first impulse is to love the people who take care of them. Sexual abuse shatters that trust, and children learn that it's not safe to respond to their most basic instincts.

Many abused children are told they're crazy, that their feelings are wrong or don't make sense. Abusers often twist reality: "This is what a loving grandfather does to his granddaughter." "This is what all fathers and sons do before they go to bed." "If you weren't so evil, I wouldn't have to do this to you." Or your perceptions may have been denied altogether: "Nothing's happening. You're imagining things." Children believe that everything adults say is true, so lies and distortions replace reality.

Although you didn't learn to trust your own feelings and instincts as a child, this chapter will help you learn to identify and listen to them now. By learning to be present, getting rid of the negative messages you absorbed as a child, discovering your inner voice, setting limits and saying no, you will clear away many of the obstacles to trusting yourself.

BEING PRESENT

In order to get in touch with your thoughts, perceptions, and feelings, you need to be present in the moment—to feel your emotions, to stay in your body, to pay attention to what's going on inside and around you. This can be a tremendous challenge for survivors, many of whom learned early on to dissociate, to disconnect from unpleasant feelings and body sensations.

When you were growing up, splitting off from your feelings and physical sensations was an effective and necessary coping skill. You couldn't stand the physical pain, the confusing sensations, the humiliation, the jumbled intensity of feelings the abuse caused. So you learned to space out. The problem is you may still be spacing out, even when you don't want to. Like other childhood coping mechanisms, the survival skill may have outlived its purpose.

Survivors tend to be at one of two extremes—spaced out and absent or hyper-vigilant, aware of everything all the time.* If you've dissociated all your life, you may not even be aware of it. Not being present may be so normal for you that you don't know you're missing anything. You may not realize that you're spacing out until someone points it out to you, or until you decide to track your own lack of attention. Then you realize you space out all the time, and it's shocking. Who was driving the car while you weren't paying attention? Who was having that conversation? Who was making love when you weren't there?

I space out ＿＿ hardly ever ＿＿ a little ＿＿ a lot ＿＿ most of the time.

I think I space out ＿＿ % of the time.

If you space out regularly, learning to be present when you want to be is an important skill. As you increase your ability to be present, your capacity to feel your feelings, think your thoughts, experience your body, and move through life with attention will dramatically increase. Such attention naturally increases your capacity for healing.

---

* A more extreme form of dissociation is the development of multiple personalities, where different parts of the self split off and form distinct personalities who are sometimes unaware of each other. If you have multiple personalities, this discussion about spacing out and being present may not adequately describe your experience of dissociation.

LEARNING TO BE PRESENT

If you want to be more present, begin by observing your current behavior. Without judgment, explore the way things are. Then set the intention to change. Decide that you are willing to be present, to feel the feelings and sensations spacing out has protected you from. Then practice paying attention. Being present is a matter of intention, willingness, and breathing.

As you begin your observations, ask yourself the following questions: Can I differentiate between the times I'm present and the times I'm not? What happens when I space out? What does it feel like inside? What thoughts run through my mind? What feelings do I have? What happens in my body? How does my behavior change? (If you don't know what you do when you space out, ask a support person to observe you and report back.)

When I space out, it feels as if   (*I'm going down the drain / I'm underwater / I'm behind a pane of glass / I'm floating on the ceiling*)

_____

_____

_____

_____

_____

I start   (*talking really fast / tapping my foot / feeling numb in my fingers*) _____

_____

_____

_____

_____

_____

I stop   *(making eye contact / breathing / feeling anything / thinking clearly)* _____

_____

_____

_____

_____

I start to think   *(I'm going to die / I don't think—that's the problem / about the multi-plication tables / about going away on a magic carpet)*

_____

_____

_____

_____

Once you're aware of the way you feel and act when you space out, begin keeping an awareness journal. Carry this book (or a small pad) around with you. Every time you catch yourself spacing out (and you won't catch them all), note the time, place, and situation. Then answer the following questions:

AWARENESS JOURNAL

Time of space-out: _____

Length of space-out (if known): _____

Place: _____

What was the last thing I remember before I spaced out? _____

What was going on? _____

_____

_____

_____

_____

Who, if anyone, was there? What were they doing? _____

_____

_____

_____

_____

What emotions was I feeling? _____

_____

_____

_____

_____

Was there anything disturbing to me at the time I spaced out? If so, what? _____

_____

_____

_____

_____

When you observe your periods of attention and inattention, you'll begin to recognize some patterns. When someone is angry with you, you space out. When you're expected to perform sexually, you disappear. When you're sad or scared, you leave. Understanding these patterns is crucial to learning to be present. When you isolate the times you space out, you can identify the need you're fulfilling, and then you can find alternative ways to meet that need.

I space out so I don't have to   *(feel angry / be sexual / say what I really think)*

_____

_____

_____

_____

Other ways I could meet this need: _____ _____

_____

_____

_____

_____

Once you've gathered information about these patterns, you have to decide if you want to change. This is a question of willingness. Are you willing to feel angry? To stand up for yourself? To feel sexual? To be present?

If you are willing to be present, some simple techniques for coming back to your body may help. Try breathing, putting your feet flat on the floor, and saying, "I'm willing to be here." You may come back immediately. Sometimes you may need other things to help you come back—looking at your surroundings, sitting or lying on the ground, moving or stretching, contact with a safe person who can help ground you, taking a walk, verbal reminders about where you are (or who you are), safe physical touch, or talking about your experience.

After you've gotten grounded again in the present, take a few minutes to figure out why you left. Record your answers in your awareness journal.

Learning to be present is a slow trial-and-error process. Often when survivors tackle this issue, they suddenly find they're spacing out more than they ever did. This can be very frustrating. Hang in there. Be patient. Keep breathing and bringing yourself back. Being present only exists in the moment. You can be present now . . . and now . . . and now.

Things to Think About:

- What has spacing out protected me from?

- What would it take for me to make a commitment to be present?

INTERNALIZED MESSAGES

When children are abused, they are told terrible things about themselves. Abusers say incredibly destructive things to them. "You're no good. You're rotten. You're stupid. You don't deserve to live. I'm sorry you were ever born. You'll never amount to anything." These messages make a deep impression on children, who believe that adults are always right.

Even if these things weren't said to you explicitly, just the fact that you were abused gave you the same message. You learned that you were of little value.

Many adult survivors still believe these messages. The litany of verbal abuse becomes internalized, and instead of hearing it from the outside, you record and store it, and end up saying the same self-hating things to yourself. When you're about to achieve a success, you get depressed and a voice inside says, "You'll never amount to anything." When you're struggling to make the commitment to heal, a voice in your head says, "What the hell do you think you're doing? You don't deserve to be alive. You should kill yourself."

These voices have nothing to do with reality. They are the regurgitated lies of the abusers. Separating out these messages and replacing them with positive, true statements about yourself is crucial to developing a positive sense of yourself. But before you can get rid of negative messages, you have to identify and isolate them.

Take a few minutes to think about the negative messages you heard when you were a child.

When I was a child, I was told:

- *You're only good for sex.*
- *You're an evil person. You have a bad seed inside of you.*
- *No one will ever love you. You're unlovable, even to God.*

- _____

_____

- _____

_____

- _____

_____

- _____

_____

- _____

_____

Being abused taught me that:

- *I'm not very important. I don't deserve any better than this.*
- *If I'm not being abused, I'm not being loved.*
- *Everything bad that happens to me is my fault.*

- _____

  _____

- _____

  _____

- _____

  _____

- _____

  _____

I still think that:

- *It's not worth it to try to change things.*
- *I'd better keep my mouth shut or I'll be killed.*

- _____

  _____

- _____

  _____

- _____

  _____

- _____

  _____

In the beginning of the healing process, you may experience negative, self-hating thoughts to the exclusion of all others. You may think terrible things about yourself and not be able to recognize that you're repeating the false messages that were thrust on you as a child. At this stage you need support people to point out the times you are lost in negative thinking.

As you surround yourself with people who affirm your strengths and your healing, the negative messages will gradually be replaced with the truth—that you are a powerful, strong survivor coming to terms with child sexual abuse. But you will still have moments when these negative messages come back and assert themselves with a vengeance. Then you need to stop and analyze why you got hooked back into the old pattern of negative thinking.

When you find yourself thinking self-hating things, answer the following questions:

When did I stop feeling good about myself?   *(Yesterday after lunch / When I woke up this morning / After I saw my father)*

_____

_____

_____

_____

What was going on at the time I started feeling bad?   *(I received a letter from my father / I was having a fight with my partner, and I got angry and stuffed it / I talked to my sister on the phone)*

_____

_____

_____

_____

_____

What was I feeling at that time? Angry? Scared? Powerless? Sad? What have I been feeling since then?

_____

_____

_____

_____

_____

What thought(s) keeps going through my mind? _____

_____

_____

_____

_____

Did I get this message (or something close to it) when I was a child?
_____ yes   _____ no   _____ I'm not sure

If yes, under what circumstances? _____

_____

_____

_____

_____

What exactly was said to me? _____

_____

_____

_____

_____

Who said it? _____

What, if anything, in the current situation reminds me of that time? _____

_____

_____

_____

_____

Identifying and tracing the roots of negative messages is a big step toward eradicating them. When you can see where your bad feelings originate, you affirm the fact that they come from somewhere, that you're not crazy or creating them to torture yourself, and that they are not, in fact, true. In the beginning, pinpointing the thoughts that make you feel bad will be a slow trial-and-error process. With practice, you will be able to search out their origins in a matter of moments.

To get rid of a negative message, you need to replace it with a positive affirmation about yourself. An affirmation is a way of stating your strengths in a powerful, declarative way: "I am a big strong woman who can defend myself." "I am a vulnerable man who can cry and still be lovable." "Just because I'm alive, I deserve love and respect." Affirmations are an effective antidote to the lies you were told.

Use the space below to write down some positive affirmations about yourself (you can add more later as you think of them):

- _____

- _____

- _____
- _____
- _____
- _____
- _____
- _____

If you have trouble coming up with positive affirmations about yourself (or even if you don't), go to two people in your support system and have each of them write down three affirmations about your strengths:

Person #1:

- _____
- _____
- _____

Person #2:

- _____
- _____
- _____

Although it may be hard to believe these affirmations at first, practice saying them. Look in the mirror and repeat them to yourself. Write them on big pieces of paper and tape them to the refrigerator. Read them over to yourself before you go to sleep at night. Gradually you'll come to believe them. With patience and practice, they can replace the old negative statements you were taught when you were growing up.

Things to Think About:

- How have internalized messages affected my sense of myself?

- How can I loosen the grip of the old damaging thoughts that linger from childhood?

- How did it feel to write down positive things about myself? To have other people write down my strengths?

THE INNER VOICE

All of us have an inner voice that can be a helpful tool in guiding our actions. Your inner voice alerts you to danger and guides you in making wise choices. When you listen to it, you can assess what you want to do in a given situation. You go out on a date and recognize cues that tell you the other person is acting like your abuser; you decide not to see that person anymore. You're walking down the street and you sense danger, so you cross the street just in time to avoid a confrontation with a violent person.

The inner voice is a quiet monitor of the choices we make in our daily lives. You have to decide whether to take a particular risk. You wonder whether to make a commitment to a relationship. You have to choose between two jobs. The inner voice can give you informaton and guidance in making such decisions.

The inner voice is not an actual voice you hear. Rather, it's a combination of sensations, thoughts, feelings, hunches, and impulses that tell you how you feel about a given situation. When people say "I had this funny feeling," or "Something was nagging at me," or "I don't know how I knew. I just knew," they're talking about their inner voice.

Most people aren't aware they have such a voice. Few of us have been trained to pay attention to our feelings and intuitions. Connecting to your inner voice requires solitude, quiet time, and introspection, qualities that aren't encouraged (or valued) in our achievement-oriented society. But your inner voice still exists. Even if you haven't paid attention to it for years, it's there. It's waiting for you to discover it.

All of us experience our inner voice differently. When you're about to make a poor decision, you might have nightmares, get a sick feeling in your stomach, have a sudden desire to binge on chocolate, lose your appetite, or be unable to sleep. Something or someone may "give you the creeps."

It will take time to learn about the ways your inner voice communicates with you. You can begin by thinking about the ways you respond to the following situations:

When I'm about to make a poor decision:

- *I feel very confused and get a gnawing feeling that something is wrong. I usually try to ignore it.*
- *I usually get a migraine headache.*
- *I can't seem to make up my mind.*

- _____

- _____

- _____

- _____

- _____

When I'm about to do something that's right for me:

- *I usually have a dream about floating in the ocean.*
- *I feel especially relaxed.*
- *Some real self-destructive thoughts always creep in at the last minute. If I ignore them, then I'm okay.*

- _____

- _____

- _____

- _____

- _____

When something is wrong:

- *I start overeating.*
- *I find myself craving alcohol and sugar.*
- *I get insomnia and can't sleep no matter what I do.*
- *I clean my house over and over.*

- _____

- _____

- _____

- _____

- _____

When I'm in danger:

- *My stomach goes into a tight knot and I start breathing fast.*
- *My stepfather's face flashes in front of my eyes.*
- *I feel like I'm eight years old and I'm about to be hit.*
- *I feel this terrible sense of immobility. I can't move or speak.*

- _____

- _____

- _____

- _____

- _____

You may not be able to pinpoint the specific ways your inner voice communicates to you right away. If you can't answer these questions now, wait until the next time you're in the situation (facing danger, doing something good for yourself), and take notes on the way you felt before, during, and after the incident.

LEARNING TO SAY NO

In "Creating Safety" on page 19, you learned about setting limits. Part of setting limits is learning to say no. Saying no is critical because it enables you to establish boundaries, to protect yourself, to make choices and decisions about your life.

"No" is one of the first things children learn to say. When children are abused, their "no" is not respected. Kids are forced to submit, to give up their free will. As an adult survivor, you may still feel you can't say no. If someone wants something from you, you have to give it to them, be it sex, work, companionship, money, favors, or anything else.

If you listen to your inner voice, you will realize that there are times you want to set limits. Respecting yourself means that you won't always give people what they want. You can refuse to take care of someone else's needs if it means neglecting your own or simply because you don't want to.

Yet saying no can be scary. If you've never done it before, you may think the world will cave in. You may be convinced that no one will like you if you say no. Chances are that some people will be angry with you for setting limits, but others will respect you for taking care of yourself.

Often when people start saying no, they feel the need to justify setting limits. You may find yourself rationalizing, apologizing, or explaining. In actuality, just saying no is enough. You don't have to qualify it.

A good place to start in learning to say no is to examine the attitudes you currently hold. Complete the following sentences:

If I say no, it would mean that _____

_____

_____

_____

If I say no, I'm scared that _____

_____

_____

_____

I'd really like to say no to _____

_____

_____

_____

I'm the most afraid of saying no to _____

_____ because _____

_____

_____

_____

_____

Here are some small ways I could say no right away: _____

_____

_____

_____

_____

When you start to say no, you will have to deal with people's reactions. If you've been someone who's said yes to everyone, expect some negative responses when you first start setting limits.

When someone gets mad at me, I _____

_____

_____

_____

_____

If someone gives me a hard time about saying no, I'm going to _____

_____

_____

_____

_____

Learning to say no takes practice. Try keeping a log of your positive and negative experiences in setting limits. In the next week, find two situations in which you can say no. Start with something small and practice from there. Record your experiences here.

What happened? *I said no to my son when he asked me if I'd work on the costumes for his junior high school play. I told him I had my own studying to do, and that his class would have to find another parent to do it.*

How did you say no? *I kind of snapped at him about something else and then slid it in at the end. "Oh, and another thing. . . ."*

What response did you get? *He told me that I was selfish and self-centered, and that I had been ever since "this incest shit" came up. That kid really knows how to push my buttons.*

Then what did you do? *I backed down and ended up promising to do more than I'd been asked to do initially.*

How do you feel about the interaction? *I felt like I'd failed.*

Is there anything you still need to do? *I need to tell him I made a mistake and say no again. Then I want to discuss with him some alternatives to my finishing the job by myself. I'd like to try to work out a solution with him instead of just laying it on him.*

What would you like to do differently the next time? *I'd like to hold my ground and not back down. I'd like to respond more directly, instead of slipping it into the conversation like I did.*

Interaction #1:

What happened? _____

_____

_____

_____

How did you say no? _____

_____

_____

_____

What response did you get? _____

_____

_____

_____

Then what did you do? _____

_____

_____

_____

How do you feel about the interaction? _____

_____

_____

_____

Is there anything you still need to do? _____

_____

_____

_____

What would you like to do differently the next time? _____

_____

_____

_____

Interaction #2:

What happened? _____

_____

_____

_____

_____

How did you say no? _____

_____

_____

_____

_____

What response did you get? _____

_____

_____

_____

Then what did you do? _____

_____

_____

_____

How do you feel about the interaction? _____

_____

_____

_____

Is there anything you still need to do? _____

_____

_____

_____

What would you like to do differently the next time? _____

_____

_____

_____

Things to Think About:

- How did it feel to say no? How did my experience change from the first situation to the second? What got easier? Harder?

- What have I learned about saying no that I can apply to other situations in my life?

SAYING NO: A WRITING EXERCISE

All of us have someone we need to say no to. It could be someone from your past (a father who didn't protect you, a family friend who abused you, a teacher who belittled you) or someone in the present (a friend who takes advantage of you, a partner who pushes you to have sex before you're ready). There may be many people to whom you need to say no.

Choose someone you need to say no to. Think about that person and all the reasons you need to say no. What do you want the person to stop doing? What do they need to hear you say? How many ways can you say it? Be creative. Be angry. Be expressive. (Be excessive!) Reread the guidelines for freewriting on page 11. Then set a timer or alarm clock for twenty minutes, and tell this person no—clearly and without apology.

REFLECTIONS: LEARNING TO TRUST YOURSELF

It is often difficult for survivors to trust their own thoughts, perceptions, feelings, and ideas. Yet each of us has an inner voice that can guide us. As you learn to pay attention and clear out the negative messages that were forced on you as a child, you make room for that clear inner voice. When you trust yourself, you pay attention to your insights and intuitions, set limits and boundaries, learn to say no, and act in your own behalf.

Here are some questions to help you assess your present feelings, goals, and needs around the issue of learning to trust yourself:

- What feelings did I have as I worked through this chapter?

- What am I feeling right now? What sensations am I experiencing in my body?

- How old did I feel as I worked through the chapter? How old do I feel right now?

- What was hard for me in this chapter? What was confusing? What didn't I understand?

- What did I learn? What commitments have I made? What steps have I taken?

- What did I do that I'm proud of?

- What's still unsettled for me? What, if anything, do I want to come back to or follow up on?

- What do I need to do to take care of myself right now?

GRIEVING
AND MOURNING

When Ellen Bass and I originally wrote the chapter called "Grieving and Mourning" in *The Courage to Heal,* we couldn't settle on a title. It seemed as if we should name the chapter either "Grieving" *or* "Mourning." Each time we worked on the chapter, we'd spend time discussing the relative merits of each title, and each time we'd fail to make a decision. So draft after draft, the title remained "Grieving and Mourning." We'd say to each other, "Oh well, we still have time to pick which name we want to use."

When we were completing the final draft of the book, we had this discussion for the last time. We were sitting together in front of the manuscript. I was holding a red pencil. We were staring at the title of the chapter. To break the deadlock, I crossed out "Grieving" and left the word "Mourning" at the top of the page. Ellen said, "I don't think that's right." So I erased the line I'd just drawn and crossed out "Mourning" instead. She looked at it for a moment, turned to me, and said, "I don't think that's right either." I put down the pencil and sighed. She sighed too. Then she turned to me and said, "You know, Laura, I think I know what it is. Survivors feel so bad when they're dealing with the pain of abuse that no one word is sufficient." So we left the title "Grieving and Mourning."

There are no exercises that will alleviate your need to grieve. Reliving painful memories and experiencing loss and loneliness are a large part of the healing process. There are no shortcuts when it comes to feeling these emotions. You will have tears—many of them. You will cry for a long time.

At every workshop, there's always one survivor who cries from the first introductions all the way through to the end. Others may not be able to cry at all, but the survivor who is crying is in touch with sadness and has hit the stage of grieving and mourning.

When you're grieving you need permission, validation, and room to feel. You need compassion and sympathy, both from yourself and from the people around you. It's a lot easier to have your loss validated when someone actually dies than when you're grieving for a lost childhood, a missing family, years lost to coping, or the struggle to survive. Because the loss you are grieving for is less tangible (for other people, not for you), you will probably find it harder to get the sympathy and understanding you deserve. That's why you have to validate your own losses and create avenues for your grief.

The exercises in this chapter will help you name your losses. You will also have the opportunity to create a grieving ritual.

NAMING YOUR LOSSES: A WRITING EXERCISE

If you're having trouble getting in touch with your grief, or if you can't justify all the sadness you're feeling, take some time to record your losses. You may be missing something quite concrete, like a grandfather for your children or the education you never received. Or you might be grieving for something more intangible—your stolen innocence or a loss of faith in God. Whatever it is you're grieving for, taking the time to mark your losses can provide relief and validation.

Take a few minutes to consider the following questions: What normal growing-up experiences did I miss? What opportunities were stolen from me? What relationships have I lost? What dreams and visions was I forced to give up because of the abuse? What areas of my life are lacking today because of what happened to me? What might my life have been like if this had never happened to me?

Reread the guidelines for freewriting on page 11. Then set a timer or alarm clock for twenty minutes, and write about the things you have to grieve for.

ACTIVITY: CREATING A GRIEVING RITUAL

In many cultures, a person in mourning dresses in black for a year after a loved one dies. Although this tradition is somewhat antiquated today, wearing black has some intrinsic value. The outward display of grief alerts the rest of the community that special care and attention must be paid to the grieving person. When someone is in mourning, external pressures and expectations are eased.

When you're mourning the ravages of child sexual abuse, there is no established way to let people know that you need extra attention. There's no outward symbol that tells people "I'm suffering a major loss in my life. I can't do as much right now. I need you to take special care of me."

I think it's time we created those means. We need to have things we can say and do to let people know we're grieving, that we're struggling to recover from a major loss. One survivor who had cut all ties with her parents went around telling everyone that they were dead. Although her parents had not literally died, they were dead to her. Saying they had died gave her some of the sympathy she needed. Another woman, who did not want to lie, took to saying "I lost my family under tragic circumstances."

Creating rituals for grieving can transform our mourning from a lonely, isolated experience into one rich in support, connection, and meaning.* In her book *To Dance with God: Family Ritual and Community Celebration,* Gertrud Mueller Nelson says that ritual gives us "a place to officially engage in our sorrows, a healthy way to suffer."† Rituals are ways to acknowledge grief, to transform fear into courage, to mark the passages and crises inherent in the healing process, to infuse despair with hope. Rituals can help build and strengthen the community of supporters who nurture your healing.

At one abuse survivors conference I attended, each survivor received a helium balloon. We were asked to imagine something we wanted

---

* Survivors who've been abused in a ritualized way or as part of a cult ritual may find it difficult or impossible to reclaim ritual in a positive way. This is completely understandable. Rituals are valuable for healing only if they feel safe and empowering. If the idea of using ritual as a way to heal doesn't feel empowering to you, skip this section. You can validate your losses in another way.

† Gertrud Mueller Nelson. *To Dance with God: Family Ritual and Community Celebration.* Mahwah, N.J.: Paulist Press, 1986. This book is an inspiring, beautifully written guide to developing rituals. It focuses on the holidays of the Christian calendar. (To order send $9.95 + $1.00 shipping to Paulist Press, 997 MacArthur Blvd., Mahwah, NJ 07430.)

to let go of, something we were grieving about, and then we released the balloons into the open air. It was a dramatic, empowering experience, a way of sharing our losses in the context of a healing community.

In a survivor workshop I led in rural Maine, we ended the day by taking down the sheets of paper on the wall marked "Name the Abuser," which were filled with the names of perpetrators. We passed them around, and each of us tore off a piece, walked over to the big wood stove that had warmed us through the weekend, and tossed the names into the flames. It was a closing ritual that gave the workshop a sense of completion and unity.

Rituals can be rooted in centuries of tradition, or they can be created in the moment. To create a personal ritual, you set aside a specific time, select a place that has special meaning, choose symbols or activities that have significance for you. You can do your ritual alone or with others, inviting only those people who will honor and respect its purpose and intent.

Spend some time thinking about a grieving ritual. The questions below can help you develop your thoughts, ideas, and plans.

What is the event or experience I want to mark? What is the transition I want to honor?

_____

_____

_____

_____

What is the theme of the ritual? _____

_____

_____

What mood do I want to express? _____

_____

_____

What is the goal of the ritual? _____

_____

_____

How do I want to feel when it is over? How do I want to be changed? _____

_____

_____

_____

Are there particular things I want to say or that I want to have said to me? _____

_____

_____

_____

_____

_____

_____

Are there particular symbols or special objects I want to include in the ritual? (photos, drums, stones, articles of clothing, mementos)

_____

_____

_____

_____

Are there any religious symbols or traditions that I want to include? _____

_____

_____

_____

Do I want my ritual to include storytelling or reading? Music? Silence? _____

_____

_____

_____

Is there any kind of movement or dancing I want as part of the ritual? If so, how?

_____

_____

_____

_____

Are there any special foods I want to serve? What are they? _____

_____

_____

_____

Where do I want the ritual to be? Should it be indoors or outdoors? _____

_____

_____

_____

_____

When should it be held? Why? _____

_____

_____

_____

Do I want other people to participate? What role do I want them to play? _____

_____

_____

_____

Do I want a leader? If so, what do I want the leader to do? _____

_____

_____

_____

Other things I want in my ritual: _____

_____

_____

_____

_____

Things to Think About:

- Have rituals been a part of my life before? If so, how?

- Have my previous experiences with ritual been positive, negative, or neutral? If they've been negative, is there a way I could reclaim the use of ritual for myself? Do I want to?

- Are there other ways I could use rituals in healing? Could I use them to note achievements, celebrate victories, mark the way, or accompany times of risk-taking?

REFLECTIONS: GRIEVING AND MOURNING

As you face the long-term effects of abuse and relive the trauma of your childhood, you will feel tremendous sadness. It's inevitable. Feeling grief is an essential part of the healing process. Until you acknowledge the losses from your past, you can't really move forward in the present.

Grief needs to be expressed. You need to name your losses and feel the anguish of mourning. Although it seems as if your sad feelings may last forever, grieving fully ensures that you will eventually move on.

Rituals can help give shape to your grief. By grieving in the context of a supportive community, your grief can be witnessed, acknowledged, and validated, thus lightening your burden.

Here are some questions to help you assess your present feelings, goals, and needs around the issue of grieving and mourning:

- **What feelings did I have as I worked through this chapter?**

- What am I feeling right now? What sensations am I experiencing in my body?

- How old did I feel as I worked through the chapter? How old do I feel right now?

- What was hard for me in this chapter? What was confusing? What didn't I understand?

- What did I learn? What commitments have I made? What steps have I taken?

- What did I do that I'm proud of?

- What's still unsettled for me? What, if anything, do I want to come back to or follow up on?

- What do I need to do to take care of myself right now?

ANGER

The most logical and appropriate response to abuse is anger. Sexual abuse is a wholly unacceptable and heinous crime. It deserves your full-blown rage. You were the victim of an atrocity. You have the right to get angry and to stay angry as long as you want.

This concept of anger as a positive, healing force contradicts most societal beliefs. Many of us (particularly women) have been taught that anger is unnecessary or counterproductive. We've been urged by family members to hurry up and get through our anger so we can get to the forgiveness part. Many forms of religion and spirituality tell us to turn the other cheek. Even well-intentioned (but misinformed) therapists have been scared by our anger and urged us to contain it.

In *The Courage to Heal* we called anger "the backbone of healing," because it can keep you going through the ups and downs of the healing process. Anger motivates you to say "I'm going to heal, no matter what. I won't give up. I won't let my abuser win." Anger is the most effective antidote to hopelessness and depression. It can inspire you to make deep and lasting changes in your life.

To be effective, anger must be directed clearly at the abuser and at the people who failed to protect you. Yet this is often very difficult for survivors, who frequently turn their anger in on themselves, lost control and lash out at others, or have no awareness of anger at all. When anger is turned inward, the results are depression, illness, addictions, self-destructive behaviors, and self-hatred. When it's misdirected toward other people, anger becomes a destructive force, one that creates barriers to intimacy and leads to further abuse. When you're unaware of anger, you can't begin to focus it or use it as a healing tool. To work for you, anger must be turned clearly and squarely at its source—the people who hurt and abused you.

The exercises in this chapter will help you assess your current experience of anger. A pair of writing exercises will help you get in touch with your anger and give you a chance to express it. You'll be asked to consider the ways anger can motivate you into action. And finally, you'll learn about the role of forgiveness in the healing process.

ANGER INVENTORY

While we were still children, many of us made choices about the way we were (or weren't) going to relate to our feelings. These early decisions may still be shaping your emotional life today. Answer the following questions about your childhood experiences with anger:*

When my mother got angry, she _____

_____

_____

_____

When my father got angry, he _____

_____

_____

_____

_____

* If you didn't grow up with a mother and a father, substitute the name of someone who took care of you when you were growing up.

When _____ (fill in the name of another household member) got angry, he / she

_____

_____

_____

When I got angry, _____

_____

_____

_____

As a result of my experience while growing up, I made the following decision(s) about anger:

_____

_____

_____

_____

Answer the following questions about your relationship to anger now:

When someone gets angry at me, I _____

_____

_____

_____

When I get angry at someone, I _____

_____

_____

_____

I'm angry at myself for _____

_____

_____

_____

I've turned anger in on myself by _____

_____

_____

_____

Turning anger inward has hurt me because _____

_____

_____

_____

I've misdirected my anger toward others by _____

_____

_____

_____

This misdirected anger has hurt me because _____

_____

_____

_____

This misdirected anger has hurt other people because _____

_____

_____

_____

I used anger effectively when I _____

_____

_____

_____

Ways anger has been empowering to me: _____

_____

_____

_____

I'd like to use my anger to _____

_____

_____

_____

FEAR OF ANGER

Fear of anger is one of the main things that stops survivors from feeling their anger and directing it at the abuser. You may be afraid that anger will take over your life, that you'll never stop being angry, that you'll lose control and kill someone, or that you'll never stop yelling once you start.

If anger is something you're scared of, complete the following:

If I really got in touch with my anger, I'm afraid I would:

- _____

- _____

- _____

I can't get angry because:

- _____

- _____

- _____

The important thing to remember when you look at these fears is that feeling enraged is not the same as acting out of rage. You can fantasize ripping your abuser limb from limb (a sweet fantasy indeed), but you don't have to act on that fantasy. Anger is a feeling, and feelings in and of themselves do not hurt anyone. It is anger that is repressed that leads to violence and loss of control. (If you have problems with violence, the book *Learning to Live Without Violence* offers a step-by-step approach to ending violent behavior.*)

What's the difference between anger and violence? _____

_____

_____

_____

Can I imagine nonviolent anger? _____ yes _____ no _____ I don't know

What would it be like? _____

_____

_____

_____

Is violence ever justified? Why or why not? _____

_____

_____

_____

---

* See "Healing Books," page 455. Although written for men, this book will be helpful for anyone struggling to stop their own violent behavior.

LETTERS TO AN ABUSER: A PAIR OF WRITING EXERCISES

Many survivors want to get angry at their abusers, but the anger doesn't seem to come. Instead of anger, you feel grief and depression. You rationalize the anger away ("Oh well, he was abused too." "She couldn't help herself"), suppress it, turn it on yourself, or simply don't feel it at all.

You may not get angry because you don't think you're worth getting angry about. You may minimize your pain ("Oh well, it wasn't that bad. It's not such a big deal") and think you don't deserve to feel the righteous anger that abuse merits.

In one workshop, where participants were having a hard time getting angry, I asked everyone to calculate the amount of money they'd spent on therapy, support groups, and other healing activities. Together, we tallied up the total and the outrageous figure prompted plenty of anger!

If you can't yet get angry on your own behalf, you may be able to get angry on someone else's. In the writing exercise in "Understanding That It Wasn't Your Fault" (page 268), you were asked to imagine a child the age you were when you were first abused, and to write to that child explaining why he or she wasn't to blame for the abuse. This exercise asks you to go a step further.

Think about that child again. Read over the letter you wrote. Imagine that the things that happened to you are happening to that child. Then think about the person who is abusing the child. Picture that person in your mind. Knowing what the abuser is doing and saying to that child, how do you feel? What would you like to say to the abuser? What do you want to do? What sort of revenge would you like to exact?

Reread the guidelines for freewriting on page 11. Then set a timer or alarm clock for twenty minutes, and write a letter to the child's abuser. Start with the words "You are miserable, rotten slime." Continue from there. Allow your anger to flow.

Once you've been able to get angry at another child's abuser, you may be able to transfer some of that anger to your own abuser. Let the momentum of your anger carry you.

Imagine yourself as a child. Think about what was done to you. Think about what you were forced to do. Consider the losses in your life. Think about the missed opportunities, the wasted years, the struggle to heal today. Then pick one person as the target of your anger, the abuser or someone who didn't protect you. Write a letter to that person. Start with the words, "I'm angry at you" or "I hate you." Set your timer for twenty minutes, and don't hold back.

If you're thinking about sending your angry letter, work through the exercises in "Confrontations," page 340, first.

ANGER INTO ACTION

Anger is a very physical emotion. It needs to be expressed and released regularly. There are many safe and effective ways to do this. You can volunteer to smash glass at a recycling center. You can take a pottery class and pound piles of clay. You can knead dough with a vengeance. You can exercise. Slapping the water as you swim, pounding softballs into the outfield, or imagining the abuser's face on the dance floor as you dance are all great ways to release anger.

Make a list of physical ways you can safely express and release your anger:

- _____
- _____
- _____
- _____
- _____
- _____
- _____
- _____
- _____
- _____
- _____

Anger is also a great motivator. By channeling your anger into action, you can make necessary changes in your life. Do you want to stop going home for the holidays? Tell your sister to protect her children from your stepfather? Report the school counselor who abused you? Quit working for an abusive boss? Stop drinking or taking drugs? End an abusive relationship? Anger can be the force that enables you to take these steps.

With my anger, I'm going to:

- _____
- _____
- _____
- _____
- _____

Anger can also motivate us to take action in the world at large. Fighting back against abuse can be incredibly empowering. Talking to children about good and bad touching, speaking out in the media, working for legislation to increase penalties for child molestation, or getting involved in survivors groups and organizations can be effective ways to channel and express your anger. Although you shouldn't rush your own healing in order to go out and save the world, taking steps to fight back against abuse can dramatically alter your sense of isolation and powerlessness.

When I'm ready to turn my attention back out into the world, I'd like to:

- _____
- _____
- _____
- _____
- _____

Things to Think About:

- What would I like to do with my anger? How could my anger serve me?

- What small thing could I do to help stop child sexual abuse?

- Am I ready to do that thing now, or do I need to stay focused on my own healing for a while?

ACTIVITY: THE BANNER PROJECT

Survivors are often invisible. To combat that invisibility, two members of an Incest Survivors Anonymous support group in Madison, Wisconsin, started the Banner Project in 1989. Survivors create individual cloth panels which use a handprint as a symbol of strength and courage. The panels are sewn together to create a banner that is displayed at rallies, public programs, and gatherings of survivors. Wherever it is displayed, the Banner Project visually dramatizes the impact of abuse and the healing power of survivors. It is a powerful way to call attention to the number of survivors and to the need for services.

A self-help project for survivors, the Banner Project is continuing to grow. Making a panel for the Banner can be a creative and empowering way to express your anger, pride, pain, and courage.

You can participate in the Banner Project in the following ways:

- Join with other survivors to start your own banner. The Banner Project will be glad to share information to assist you.

- Send in your own banner section. It will be added to the original Banner and included in future displays. (If you're in a support group, you might want to do it as a group activity.)

- Organize to display the Banner in your community.

INSTRUCTIONS FOR MAKING A BANNER SECTION

Any survivor, male or female, of any age, or anyone who suspects they might be a survivor, even if they're not sure, is invited to make a banner section.

Your banner section should be made out of fabric, with a finished size of 11 inches wide and 8½ inches tall (the size of a sheet of paper turned sideways). Draw, embroider, appliqué, paint, or otherwise imprint your handprint on the fabric. You may add any other words, design, image, or message that you wish to personalize your section. You may put your name or initials on it, but it is not necessary. Leave a half-inch margin on the sides so the sections can be sewn together (please do not use fabrics that are too heavy to sew). Indicate which way is up by using an arrow on the back.

Mail your completed banner section to: The Banner Project, Wisconsin Committee to Prevent Child Abuse, 214 N. Hamilton St., Madison, WI 53703, (Attn. Sally Caspar), (608) 256-3374; fax (608) 256-3378, e-mail: wcpca@juno.com. (Banner sections become the property of the Banner Project and cannot be returned.)

If you are able to, please send a donation of help pay for organizing costs. Any amount will be appreciated. Checks should be made payable to The Banner Project.

The confidentiality of all survivors will be protected.

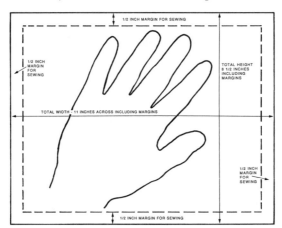

FORGIVENESS?

Whenever I talk to people about anger, they inevitably bring up forgiveness. For many people the two concepts are inextricably linked. Anger, if it has any viable purpose at all, is seen as a prelude to forgiving the abuser. This kind of thinking hurts survivors. It's also dead wrong.

Some things in life are unforgivable. Period. Child sexual abuse is one of them. *You don't have to forgive your abuser in order to heal.*

This single concept—that you don't have to forgive—has been one of the most liberating concepts in *The Courage to Heal*. Wherever we went promoting the book, someone in the audience would stand up and say, "Could you just repeat that part about forgiveness again?" And we would. And I will: You don't have to forgive your abuser in order to heal.

In *The Courage to Heal* we took some time to analyze exactly what forgiveness is. I want to repeat that discussion here, because it's essential to understanding what is and isn't necessary in terms of forgiveness:

> To find out exactly what forgiveness is, we looked in the dictionary and found these definitions: (a) to cease to feel resentment against an offender; (b) to give up claim of requital from an offender; to grant relief from payment.
>
> There are, then, two elements in what we call forgiveness. One is that you give up your anger and no longer hold the abuser to blame; you excuse them for what they did to you. The other element is that you no longer try to get some kind of compensation from the abuser. You give up trying to get financial compensation, a statement of guilt, an apology, respect, love, understanding—anything. Separating these two aspects of forgiveness makes it possible to clarify what is and what is not necessary in order to heal from child sexual abuse.
>
> It is true that eventually you must give up trying to get something back from the abuser. This process need not be hurried. It is appropriate and courageous to fight back any way you choose. However, at some point, trying to get from abusers what they aren't going to give keeps you trapped. There comes a time when what you feel about the abuser is less important than what you feel about yourself, your current life, and your future. The abuser is not your primary concern. You say, "*I* am my primary concern. Whether the abuser rots or not, I'm going on with my own life." . . .
>
> This stance is not incompatible with anger. And none of this pardons or excuses the abuser.
>
> When a friend inadvertently hurts our feelings and apologizes, we forgive her. We no longer blame her. The relationship is mended. We are reconciled and we continue with trust and respect, without residual anger between us. This kind of forgiveness—giving up anger and pardoning the abuser, restoring a relationship of trust—is not necessary in order to heal from the trauma of being sexually abused as a child.*

---

* Ellen Bass and Laura Davis, *The Courage to Heal* (New York: Harper and Row, 1988), p. 150.

If at some point in your healing, you come to feel compassion or understanding for your abuser, that's fine. It's a personal decision, not the goal of healing. It is not essential to your own recovery.

There is only one essential forgiveness you must have to heal from child sexual abuse, and that is forgiveness for yourself. If you're struggling with shame, you will need to forgive the child inside of you for having been vulnerable, for having needed attention and affection. You'll have to forgive your adult self for the ways you coped, for the mistakes you've made. But you do not have to forgive your abuser.

Most of us have been indoctrinated with strong ideas about forgiveness. Examining those messages is the first step in coming up with your own understanding of forgiveness.

Messages I've received from my religion about forgiveness:

- _____

  _____

- _____

  _____

- _____

  _____

- _____

  _____

Messages I've received from my family about forgiveness:

- _____

  _____

- _____

  _____

- _____

  _____

- _____

  _____

Messages I've received from other people about forgiveness (name them):

- _____

  _____

- _____

  _____

- _____

  _____

- _____

  _____

For me, forgiveness is _____

_____

_____

_____

_____

_____

I still need to forgive myself for:

- _____
  _____

- _____
  _____

- _____
  _____

- _____
  _____

I can forgive myself by:

- _____
  _____

- _____
  _____

- _____
  _____

- _____
  _____

REFLECTIONS: ANGER

As you start to face the long-term effects of abuse in your life, the natural response is anger. Many survivors have turned their anger in on themselves or lashed out at others. To heal, you need to redirect your anger directly and clearly at the abuser and the people who failed to protect you. When you respect your anger and channel it into action, it motivates and empowers you, sparking tremendous healing and change.

One of the least understood aspects of the healing process is forgiveness. Many people think survivors need to forgive their abusers, but this is not true. The only essential forgiveness is for yourself.

Here are some questions to help you assess your present feelings, goals, and needs around the issue of anger:

• **What feelings did I have as I worked through this chapter?**

- What am I feeling right now? What sensations am I experiencing in my body?

- How old did I feel as I worked through the chapter? How old do I feel right now?

- What was hard for me in this chapter? What was confusing? What didn't I understand?

- What did I learn? What commitments have I made? What steps have I taken?

- What did I do that I'm proud of?

- What's still unsettled for me? What, if anything, do I want to come back to or follow up on?

- What do I need to do to take care of myself right now?

CONFRONTATIONS

In a confrontation, you stand up as an adult and face the people who hurt you as a child.* You name your experience as sexual abuse, express your feelings, and talk about the way the abuse has affected you. Confrontations can be incredibly empowering because you learn that you are strong and powerful. You experience the freedom of telling the truth and you break the silence that has bound you. Confrontations give you the opportunity to get information about your past, protect children in the present, gain support for your healing, and give up false hopes that keep you tied to damaging relationships.

At the same time, confrontations can be overwhelming and disappointing. It is terrifying to confront the abuser or to risk the condemnation of your family. Even with preparation and support, confrontations can be shattering.

Unlike other parts of the recovery process, confrontations are not essential to healing. The choice to confront is a personal one. If your abuser is dead or unknown, if you don't want to be called crazy or a liar, if you don't want to risk physical injury from a potentially violent person, or if you simply don't want to, you don't have to confront. You can heal without it.

---

* A confrontation happens quickly, and then it's over. It has a distinct beginning and end. Your relationships with family members, however, develop and change over the years. This chapter deals with the specific issues surrounding the actual confrontation itself. The next one, "Dealing with Your Family Now," can help you deal with the implications of confrontations on family relationships over time.

In "Breaking Silence" (page 234), you learned about talking to supportive people about your abuse. In this chapter you'll gain skills in confronting people who are more likely to be threatened or upset when you talk about having been sexually abused. The exercises in this chapter are designed to help you decide whether a particular confrontation is right for you. You'll have the opportunity to explore your fears and expectations, to weigh the pros and cons of a particular confrontation. If you decide to confront, you'll learn how to design a plan for doing so. If you don't, "The Other Eulogy" on page 361 will give you an opportunity to express your feelings without confronting directly.

WHAT HAVE I DONE ALREADY?

You may be considering the idea of confrontation for the first time or you may already have done a confrontation. You may be wondering if you want to confront a particular person or you might already have decided to go ahead; you need help with planning and strategies.

Start by assessing where you are right now. Have you already started the process of confrontation? Are there people you've already ruled out as far as confrontations go? Is there anyone you're actively considering confronting at the present time?

People I've already confronted:

_____   _____

_____   _____

_____   _____

People I'm thinking of confronting:

_____   _____

_____   _____

_____   _____

People I don't want to confront:

_____   _____

_____   _____

_____   _____

People I'm uncertain about:

_____   _____

_____   _____

_____   _____

If you've already experienced a confrontation and are considering another, it can be helpful to assess your initial experience(s). You can complete the following for each confrontation you've done:

I confronted _____

As a result of that confrontation, _____

_____

_____

_____

_____

How did I feel about the confrontation when I did it? How do I feel about it now?

_____

_____

_____

_____

If I could do the confrontation over, I would _____

_____

_____

_____

I don't feel finished with that person. I still need to _____

_____

_____

_____

Things to Think About:

- What can I learn from the confrontations I've already done?

- What are my current goals regarding confrontations?

- (If you're considering a confrontation) What do I stand to lose if I confront? If I don't? What are the risks involved?

SHOULD I CONFRONT?

This exercise will help you decide whether you want to confront a particular person at this time. You can repeat it as many times as necessary. You may decide that you don't want to confront now, but you do later on. You may decide to confront your brother and not your grandfather. You may want to confront everyone involved in your abuse in any way. Or you may decide you don't want to confront anyone. Take the time to make an independent, separate decision about each potential confrontation.

Choose a particular person you're considering. On the left side of the page below, write down the reasons you want to confront (It wouldn't be hanging over my head anymore / I'm sick of the silence in my family. I want to protect my nephews / I won't have to come up with fake excuses about not visiting anymore / I want to set an example for my son that these things can be talked about). On the right side of the page, write down the reasons you don't want to confront (I'm afraid I won't be able to see my nephew again / I'm scared Dad will have another heart atttack / My support system isn't strong enough yet / I don't want to be told I'm crazy one more time / My stepfather might get violent / I don't think my sister can take it / I don't want to make waves or upset people).

I'm thinking about confronting _____

Reasons I want to confront   **Reasons I don't want to**

_____   _____

_____   _____

_____   _____

_____   _____

_____   _____

_____   _____

Reasons I want to confront　　　　　**Reasons I don't want to**

_____　　_____

_____　　_____

_____　　_____

_____　　_____

_____　　_____

_____　　_____

Go back to both lists and write the appropriate initials next to each response:

- **PF** (protecting family): reasons that have to do with not upsetting your family

- **PS** (protecting self): reasons that have to do with protecting yourself

- **PC** (protecting children): reasons that have to do with protecting children

- **F** (fear): reasons that stem from fear

- **S** (shame): reasons that are rooted in shame

- **E** (empowering): reasons that are empowering to you

While there are good reasons for not confronting, protecting a sick family or feeling too ashamed is not among them. Go back and cross out all the reasons marked **PF** or **S**. Now go back and list the reasons you marked **F**, those rooted in fear:

_____　　_____

_____　　_____

_____　　_____

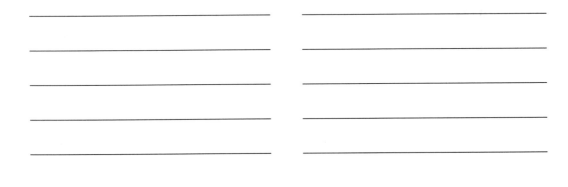

There are three kinds of fear to look at when considering a confrontation. The first is fear you carry over from childhood—childhood fear **(CF)**. (My Dad said he'd kill me if I told / The world will end if I tell / My words have the power to destroy people.) These fears are usually distorted or false.

The second kind of fear is realistic fear **(RF)**. It is based on a possible or probable outcome in the present. (My sister might not let me see my niece / I might get disinherited / My uncle might not talk to me anymore / My stepfather is psychotic and unpredictable and he might get violent.) These fears need to be considered in weighing your alternatives.

The third kind of fear is the inevitable fear that accompanies any courageous act. I call this warrior fear **(WF)**—the fear that accompanies great acts of courage and healing. Deciding to confront a wall of denial or a hostile family is terrifying. That doesn't mean it isn't worthwhile. Fear is sometimes worth pushing through (see "Preparing for Change" on page 170).

Go through your list of fears and categorize them, just as you did the last list. This time, use the following set of initials:

- **CF**: fears based on childhood messages

- **RF**: fears that are realistic

- **WF**: fears that accompany any act of courage

Take your list of fears and cross out the fears marked **CF**, so that only **WF** (warrior fear) and **RF** (realistic fear) remain.

Go back to your original lists. Cross out the **CF** statements there too. The remaining list should be limited to things that protect you, empower you, protect children, or are realistic or warrior fears. Although the reasons you crossed out may still affect your thinking about a given confrontation, the pros and cons that remain are the most realistic and empowering reasons on which to base your decision.

When you've finished examining your reasons, complete the following:

What was the scariest / hardest thing to cross out? Why? _____

_____

_____

_____

_____

Am I ready to let go of the things I crossed out? Or do I need to keep them as part of my decision-making process?

_____

_____

_____

_____

_____

Can I go ahead with the confrontation even though my realistic fears might be realized? Why or why not?

_____

_____

_____

_____

_____

If my worst fears were realized, how would I live with the result? _____

_____

_____

_____

_____

Did I cross out most of the reasons on my original list? Or only a few? What does this tell me?

_____

_____

_____

_____

_____

Things to Think About:

- What was clarified as a result of this exercise?

- Am I any clearer about the particular confrontation I'm considering? If so, how?

Many survivors secretly (or not so secretly) enter into a confrontation hoping that things will magically be set right. Your sister will divorce your brother-in-law. Your cousin will apologize and pay for your therapy. The principal will fire the teacher. Everyone will believe you and comfort you, offering the kind of nurturing and support you've always longed for. Except in rare circumstances, these outcomes are fantasies. What's more likely is that you will be discounted, called crazy or a liar, ignored, scapegoated, or attacked.

It is crucial that you enter a confrontation because it will strengthen and empower you, not because you're hoping for a particular response. As a child, you could not protect yourself. Now you can. As an adult, you can assess the situation realistically, form realistic expectations, set self-protective ground rules, and say what you want to say directly and powerfully.

To prepare effectively for a confrontation, you will have to recognize and relinquish, to the greatest extent possible, any unrealistic expectations you're carrying. It may be impossible for you to give up all of your fantasies before you confront—sometimes only repeated confrontations and disappointments make it possible to finally let go. But try to eliminate as many false hopes as you can ahead of time. The following exercise will help you identify and weed through your expectations.

Finish the following sentences as honestly and completely as you can. Admitting your fantasies is the first step in letting go of them. Include your deepest, most far-flung fantasies:

When I confront   *my mother,*   I hope that she   *begins to cry, rushes toward me, puts her arms around me, says, "There, there. I'm so sorry this happened. I'll kill the bastard. Tell me what I can do. I'll do anything to help you."*

When I confront   *my ex-therapist,*   I hope that he   *shrivels up and dies on the spot.*

When I confront   *my brother,*   I hope that he   *says he did something terrible and that he will do anything he can to help me heal. He'll offer to pay for my therapy and go to therapy himself, but promises never to rush me in my healing process.*

When I confront _____,

I hope that he / she _____

_____

_____

_____

_____

When I confront _____,

I hope that he / she _____

_____

_____

_____

_____

When I confront _____,

I hope that he / she _____

_____

_____

_____

_____

When I confront _____,

I hope that he / she _____

_____

_____

_____

_____

When I confront _____,

I hope that he / she _____

_____

_____

_____

_____

When I confront _____,

I hope that he / she _____

_____

_____

_____

_____

Go back over your responses. Using a different color pen or pencil, categorize each part of your response using the following code:

P: definitely possible
U: unpredictable or unlikely
F: fantasy or wishful thinking

How many of your hopes and expectations were realistic? _____

How many were unpredictable or unlikely? _____

How many were in the realm of fantasy? _____

Things to Think About:

- How do I feel about giving up the hopes I judged to be fantasies?

- What would my life be like without them?

- Is it easier for me to give up hope with some people than with others? Who is easier? Who is harder? Why?

MAKING A CONFRONTATION PLAN

In a confrontation, you clearly and directly tell someone about your abuse: what happened, how it hurt you, and how you feel about it. You can express your feelings, give information, set limits, and ask for things you want. Confrontations can be done in a variety of ways—in person, on the phone, in a letter, through a messenger. A confrontation is not a discussion. It is a statement of fact. You control how long it lasts, where it takes place, and what you say. You are the one in charge.

Yet facing someone who abused you, didn't protect you, or doesn't want to hear what you have to say can easily flip you into childhood feelings of powerlessness. Naively, many survivors begin a confrontation unprepared, with no sense of what they're going to do or say. In doing so, they relinquish control and slip back into the role of the powerless child, waiting for Mommy or Daddy or the official in charge to take control. When you're confronting a dysfunctional family or an indifferent bureaucracy, this attitude can be disastrous. I call it the "lamb to slaughter" school of confrontation. I've done it myself, when I didn't know better, and I regret it. I wish I'd taken the time to prepare. It's much more effective and self-loving to have a plan.

It may feel strange to set out a concrete plan for something that is so charged and emotional, but that's precisely why you need one. Your plan will give you a framework to lean on when you start feeling out of control or panicked. Things may not (and probably won't) go exactly according to your plan since you're dealing with other (unpredictable) people, but if you take the time, you can think through various potential outcomes and come up with strategies for handling each one.

Walk through each step of the confrontation, from beginning to end. What do you want to say? How do you want to say it? What are you going to do to take care of yourself?

If at all possible, involve other people in planning your confrontation. Talking to other survivors who've done it before, brainstorming with a friend, or working it out with your therapist can help you clarify your goals. Support people can make specific suggestions (Why don't you ask your sister to come here instead of going to where she lives?), offer practical assistance (I'll go with you. I'll sit with you while you call), and point out holes in your plan (But what if your father refuses to leave the room?).

Consider the following questions:

How do I want to confront?   *(in a letter / in person / on the phone)* _____

_____ Why have I chosen this method?

_____

_____

_____

_____

_____

_____

If I'm choosing to do the confrontation in person, where do I want to do it? Why is it the best choice? Have I considered other alternatives?

_____

_____

_____

_____

_____

_____

Do I want anyone else be present? Why or why not? _____

_____

_____

_____

_____

_____

When will I do the confrontation? Why have I chosen this time? _____

_____

_____

_____

_____

_____

_____

How long will the confrontation last? How will I know when it's over? _____

_____

_____

_____

_____

_____

This is what I want to say and do: _____

_____

_____

_____

_____

_____

_____

_____

_____

_____

_____

_____

_____

_____

_____

_____

_____

_____

(Use additional pages as needed. Sometimes, writing out an entire plan or an actual script can be helpful.)

This is what I'm going to ask for: _____

_____

_____

_____

_____

_____

_____

_____

When it's over, I'm going to: _____

_____

_____

_____

_____

_____

_____

If I start to lose myself, I will: _____

_____

_____

_____

_____

To take care of myself, I'm going to: _____

_____

_____

_____

_____

My backup support people are: _____

_____

_____

_____

I'm going to ask them to: _____

_____

_____

_____

_____

Things to Think About:

- How will I respond if the person I confront denies or minimizes the abuse?

- How will I respond if I get a hostile reaction? What if I'm ignored and get no reaction at all?

- How could I make the confrontation valuable no matter what reaction I get?

AFTER THE CONFRONTATION

You can assess how the confrontation went by asking yourself the following:

How do I feel now? _____

_____

_____

_____

_____

Was I able to take care of myself? If not, what got in my way? _____

_____

_____

_____

_____

Did I say what I wanted to say? If not, what was left unsaid? _____

_____

_____

_____

_____

How would I do things differently if I had another chance? _____

_____

_____

_____

_____

Is there anything I've learned from this confrontation that I could apply to another one?

_____

_____

_____

_____

_____

What am I proud of? _____

_____

_____

_____

_____

Things to Think About:

• Was the confrontation worthwhile to me? Why or why not?

• Is there anything unfinished about this confrontation? If so, what do I need to do about it?

• What kind of contact, if any, do I want with this person now?

THE OTHER EULOGY: A WRITING EXERCISE

Survivors often despair of healing because their abusers are dead or otherwise unavailable for a confrontation. But it is possible to confront in absentia. You can write a letter, say what you have to say to a pile of pillows at your therapist's office, role-play with another survivor, or confront symbolically. That is what I chose to do.

My grandfather died six years before I remembered his assaults, so I never had the opportunity to confront him in person. But I still felt the need to get the anger out. I was furious that he had the nerve to die before I remembered. I had, in fact, written a eulogy for my grandfather, about the vibrant Eastern European heritage he passed on to me. I had talked about his immigrant roots and his struggles in coming to America. I talked about the richness I had gained from his culture and his individuality. I had put this man, who had forced me to suck his penis, who had raped and violated me, on a pedestal. I felt sick inside. I'd let him get away with it.

One day I had an idea at a writing workshop. I started writing furiously. At the top of the page I wrote *The Other Eulogy*. Then I started out: "There were a few things you gave me that I forgot to mention the last time around. . . ." And from that point on, I wrote nonstop, pouring out page after page of my indignation, my rage, my grief; page after page naming his violations. It was a most satisfying exercise. My voice shook as I read it out loud in that circle of women. It was terrifying and empowering to finally tell the truth, to graphically set out the things he'd really given me. I never read *The Other Eulogy* outside of that group, but the writing and the telling were a powerful catharsis nonetheless. It was the confrontation I'd longed for.

Reread the guidelines for freewriting on page 11. Then set a timer or alarm clock for twenty minutes, and write a eulogy for your offender. Imagine your offender dead (if he or she isn't already). Imagine standing up at the funeral. How do you want your abuser remembered? What's the legacy he or she left behind? What was his or her real impact in the world? On your life? Imagine the power of having an audience hanging on your every word. This is your chance to set the record straight. Spare nothing.

REFLECTIONS: CONFRONTATIONS

Confronting your abuser(s), members of your family, or other people connected to your abuse can be incredibly empowering. Confrontations can make you feel like a strong adult in the face of people who have always treated you like a powerless child. They can liberate you from false beliefs about your family and free you to get on with your life. But confrontations can also be stressful and terrifying.

If you choose to confront, it's unlikely that you'll get a satisfying reaction. Most survivors experience denial, minimizing, anger, and rejection when they confront. It's only in rare instances that you actually get the support you deserve. Therefore it's essential that the confrontation be for you, not because you're hoping for a particular response.

If you're considering a confrontation, weigh your motives carefully and take the time to prepare. Knowing what you want to say and how you want to say it is crucial. It's also important that you get adequate support. Never underestimate the impact of a confrontation. They can free you, but they can also shake you to your roots.

It is possible to heal without a face-to-face confrontation. The decision to confront is a personal one. Confronting is only one of the many ways you can express your feelings about what happened to you.

Here are some questions to help you assess your present feelings, goals, and needs around the issue of confrontations:

- What feelings did I have as I worked through this chapter?

- What am I feeling right now? What sensations am I experiencing in my body?

- How old did I feel as I worked through the chapter? How old do I feel right now?

- What was hard for me in this chapter? What was confusing? What didn't I understand?

- What did I learn? What commitments have I made? What steps have I taken?

- What did I do that I'm proud of?

- What's still unsettled for me? What, if anything, do I want to come back to or follow up on?

- What do I need to do to take care of myself right now?

DEALING WITH YOUR FAMILY NOW

Families are supposed to give solace in time of need, to be there in hard times, to rally around in a crisis. When you're struggling to heal from child sexual abuse, you desperately need this kind of nurturing, encouragement, and practical assistance. But the family you grew up with is not likely to give it to you.* If you approach your family with vulnerability and an open heart, you are likely to be belittled, ignored, or attacked. Instead of being supportive, your family will probably minimize or deny the abuse.†

Sometimes family members support you in one way but undercut you in another. Your father pays for your therapy but expects to be forgiven. Your mother says she supports you but tells you to hurry up and put it in the past. Your brother says he's sorry but continues making inappropriate sexual remarks whenever you're around. In these cases the lack of support isn't as blatant, but it still undermines you.

---

* Anyone who was significant to you during your childhood or adolescence qualifies as family, whether they're blood relatives or not. If the extended family or alternative family you grew up with doesn't fit the examples in this chapter, just change the words to fit your circumstances. For the purposes of this book, the people you grew up with will be referred to as your "family of origin."

† This is particularly true in families where incest took place. People abused by a stranger or someone outside the immediate family circle are more likely to get support from their families, although this is not always the case.

There are exceptions to this. Family members have been known to be supportive, loving allies; it's just that it's rare. If one out of every hundred survivors has support from his or her family, you, of course, want to be that exception—and are crushed when you're not. When approaching your family, it's safer to expect hostile responses, silence, lack of respect, denial, and ambivalence, because that's what you're most likely to get. And if you're lucky enough to find a true supporter in your family, you'll have unexpected cause to celebrate.

Although you probably won't get the support you want, there are other good reasons for having contact with your family. Interactions with your family can be excellent opportunities to gain information, to validate how far you've come, to test your perceptions, and to practice setting limits. Bumping up against a lack of support in your family can motivate you to build a stronger, more responsive support system elsewhere.

It's important that you approach your family with realistic expectations. This isn't easy. Many of us have to butt our heads against our families many times before we realize we're not going to get what we want. Coming to terms with your family can take years. No matter how willing and prepared you are, dealing with an unsupportive family usually leads to a painful cycle of hope, disappointment, loss, and revised expectations. Even in families where relationships improve over time, the process is frequently painstaking and slow.

In the preceding chapter you read about planning an initial confrontation with people in your family, but a confrontation is only a moment in time. This chapter expands on the issues introduced in "Confrontations," focusing on strategies for dealing with your family of origin over the long haul. You'll define what a family is and assess the quality of your family relationships today. You'll assess which connections, if any, you value and want to keep with members of your family. You'll use writing as a way to let go of unrealistic fantasies. And finally, you'll develop your own set of ground rules for family contact. The chapter closes with a discussion of what to do if your ground rules aren't respected.

WHAT IS A FAMILY?

Our expectations about family life are directly related to our childhood experiences. As a result, those of us who grew up in abusive homes often have a distorted, unhealthy picture of what a family is.

Abusive families are called dysfunctional families, because they don't function properly. Instead of trust, there is fear and betrayal. Instead of encouragement, there is humiliation and neglect. Mixed in with the love is manipulation and violence. Along with affectionate cuddling is sexual abuse. And so on.

In the space below, make a list of characteristics that typically occur in a dysfunctional family (secrecy / lack of trust or respect / poor communication / name-calling / unrealistic expectations / severe punishments / inadequate nurturing / humiliation).

This is an excellent exercise to do in a group setting, with everyone compiling the lists together. As individuals we don't have much information about families that do and don't work; a group can help you round out your answers. If you're not in a group, talk to friends, your counselor, or another support person for ideas about what is and isn't healthy in a family.

CHARACTERISTICS OF AN UNHEALTHY FAMILY

_____ _____

_____ _____

_____ _____

_____ _____

_____ _____

_____ _____

_____ _____

_____ _____

_____ _____

_____ _____

Now think about any relationships (between adults or between parents and children) that you respect. Take some time to identify the common characteristics that exist in those relationships. What are the qualities that make those families work?

Below is a list of qualities that exist in healthy families. Check off those that are most important to you. Add any others you can think of.

CHARACTERISTICS OF A HEALTHY FAMILY

_____ Has fun

_____ Loves me no matter what

_____ Is willing to work through conflicts

_____ Encourages the abilities of every member

_____ Cooperates together

_____ Respects one another

_____ Expresses anger safely

_____ Respects and talks about feelings

_____ Is willing to negotiate and compromise

_____ All members have power according to their age and ability

_____ Girls and boys are treated equally

_____ Small accomplishments are noted and celebrated

_____ It's okay to make mistakes

_____ People can freely say "I was wrong"

_____ Punishments are fair and appropriate

_____ People really listen to each other

_____ Resources are shared equally

_____ Family members are affectionate and warm, but never intrusive

_____ Privacy is respected

_____ Mealtimes are calm and enjoyable

_____ Individual differences are respected and encouraged

_____ Can be silly

_____ Family members are honest with each other

___ _____

___ _____

___ _____

___ _____

___ _____

___ _____

___ _____

___ _____

___ _____

When I look at this list of positive family characteristics, I feel _____

_____

_____

_____

_____

Can I imagine a family having the positive characteristics I just identified?
_____ yes   _____ no   _____ I don't know

Why or why not? _____

_____

_____

_____

EVALUATING MY FAMILY OF ORIGIN

Fill out the following table. In the left-hand column, list the characteristics of a healthy family that you identified in the last exercise. Across the top of the table, write the names of people in your family (parents, stepparents, siblings, grandparents, other signficant relatives or caretakers). Then check off the characteristics that apply to each person.

CHARACTERISTIC	NAME					

(Continued)

This exercise often surprises people because there may be very few checkmarks on the page. It's likely that a lot of blank space is staring back at you. Even though you may know that you have poor relationships with your family members, seeing it graphically can be jarring.

Look over the things you've checked (or haven't checked) and then answer the following questions:

What do I notice when I look at my table? _____

_____

_____

_____

_____

How did the results match my expectations? _____

_____

_____

_____

_____

How did the results differ from my expectations? _____

_____

_____

_____

_____

Do the people in my family have many of the characteristics of a healthy family? Why or why not?

_____

_____

_____

_____

_____

Who had the most healthy characteristics? _____

Who had the least? _____

What does this exercise show me about my family? _____

_____

_____

_____

_____

REDEFINING FAMILY

If this exercise showed you that your family of origin isn't very healthy, you'll need to create an alternative. Families are formed through shared experiences, common values, consistent mutual caring, weathering crises, and love. Blood is not all that determines family ties. If your family hasn't been there for you, you have a much better chance of getting your needs met by an alternative family you create for yourself.

Repeat the preceding exercise, but instead of the names of family members at the top of the table, list names of people in your support system today. You can use the list you came up with on page 37. If you have a partner, include your partner. If someone in your original family does support you, include that person as well. Add anyone else you can think of. Borrow a friend's mother, your neighbor's father. It's okay if the people on your list aren't related or don't know each other.

CHARACTERISTIC

NAME

(Continued)

Look over this table. Compare it to the previous one. It's likely that there's been a dramatic increase in the number of check marks.

If you're still pretty isolated, it may because you didn't have many names to put across the top of the second table. This can be tough. Go back to "Building Your Support System" (page 35) for suggestions on broadening your base of support.

What do I notice when I look at this second table? _____

_____

_____

_____

_____

What do I notice when I compare the two tables? _____

_____

_____

_____

_____

When I look over both charts, who best fills my need for a supportive, healthy family? Why?

_____

_____

_____

_____

What, if anything, do I need to do to strengthen the relationships shown on the second chart?

_____

_____

_____

_____

_____

(If you included a partner in the assessment) What did I learn about the quality of my relationship with my partner?*

_____

_____

_____

_____

_____

Things to Think About:

- What surprised me about these exercises? What did I learn?

- Have these exercises shifted my attitude about family? If so, how?

---

* If your partner doesn't have many of the characteristics healthy families should have, you may not be getting the support and caring you deserve in that relationship. Many survivors are drawn into abusive or unsatisfying relationships because they duplicate childhood dynamics. Although it is beyond the scope of this workbook to do a full assessment of your current relationship, it's essential that you get help if you're in an abusive relationship. See "Resources," page 453, for help in assessing your situation and getting out if necessary.

LOOKING AT INDIVIDUAL RELATIONSHIPS

We tend to think of our families as a single unit. Although there are patterns and behaviors that bind the family together, there are also individual qualities that make people unique, that make certain relationships more viable for us than others. Realistically assessing your relationships with individual family members can help you take control of the way you relate to your family.

Take the list of family members you used in the first exercise (or other ones, if you'd prefer). For each person, fill out the following:

1. When I see (or talk to) _____, I feel _____

_____

_____

_____

_____

The good things about this relationship are _____

_____

_____

_____

_____

The bad things about this relationship are _____

_____

_____

_____

_____

I stay in this relationship because _____

_____

_____

_____

_____

The things I gain from this relationship are _____

_____

_____

_____

_____

2. When I see (or talk to) _____, I feel _____

_____

_____

_____

The good things about this relationship are _____

_____

_____

_____

_____

The bad things about this relationship are _____

_____

_____

_____

_____

I stay in this relationship because _____

_____

_____

_____

_____

The things I gain from this relationship are _____

_____

_____

_____

_____

3. When I see (or talk to) _____, I feel _____

_____

_____

The good things about this relationship are _____

_____

The bad things about this relationship are _____

_____

_____

_____

_____

I stay in this relationship because _____

_____

_____

_____

_____

The things I gain from this relationship are _____

_____

_____

_____

_____

4. When I see (or talk to) _____, I feel _____

_____

_____

The good things about this relationship are _____

_____

_____

_____

_____

The bad things about this relationship are _____

_____

_____

_____

_____

I stay in this relationship because _____

_____

_____

_____

The things I gain from this relationship are _____

_____

_____

_____

_____

5. When I see (or talk to) _____, I feel _____

_____

_____

The good things about this relationship are _____

_____

_____

_____

_____

The bad things about this relationship are _____

_____

_____

_____

_____

I stay in this relationship because _____

_____

_____

_____

The things I gain from this relationship are _____

_____

_____

_____

_____

6. When I see (or talk to) _____, I feel _____

_____

_____

The good things about this relationship are _____

_____

_____

_____

_____

The bad things about this relationship are _____

_____

_____

_____

_____

I stay in this relationship because _____

_____

_____

_____

_____

_____

The things I gain from this relationship are _____

_____

_____

_____

_____

Things to Think About:

- What differences emerged between the relationships I looked at?

- Which relationships hold the most promise? Why?

- Which relationships seem difficult or impossible?

- What changes, if any, do I want to make as a result of this exercise?

SETTING THE GROUND RULES

In "Creating Safety" (page 19), you were introduced to the concept of ground rules. If you want to take control of your relationship with your family, it's essential that you set ground rules about what is and isn't acceptable to you.

Many survivors have few defenses and boundaries when they interact with family members. You may find yourself manipulated, scapegoated, or ignored, feeling crazy and out of control, unable to set limits or decide what you want. Setting ground rules regarding family interactions can help prevent this kind of collapse. Your limits may not be respected by your family, but at least you will have information by which you can gauge whether these relationships are viable.

Setting ground rules can have major implications in your life. If someone in your family doesn't respect the guidelines you've set, you will be faced with difficult choices about the value of that relationship. Setting ground rules can be frightening; it means that you are willing to take a stand, to consider the possibility of letting go.

I _____ am _____ am not   ready to risk setting ground rules at this time.

Why? _____

_____

_____

_____

If you're not ready to set ground rules right now, take your time. Setting limits with your family is not something to be rushed. Wait until you're ready. Then come back to this exercise.

If you decide you are ready, complete the following:

These are the things I won't do with my family anymore: *(take care of my father when he's drunk / go home for Thanksgiving dinner)*

● _____

_____

- _____

_____

- _____

_____

- _____

_____

These are the things I won't discuss with my family anymore: *(my weight / anything to do with sex or sexual preference / whether the abuse really happened)*

- _____

_____

- _____

_____

- _____

_____

- _____

_____

If I visit, it must be under the following conditions: *(They come here / I only stay for the afternoon / We meet on neutral turf / I bring a friend with me / I visit only when Dad's not there)*

- _____

_____

- _____
  _____

- _____
  _____

- _____
  _____

These are the other things I'm going to do to create boundaries between me and my family: *(Have my partner read letters from my family / Install a phone machine and screen my calls)*

- _____
  _____

- _____
  _____

- _____
  _____

- _____
  _____

Once you've written your ground rules, think about the way you want to communicate them to your family. You can do this in a letter, on the phone, in person, through a third party, or simply through your behavior. Think about what would work best for you.

I'm going to communicate my ground rules by _____

_____

_____

_____

_____

Some of the ground rules you've listed are things you can control (like whether your phone number is unlisted), but most of them will require cooperation from the people in your family. Go back to your list of ground rules and **star (★)** the ones that require a cooperative response.

ASSESSING THE RESPONSES

Once you've communicated your ground rules, you have to wait and see if they're respected. This is often the hardest part of the process because you need to decide how you're going to respond if people refuse to go along with them.

If my ground rules aren't respected, I'll *(limit the relationship / modify my ground rules and try again / think about letting go)*

- _____

  _____

- _____

  _____

- _____

  _____

- _____

  _____

- _____

  _____

You can use the following exercise to help you assess the response you get to your ground rules from individuals in your family (their responses may be very different from one another and may change over time):

1. When I communicated my ground rules to _____,

he / she _____

_____

_____

_____

As a result, I _____

_____

_____

_____

_____

2. When I communicated my ground rules to _____,

he / she _____

_____

_____

_____

As a result, I _____

_____

_____

_____

_____

3. When I communicated my ground rules to _____,

he / she_____

_____

_____

_____

As a result, I _____

_____

_____

_____

4. When I communicated my ground rules to _____,

he / she_____

_____

_____

_____

As a result, I _____

_____

_____

_____

5. When I communicated my ground rules to _____ ,

he / she _____

_____

_____

_____

As a result, I _____

_____

_____

_____

6. When I communicated my ground rules to _____ ,

he / she _____

_____

_____

_____

As a result, I _____

_____

_____

_____

Things to Think About:

- Was there any room for compromise in my ground rules? Why or why not?

- Is there anyone else in my life I need to set ground rules with?

PLANNING FOR FAMILY CONTACT

Survivors frequently revert to old childhood patterns when they have contact with their families. A visit to your sister, a phone call with your father, or a letter from your stepmother can leave you devastated and reeling. The next time you're considering a visit, phone call, or other interaction with someone in your family, fill out the following:

The reason for this interaction is _____

_____

_____

My personal goals for this interaction are _____

_____

_____

_____

_____

The things I want to observe during this interaction are _____

_____

_____

_____

_____

The information I want to gain is _____

_____

_____

_____

_____

The questions I'm going to ask are _____

_____

_____

_____

_____

_____

_____

_____

To protect myself, I'm going to   *(keep a journal / stay at a motel / hang up if necessary)*

_____

_____

_____

_____

_____

If I start to lose it, I'm going to   *(leave / call my therapist / take a walk)* _____

_____

_____

_____

After an interaction with your family, evaluate how things went. Congratulate yourself for the things you did well, and decide how you want to handle things differently the next time (if there is a next time).

The following questions can be a guide:

How did I feel before the interaction? _____

_____

_____

How did I feel during the interaction? _____

_____

_____

How do I feel now? _____

_____

_____

How old did I feel:

- before the interaction? _____
- during the interaction? _____
- how old do I feel now? _____

Were my expectations fairly accurate or was I taken by surprise? What surprised me?

_____

_____

_____

_____

_____

Did I accomplish my goals? If so, how? _____

_____

_____

_____

_____

If not, why not? _____

_____

_____

_____

_____

What did I learn? _____

_____

_____

_____

_____

_____

What strengths do I see in myself as a result of this interaction? _____

_____

_____

_____

How did I succeed in taking care of myself? _____

_____

_____

_____

How did I fail to take care of myself? _____

_____

_____

_____

_____

What would I do differently next time? _____

_____

_____

_____

_____

Do I want there to be a next time? Why or why not? _____

_____

_____

_____

_____

How do I need to foilow up this interaction? _____

_____

_____

_____

_____

DEVELOPING REALISTIC EXPECTATIONS

Even after repeated failures and disappointments with family members, many of us still hold on to hurtful relationships. We believe in a fantasy that someday things will magically change.

In "Confrontations" you looked at your fantasies in terms of one-time confrontations (page 340). If you haven't done that exercise yet (or even if you have), try it again in the space below, substituting the names of family members you pin your deepest hopes on:

I wish *my mother* would:

- *Believe the abuse happened.*
- *Tell me she's sorry she didn't protect me. Ask me how she could help.*
- *Stop protecting my father.*
- *Stop drinking and stop telling me her problems.*

I wish _____ would:

- _____

- _____

- _____

- _____

I wish _____ would:

- _____

- _____

- _____

- _____

I wish _____ would:

- _____

- _____

- _____

- _____

I wish _____ would:

- _____

- _____

- _____

- _____

I wish _____ would:

- _____

- _____

- _____

- _____

I wish _____ would:

- _____

- _____

- _____

- _____

Go back over the list of wishes you just wrote for each person. In the margin to the left, rate your wishes as follows:

P: definitely possible
U: unpredictable or unlikely
F: fantasy or wishful thinking

Look over your ratings. Then answer the following questions:

- How many of your hopes and expectations were realistic? _____

- How many were unpredictable or unlikely? _____

- How many were in the realm of fantasy? _____

GIVING UP THE FANTASY: A WRITING EXERCISE

It's important to let go of the fantasies you still hold on to about your family so you can turn your attention to building a support system that can provide real closeness and intimacy in your life today. One of the most dramatic ways to do that is to face the discrepancy between what you wish your family would say to you and what they actually do say.

Pick your abuser or someone in your family that you are currently struggling with. Choose the person on which you pin your secret hopes for reconciliation. Compose the letter you wish they would write to you. Use their phrasing, their language, their writing style.

> *Dearest Sandy,*
> *This letter is long overdue. When you were a child, I did unspeakable and unforgivable things to you. I know now that I was wrong, that I never should have violated you to satisfy my own selfish desires. There is no excuse for what I did to you . . .*
> *. . . Love and continuing wishes for your recovery,*
> *Uncle Phillip*

Reread the guidelines for freewriting on page 11. Then set a timer or alarm clock for twenty minutes, and write your own letter. Express all your secret hopes and dreams, no matter how unrealistic.

Dearest _____,
(your name)

LETTING GO: AN ACTIVITY

As you grow and change, there's no guarantee your family will grow with you. The only thing you can control is your side of the relationship. And as you come to respect yourself more, the way your family (or a particular family member) responds to you may become increasingly unacceptable.

If you set ground rules and they aren't respected, if your visits with your family leave you desolate, depressed, and despairing, you may need to cut ties or drastically limit your connections with some family members. These changes can be temporary or permanent, but they are always agonizing. One way to ease the loss is to create a grief ritual.* One woman took an image of her uncle and set it to sea in a boat. Another survivor wore black for a year to symbolize the loss of his parents.

Read over "Creating a Grieving Ritual" (page 307) and reanswer the questions. Consider designing a ritual that deals specifically with the loss of your family.

---

* If the idea of ritual is difficult or disturbing to you, reread the footnote on page 307.

ENJOYING YOUR NEW FAMILY: A WRITING EXERCISE

As you let go of family relationships that don't support you, it's essential that you build a healthy alternative with people in your life today. Let yourself imagine what a truly supportive family would be like. Reread "Creating a Support System" on page 37. Look through your answers to the exercises in "What Is a Family?" on page 368. Think about the alternative family you are creating (or would like to create). Who is part of that family now? Who would you like to be part of it? How do you treat each other? How do you spend time together? What kind of things do you like to do? How do you have fun?

Imagine a family gathering with the members of your new family. You're coming together to celebrate. You create the setting, the theme, the conversation, the activities, and the reason for your celebration. (Your team won the World Series. You had a story accepted for publication. Your abuser died. It's your birthday.) Let your imagination go. This is your fantasy.

Reread the instructions for freewriting on page 11. Then set a timer or alarm clock for twenty minutes, and describe your celebration.

REFLECTIONS: DEALING WITH YOUR FAMILY NOW

When you're struggling to heal from child sexual abuse, the last thing you want to deal with are problems with your family of origin. Yet many survivors find themselves having to make decisions about holidays, family visits, and relationships with family members.

This chapter has been designed to help you develop realistic expectations and practical strategies for dealing with your family. You've had a chance to explore what a family is, to assess individual relationships, to give up your fantasy family, and to work out a plan for interactions. As a result, you may have shifted your expectations and plans for relating to your family. This may involve some very painful letting go. If it does, it's important to acknowledge the losses and to reach out for support from the people who truly support you in your life today.

Here are some questions to help you assess your present feelings, goals, and needs around dealing with your family:

• What feelings did I have as I worked through this chapter?

• What am I feeling right now? What sensations am I experiencing in my body?

• How old did I feel as I worked through the chapter? How old do I feel right now?

- What was hard for me in this chapter? What was confusing? What didn't I understand?

- What did I learn? What commitments have I made? What steps have I taken?

- What did I do that I'm proud of?

- What's still unsettled for me? What, if anything, do I want to come back to or follow up on?

- What do I need to do to take care of myself right now?

RESOLUTION AND MOVING ON

As you move through the healing process, you will eventually reach the stage of resolution and moving on. This is when the intensity of dealing with sexual abuse begins to subside and you gain the capacity to just live life. Your feelings and relationships start to stabilize, and your attention shifts from resolving traumas of the past to living in the present. You begin to think about things besides sexual abuse. You start having more fun. Life broadens.

Reaching a place of resolution doesn't mean that you don't have problems or crises anymore; everyone does. It means that you start to make choices that relate to improving the quality of your life, not just to healing and survival. You set goals for yourself that don't have to do with fixing yourself in some way. As I say to people in my workshops, "This is the stage where you get to be a normal neurotic, just like everybody else."

Resolution cannot be rushed. It is the natural result of moving through the stages of the healing process, over and over again. Until you have met your anger, felt your pain, and experienced your vulnerability, you can't move on. If you try to do so prematurely, you will be running away, not healing.

If you have worked through a lot of the exercises in this workbook, you will be closer to a place of resolution than you were when you began. Because healing is not linear, with a clear beginning, middle, and end, you may still have more to do, but you will have made substantial progress. In this chapter you will take stock of your accomplishments and get some perspective on the work you've done so far. You'll set new goals for yourself. And you'll have the opportunity to design a closing ritual to celebrate your courage, determination, and progress.

HOW FAR HAVE I COME? A WRITING EXERCISE

In "Marking the Way" (page 98), you assessed where you were in the healing process. Do so again, but this time take the long view. Talk to people who've known you since you first made the commitment to heal. Think about the concrete ways your life has changed. Read back through what you've written in this book. Spend some time talking to survivors who are new to healing. These things will give you a sense of movement and change that you may not be able to recognize otherwise.

As you do this self-assessment, focus on the progress you've made, not on what you still have to do. Ask yourself: What have I learned? How have I changed? How is my life different than it was when I began?

Reread the instructions for freewriting on page 11. Then set a timer or alarm clock for twenty minutes, and write with pride about how far you've come.

WHY HAS IT BEEN WORTH IT?

When I was interviewing women for *The Courage to Heal,* this was my favorite question. I was struggling through the emergency stage and I needed to know why I should keep struggling. When I asked survivors what made it worth it for them to heal, I heard answers that enabled me to keep going. One woman said she could hear the birds and see the flowers for the first time. Another said she didn't have to be lonely anymore. A third said she finally liked herself. At the time, these were small jewels that held out some hope for me.

Why has it been worth it for you to heal?

WHY IT'S BEEN WORTH IT

- _____

- _____

- _____

- _____

- _____

- _____

- _____

- _____

- _____

- _____

- _____

- _____

- _____

- _____

TOOTING YOUR OWN HORN

In our culture someone who brags is seen as self-centered and boring. But in the context of healing from child sexual abuse, pride is an appropriate affirmation of accomplishments. You should brag, and brag often.

Make a list of things you're proud of. (If you get stuck, read your answers to the question on pride in the "Reflections" section at the end of each chapter.)

THINGS I'M PROUD OF

- _____
- _____
- _____
- _____
- _____
- _____
- _____
- _____
- _____
- _____
- _____
- _____
- _____
- _____

THINGS I LIKE ABOUT MYSELF

Part of the healing process is learning to love yourself. When you feel like a victim, when you blame yourself and feel ashamed, there's little room to like yourself. But as you heal, you notice things about yourself that are special, ordinary, quirky, or just plain lovable.

Make a list of things you like about yourself (they don't have to be big things):

THINGS I LIKE ABOUT MYSELF

- _____
- _____
- _____
- _____
- _____
- _____
- _____
- _____
- _____
- _____
- _____
- _____
- _____
- _____
- _____

THINGS I'VE DREAMED OF DOING AND BECOMING

Abused children (and adult survivors in crisis) rarely have the chance to explore their interests. When you're focused on keeping yourself alive or on healing from child sexual abuse, it can be impossible to see beyond your day-to-day struggles. But once your life starts to stabilize, you can see beyond your pain to the bigger world. You can lift up your head and say, "Well, I've been dealing with sexual abuse for a long time. I'm beginning to feel more solid. I'm starting to think about other parts of my life. Now what do I want to do?"

As an adult with some healing behind you, ask yourself, "Are there things I've always wished I could try? What are the things I've always been interested in? Do I have any secret fantasies I'd like to fulfill? Is there a way I want to have an impact on the world? What do I have that I can give back to the world? What things would I like to help change?"

Let yourself live with these questions. Give yourself time to find the answers. Then list your goals here.

THINGS I'D LIKE TO DO IN MY LIFE

- _____
- _____
- _____
- _____
- _____
- _____
- _____
- _____
- _____
- _____
- _____

- _____

- _____

ACTIVITY: CREATING A CELEBRATION RITUAL*

In "Grieving and Mourning" and again in "Dealing with Your Family Now," you were asked to design rituals for grieving and letting go. Now it's time to create another kind of ritual—one that celebrates your accomplishments, your courage, and your persistence. Even though you may still have a long way to go, you have come far and you deserve a rest. Let yourself enjoy the fact that you've grown and that you actually are healing. Allow yourself to receive acknowledgment and pampering.

Think about the accomplishments you've listed in this chapter. How can they best be celebrated? What would make you feel truly acknowledged for the hard work you've done?

Read over "Creating a Grieving Ritual" (page 307) and reanswer the questions, this time thinking through ways to design a celebration.

You already made a list of celebration possibilities on page 106. Go back and look at them now. Which of those things could you incorporate into a celebration ritual?

Things to Think About:

- Can I imagine celebrating my progress even if I'm not completely "finished"? Why or why not?

- Can I take a breather, now that I've come to the end of this workbook? If not, what's stopping me?

- Which of the things I've listed in this chapter makes me the most proud? Why?

---

* If the idea of ritual is difficult or disturbing to you, reread the footnote on page 307.

REFLECTIONS: RESOLUTION AND MOVING ON

As you move through the spiral of healing, you eventually reach the stage of resolution and moving on. Sexual abuse stays part of your history, but it no longer dwarfs or diminishes the rest of your life. As you reach a place of resolution, you gain a perspective on where your healing journey has led you. You appreciate yourself for the hard work you've done and begin to see the ways the work has been worthwhile.

Since healing is not a linear process, there is no clear finish line. The fact that you've come to the end of this workbook doesn't signify that you're through with healing. There's no graduation certificate or diploma. You may be in the first round of the spiral, or you may be on your third time through. You may want to rework sections of this workbook again and again. Or you may be ready to put it away.

Wherever you are in the process right now, you have demonstrated commitment and courage in your pursuit of healing. You've made valuable changes and gains. You haven't let the abusers win. You've joined a brave, admirable group of survivors who are fighting back and reclaiming their lives. They stand with you now.

Keep up the good work.

Here are some questions to help you assess your present feelings, goals, and needs around the issue of resolution and moving on:

• What feelings did I have as I worked through this chapter?

• What am I feeling right now? What sensations am I experiencing in my body?

- How old did I feel as I worked through the chapter? How old do I feel right now?

- What was hard for me in this chapter? What was confusing? What didn't I understand?

- What did I learn? What commitments have I made? What steps have I taken?

- What did I do that I'm proud of?

- What's still unsettled for me? What, if anything, do I want to come back to or follow up on?

- What do I need to do to take care of myself right now?

APPENDIX: GUIDELINES FOR HEALING SEXUALLY

Although this workbook has not delved extensively into areas of intimacy and relationships, I wanted to share with you some of the exercises I've developed for my sexuality workshops.

The sexuality workshops have been for women only, so many of the examples in this chapter reflect women's experiences. However, male survivors share many of the same sexual problems and concerns and can find these exercises equally valuable.

The exercises in this section are by no means comprehensive. In fact, they may not even touch on the sexual issues you're currently facing. But hopefully they will encourage you to think about sex in a new way.

In my work with survivors, I've witnessed more despair about healing sexually than about any other aspect of the healing process. Why? Because the contrast between what you're "supposed to feel" and what you do feel is often extreme. Sex is the arena in which the past can most clearly and directly impinge on the present. And sex is physical. You can't think your way through flashbacks and body memories.

Without role models, without someone telling you it's possible, it's easy to feel hopeless about sex. For that reason, whenever I talk to survivors about the process of healing sexually, I always begin with my own story.

Before I had my first memories of being sexually abused, I enjoyed sex. I was never really present, it's true, but in my own way I enjoyed it. I'd be up on the ceiling, lost in a fantasy, or thinking about what I was going to make for breakfast, but I still had a good time. I thought spacing out was normal. Isn't that what everybody did?

When I remembered the incest, everything changed. I shut down totally. Activities that had been okay or even pleasurable before were suddenly impossible. I couldn't stand to be touched. I was having flashbacks all the time. Sex was out of the question. My partner and I fought about sex constantly, and six months after I had my first memories, we broke up. I felt devastated and abandoned. I knew I was a failure, that I was hopelessly damaged, that I'd never make love again.

Whenever I heard a survivor talk about having a supportive partner or about enjoying sex, I would start sobbing. I couldn't imagine anyone being there for me. I couldn't imagine sex ever feeling good. But I was wrong.

In the years since then, I've had wonderful, supportive partners. I've learned to be both emotionally and sexually close with the same person. I set limits in which lovemaking was possible, and then I expanded those limits. I communicated honestly and clearly about my sexual desires and needs. And making love began to feel good.

Incest still influences my sexuality, but that influence is no longer incapacitating or frequent. When old feelings or memories come up, I know how to take care of myself. I know what to do. And most important, I no longer feel ashamed or damaged when it comes to sex. I may be unique or a little different, but I no longer think there's something wrong with me.

This last part, overcoming shame and accepting myself, was at the core of my sexual healing. I had to come to the realization that every one of the sexual problems I was experiencing had a certain inner logic. Each one was directly connected to something that had happened to me as a child. The problems I had with sex had been forced on me as surely as the incest. They weren't my fault!

The fact is I'd been robbed of the opportunity to develop my sexuality at my own pace. To heal, I had to give myself that chance as an adult woman. I learned to say no to sex I didn't want. I stopped—even if it was in the middle of making love—whenever I could no longer connect with my feelings in the present. I made commitments to myself about what was and wasn't acceptable to me sexually, and I stuck with them. I expected and demanded more from my partners. And my persistence paid off.

To change sexually requires this kind of consistency and dedication. You will need an attitude of self-love and self-acceptance, commitment over the long haul, a tremendous amount of patience, and a lot of creativity. It is slow going, full of steps forward and backsliding, but it is worth it.

Although you won't be able to complete your sexual healing by filling out a few pages in a workbook, the exercises in this chapter will give you a starting place. You'll look at your motives for wanting to explore your sexuality at this time and reexamine your definition of sex. You'll define the sexual activities that are possible for you through the use of safe sex guidelines and sexual ground rules, and you'll have a chance to imagine how you'd like to experience sex in the future.

FOR WHOM AM I DOING THIS?

Survivors are frequently under pressure from their partners to hurry up and "get fixed" sexually. When you are afraid of risking the loss of someone you love, it's natural to try to accommodate that person's needs. It's important to respect your partner's feelings and to think about the impact your choices will have on your relationship. But if you focus on sexual issues solely because of outside pressures, or force yourself to go at a pace that is not your own, your efforts will backfire.*

As a child, you experienced sex on someone else's timetable. Repeating that pattern is a mistake. If you force yourself to work on sexuality issues before you're ready, it will just be one more layer of abuse added to what you've already experienced.

If you're just beginning the healing process, you may not be ready to work on your sexuality. You may be inundated with memories, coping with suicidal feelings, struggling just to keep your head above water. These are survival issues. Sex is not. Wait until you're ready to focus on sexuality. Don't do it solely because your partner wants you to. Wait until you have your own reasons. Readiness is crucial to sexual healing. In six months you may be able to tackle issues you're not capable of handling now. Allow yourself to set a pace that you can live with.

Complete the following sentences:†

I want to work on my sexuality right now because:

- *I'm ready.*
- *Jackie will leave me if I don't.*

---

* Thanks to JoAnn Loulan for the insights at the core of this exercise.

† If you don't have a partner and are considering exploring your sexuality on your own, you can still use this exercise to determine your readiness.

- *I want my body back. I don't want my abuser in my bed.*
- *My marriage is at stake.*

- _____

_____

- _____

_____

- _____

_____

- _____

_____

- _____

_____

- _____

_____

Go back and **circle** any reasons that indicate your own internal readiness. Put a **star (★)** next to those that are based primarily on outside pressures. Then complete the following:

I don't want to work on my sexuality right now because:

- *I have more urgent things to deal with in my healing.*
- *I'm sure nothing will change.*
- *I'm afraid of having flashbacks.*
- *I'm not ready.*

- _____
  _____
- _____
  _____
- _____
  _____
- _____
  _____
- _____
  _____
- _____
  _____

Compare both sets of answers and then respond to the following:

Which set of reasons is more compelling to me? _____

Why? _____

_____

_____

Do I feel pressured to heal sexually? _____ If so, by whom? How?

_____

_____

_____

Does that pressure remind me of the abuse? If so, how? _____

_____

_____

_____

Am I ready to focus on sexual issues? ____ yes ____ no ____ I don't know

If yes, at what pace?   _(I'm ready to explore sex on my own / I think I could talk about sex with a counselor / I'm ready to have sex that isn't genital)_

_____

_____

_____

If no, how much time off do I want from sexual demands of any kind? _____

_____

_____

WHAT IS SEX?

At a recent workshop on sexual healing, an incident took place that really brought me back to the basics. It was the morning of the second day. We'd already spent a whole day talking about sexuality and healing sexually. We'd met in big groups and small groups. We'd done writing exercises and shared personal experiences. I thought we were pretty far along. But during our morning check-in, one woman raised her hand. She had a very puzzled look on her face. "You know," she said bravely to the group, "I don't have any idea what you're talking about. What is sex, anyway?"

This confusion isn't uncommon. Our culture flaunts sex, exalts sex, and is ashamed of sex, all at the same time. The media see it as a commodity. Men and women have confusing and contradictory sexual roles. In addition to these pressures, we were initiated into sex by an abuser. Abusers taught us that sex was about pain, shame, betrayal, and someone else's power over us. No wonder we're confused.

Defining sex is a clarifying place to begin. If you're doing this exercise in a group setting, you might want to put a big sheet of paper on the wall and brainstorm together, calling out answers and having someone write them on the paper. If you're doing it on your own, write down anything that comes to your mind, positive or negative, in the space provided.

Take the next five minutes to finish this sentence in as many ways as you can: "Sex is . . ."

SEX IS...

_____   _____

_____   _____

_____   _____

_____   _____

_____   _____

_____   _____

_____   _____

_____   _____

_____   _____

_____   _____

_____   _____

_____   _____

_____   _____

_____   _____

_____   _____

_____   _____

_____   _____

_____   _____

Things to Think About:

- What influenced my responses the most? Cultural beliefs? My own desires? Messages I received about sex when I was a kid?

- Were most of my responses positive or negative? What does that tell me?

- What, if anything, surprised me about my answers?

Our culture gives us a narrow, limited definition of sexuality. Sex is what men and women do together in bed to make babies. The man is on top. The woman is on the bottom, and at least one person (the man) has an orgasm. Not only is this perspective homophobic and sexist, it's also boring. Sex is more than genital stimulation and muscle contractions. It's more interesting than that. It's about intimacy, communication, pleasure in your body, feeling good, and fun.

Have you ever held a new kitten to your face? Eaten an ice cream cone on a hot summer day? Danced slow and close with someone special? Felt the warmth and release in your muscles after good hard exercise? Told an erotic story? Eaten raspberries and cream in bed? Worn something soft and cozy, even when you were spending the evening alone? Taken a long, hot bath by candlelight? These are all things that you can enjoy with your body. Sensual experiences—anything that pleases your senses—are just as much a part of sex as genital or partner sex.

There is a rich continuum of sensual and sexual experiences that you can experience alone or with a partner. Some of these will feel good (or safe) to you, and others will be laden with negative memories and painful feelings. If you broaden your concept of sex, you will find that there are at least a few body-related pleasures that you can actually enjoy.

One survivor hadn't had sex in almost thirty years. She couldn't relate to sex at all, except as a terrifying, terrible experience. When I asked her if there was anything at all that she enjoyed with her body, she said no. I asked her to think about it some more. "Isn't there anything, even a small, insignificant, little thing that ever feels good to you?" She thought about it for a long time. Finally she said yes, there was one thing. She liked to take off her clothes and dance when the full moon shone through her window. "Good," I said, "you have a place to start." I encouraged her to begin her sexual healing by dancing and exploring movement.

Healing sexually is about integrating our attention, our feelings, and our bodies, all at the same time. If you start with the experiences that threaten you the least, you can begin to have positive experiences in your body. They will reinforce your interest in reclaiming your sexuality. You can take greater risks and expand the possibilities from there.

Take the next few minutes to come up with a list of sense-related experiences that you currently enjoy. Don't limit yourself to the few things you've been taught to think of as sexual (but feel free to include them if you genuinely enjoy them). Be creative. Include as many senses as possible—hearing, seeing, smelling, tasting. If your list includes tactile (touch) sensations, that's fine. If it doesn't, that's okay too.

I EXPERIENCE PLEASURE WHEN I...

_____   _____

_____   _____

_____   _____

_____   _____

_____   _____

_____   _____

_____   _____

_____   _____

_____   _____

Things to Think About:

- What's the relationship between sensuality and sexuality?

- Is sensuality more or less threatening to me than "traditional" sex? Why?

- Did I minimize the "nonsexual" things on my list? Was it hard for me to see that they counted?

- What new thoughts (if any) do I now have about pleasure?

SEXUAL GROUND RULES

As survivors, we've been conditioned to be victims sexually. Many of us have never learned to say no or to set limits on our sexual activities. Sex happens because someone else wants it. To heal, it's important that we take control, that we make active choices concerning if, when, and how we want to explore our sexuality. Especially in the beginning, you need to put your own needs about sex ahead of anyone else's.

This can be terrifying. You may fear losing your partner, your ability to get aroused, or your capacity to have sex at all. But to reclaim your sexuality, you have to start the rebuilding process from where you really are. If you need to begin with holding hands or just flirting for a while, begin with that. If you need to say no to sex entirely, say no to sex. If you don't set limits, you'll never feel safe enough to explore your sexuality. You have to go through a period of changed sexuality in order to heal.

Use the questions below to guide you in formulating ground rules for exploring your sexuality. Be as realistic as you can. What can you live with today? When you stop thinking about your partner and only think about yourself, what is it that you want?

Under what conditions will I be sexual?

I won't make love with strangers / I will have sexual contact only with people who respect me / I won't make love in the middle of the night / I will masturbate only when I can do so in a loving and gentle way.

_____

_____

_____

_____

_____

_____

_____

What are the boundaries and limits I want to set?

I will say no to sex I don't want / I will be celibate for the next six months; then I'll reevaluate / I will say no to orgasmic sex and develop my more sensual side instead / I won't masturbate to abuse fantasies anymore / I will tell my partner that I don't want my ears touched / When I want to have sex, I'll stop and ask myself what I really want; I'll see if there's a better way I could meet my needs.

_____

_____

_____

_____

_____

_____

_____

_____

Are there any commitments I can make to myself that will help me take care of myself when I'm in a sexual situation?

I will stop, even if it's in the middle, if I stop being present / I will tell my partner exactly what I experience when we make love / I won't fake it anymore / When I start to fall back into an old abusive fantasy I will stop masturbating / I will come up with a strategy for dealing with flashbacks.

_____

_____

_____

_____

_____

_____

_____

_____

_____

Things to Think About:

- How did it feel to write down specific ground rules?

- How do I feel about the ground rules I came up with? Will I be able to stick with them? Why or why not?

- What kind of support do I need in order to stick with my ground rules? Do I have that kind of support in my life? If not, what do I need to do to get it?

- Whom do I want / need to share these ground rules with?

SAFE SEX GUIDELINES

The advent of AIDS has dramatically upped the stakes when it comes to sexually transmitted diseases. The potentially deadly virus has forced millions to radically examine and change their sexual behavior. We are all being urged to use condoms. Condom dispensers have turned up in airport bathrooms. The gay men's community, one of the hardest hit high-risk populations in the United States, has pulled together to create effective educational materials to stop the spread of the AIDS virus. At the cornerstone of this educational effort are guidelines for safe sex. These guidelines specify which sexual activities spread the AIDS virus and which do not. Safe sex guidelines usually divide sexual activities into three categories: safe, possibly safe, and unsafe. By looking at these guidelines, an individual can responsibly choose sexual activities that prevent the possible transmission of the AIDS virus.

One day when I was looking at a list of safe sex guidelines, it occurred to me that survivors could benefit from designing similar guidelines for themselves. What activities are totally unsafe (certain to bring up terror, disgust, memories of abuse)? Which are safe (likely to be positive, present-oriented, disconnected to unpleasant memories or sensations)? Which are possibly safe (okay sometimes, but not okay other times)?

This exercise can benefit you whether you're exploring sexuality on your own or with a partner. Your responses will shift and change over time, and they will be highly individual. You may have very few safe activities and many that are unsafe. Or vice versa. What is safe for one person may be unsafe for another. A warm bath with candles may be erotic and pleasurable for you. A survivor who was abused in the tub may find baths terrifying.

There are no right or wrong answers. Answer as honestly as you can. These guidelines are for you. (If you have a partner, you can both do the exercise and then discuss your answers together.)

Here's what one survivor came up with for her safe sex guidelines:

Safe	Possibly Safe	Unsafe
cuddling	*having my breasts touched*	*kissing or touching my ears*
free-form dancing	*dancing close with a partner*	*penetration of any kind*
reading erotica (if it isn't about abuse or violence)	*making out*	*my partner initiating sex*
backrubs	*sex if I initiate and if we talk about what we're going to do first*	*sex when I'm expected to (romantic occasions, anniversaries, etc.)*
phone sex	*sex out of the house*	*sex in the morning*
talking dirty	*anal penetration with a finger*	*quiet sex (no talking)*

Safe	Possibly Safe	Unsafe
erotic dinners	*oral sex (having it done to me)*	*oral sex (doing it to my partner)*
kissing standing up with clothes on	*sharing fantasies*	*being approached from behind*
flirting	*saying yes after being told I can say no*	*being held down in any way*
walking barefoot on the beach	*being held after a flashback*	*being told "I need you" or "You have to . . ."*
petting my cat	*looking in my partner's eyes*	*sex in the dark*
holding hands	*wearing sexy clothes*	*any weight on top of my body*

Design your own safe sex guidelines. You can include activities that are anywhere on the continuum between sensuality and sexuality. Anything that gives you pleasurable feelings in your body counts. You can list activities that include a partner or those that are for you alone. If you're not ready for anything that is traditionally thought of as "sexual" —kissing, caressing, licking, touching, or rubbing body parts together— you can still find physical or sensual activities that feel good to you. (Feel free to go back and use the "I Experience Pleasure" list you made on page 437 as the basis of your safe sex category.) Starting with what's safe for you, no matter how small, is the best place to begin.

If you spend the majority of your time focusing on the activities on your "safe" list, you'll begin to build a series of successful experiences regarding sexuality. When you're ready, you may want to push yourself a little (remember, only a *little*) to try some of the things that aren't as safe for you. Working through the feelings that come up when you are doing things on your "possibly safe" list can be healing too. But make sure you give yourself permission to stop if you get too scared or start to feel out of control.

Reassess these lists periodically. As you continue healing, what's safe and not safe will shift.

MY SAFE SEX GUIDELINES		
Safe	Possibly Safe	Unsafe

Take a few minutes to complete the following:

The hardest part of this exercise was _____

_____

_____

_____

_____

I was surprised that _____

_____

_____

_____

_____

I learned _____

_____

_____

_____

_____

I wish _____

_____

_____

Things to Think About:

- Was I able to isolate things that were specifically safe or unsafe? Why or why not?

- Are there direct connections between the things on the unsafe list and my abuse? What are they?

- How can I utilize these guidelines to promote my sexual healing?

- Will I be able to set limits based on these guidelines? If not, what's standing in my way?

ACTIVITY: MASSAGING HANDS

Through the sexuality workshops I've met many survivors who have been celibate for long stretches of time, some of whom have not been touched in years. Other survivors have been sexual but have never allowed themselves to be present, to feel that touch. I began using this simple exercise as a safe way to explore touch. Allowing yourself to touch and be touched in a conscious way is necessary if you want to explore physical closeness with another person. If physical intimacy with another person isn't your goal right now, or if this exercise feels too scary, feel free to skip it. Don't force yourself.

You will need a partner for this exercise. If at all possible, choose someone other than your sexual partner. If your sexual partner is the only person available, make a commitment that this exercise will not be a prelude to sex. Although sexual feelings may come up when you touch each other's hands, it is important to keep this touching safe—devoid of sexual pressure or expectations.

Sit next to your partner and massage his or her hand for five minutes. It doesn't matter if you know anything about the principles of massage or if you've ever massaged anyone before. To start, you can just hold or stroke your partner's hand. Talk about how it feels for you to do the touching. Say whatever comes into your head. (I feel like I'm coming on to you / Your hand is smooth and soft / This is really scary / I feel like I'm masturbating my father's penis.) At the same time, the person whose hand is being massaged should also talk about his or her experience. (It doesn't feel like you're coming on to me / I don't like you touching the top of my hand—would you try the bottom? / I keep wanting to space out and leave my body / Your touch is warm and reassuring.) Either participant can say "stop" at any point. If one person asks for the touch to change, or for the touching to stop, that request should be honored immediately. After five minutes, switch roles so that the person who was doing the massage becomes the receiver and the receiver becomes the one doing the massage.

Although it seems simple, this exercise can bring up extremely strong feelings. If you've never been in your body when you've been touched, have never experienced nonsexual touch, or start to have memories of your abuse during the massage, this can be a very powerful experience. You may feel sad or angry that you've never had safe touching before. You may experience flashbacks to your abuse. You may have unfamiliar feelings and body sensations. Remember, you can stop at any time, even if you're just "a little" uncomfortable.

When you've both had a turn, discuss the following questions:

- Was it easier to touch or be touched?

- What did it feel like to stay in your body while you were being touched? While you were doing the touching?

- Were you able to pay attention to the sensations in your body? What did they tell you?

- Did you experience sexual feelings at any point? If so, how did you handle them?

- Did any unpleasant memories come up? What did you do?

- Were you able to express your thoughts and feelings?

- Could you ask for what you wanted? If you wanted to say no, were you able to?

- What was it like to experience nonsexual touch? To have your boundaries respected?

SEXUAL HOPES: A WRITING EXERCISE

When you're caught up in day-to-day struggles around sex, it's sometimes hard to remember why you're going to the trouble. It's helpful to have a vision of sexuality that you're working toward. If you can't imagine a positive experience of sexuality, talk to friends who feel good about their sexuality and ask them what they experience. You'll probably start to get a sense of the possibilities. When you've talked to a few people, think about the kind of experience of sexuality you'd like to have. How would you like your perceptions or feelings about sex to change? How would you like to feel about sex a year from now? In five years? What would your sexuality be like if you could overcome the effects of abuse?

Reread the guidelines for freewriting on page 11. Then set a timer or alarm clock for twenty minutes, and write about your hopes for your sexuality.

REFLECTIONS: SEXUALITY

Healing sexually is a long-term, complex process. It requires that you accept and start where you are, and that you build slowly, one small step at a time. You may be starting from a place of being disconnected and frightened of your sexuality. You might be having sex you don't really want. Or you might be functioning well sexually, having problems only in a few key areas. Wherever you are in the process, the core of sexual healing is flexibility, honesty, creativity, and patience.

Sexuality is misunderstood and misrepresented in our culture. If you broaden your definition of sexuality, set limits and boundaries that accurately reflect where you are, you will often find a place from which you can start to reclaim your experience of sex.

Here are some questions to help you assess your present feelings, goals, and needs around the issue of sexuality:

• What feelings did I have as I worked through this chapter?

• What am I feeling right now? What sensations am I experiencing in my body?

• How old did I feel as I worked through the chapter? How old do I feel right now?

- What was hard for me in this chapter? What was confusing? What didn't I understand?

- What did I learn? What commitments have I made? What steps have I taken?

- What did I do that I'm proud of?

- What's still unsettled for me? What, if anything, do I want to come back to or follow up on?

- What do I need to do to take care of myself right now?

THE COURAGE TO HEAL WORKBOOK RESOURCE GUIDE

NATIONAL HOTLINES

RAINN
(800) 656-HOPE

A free 24-hour-a-day hotline for survivors of sexual assault, sexual abuse, rape, and domestic violence. When you call RAINN, a computer instantly connects you to the nearest rape crisis center.

Childhelp USA National Child Abuse Hotline
(800) 4-A-CHILD
(800) 422-4453

Counselors are available 24 hours a day offering crisis intervention, information regarding child abuse, resources for survivors, help with parenting, and referrals.

ORGANIZATIONS

The following organizations have resources of interest to survivors of child sexual abuse. Inclusion on this list does not necessarily indicate a recommendation or endorsement. What is helpful to another survivor may not be right for you. As always, use your own judgment when contacting any of these organizations.

The Healing Woman Foundation, P.O. Box 28040, San Jose, CA 95159, (408) 246-1788; fax (408) 247-4309; e-mail: HealingW@aol.com or on the web: http://www.healingwoman.org/

   A good starting place for information, self-help support, and a pen pal program, as well as inspiration for advanced healing.

VOICES in Action, P.O. Box 148309, Chicago, IL 60614-8309, (800) 7-VOICE-8; (773) 327-1500 (international calls); calls returned collect; fax (773) 327-4590; e-mail: voices@voices-action.org or on the web: http://www.voices-action.org

National network of incest survivors and supporters, founded in 1980. Referrals to therapists, legal resources, agencies, and self-help groups. Members receive a survival packet of excellent resources and a subscription to *The Chorus.*

Survivors of Incest Anonymous (SIA), P.O. Box 21817, Baltimore, MD 21222-6817, (410) 282-3400.

A twelve-step program which provides literature, a bimonthly newsletter, and a pen pal program. Call for groups in your area.

Incest Survivors Resource Network International, P.O. Box 7375, Las Cruces, NM 88006-7375, (505) 521-4260 (2–4 p.m. or 11–12 p.m. EST Monday–Saturday); e-mail: IRSNI@zianet.com or on the web: http://www.zianet.com/ISRNI/

Since 1983, ISRNI has operated an international helpline for survivors and professionals answered by incest survivors.

Incest Resources at The Women's Center, 46 Pleasant St., Cambridge, MA 02139, (617) 354-8807 (TTY/V).

Founded in 1980 by and for survivors. Provides excellent low-cost literature, information, and referrals nationally.

One Voice: The National Alliance for Abuse Awareness and its public policy project, **The American Coalition for Abuse Awareness (ACAA),** P.O. Box 27958, Washington, D.C. 20038-7958, (202) 667-1160 or (202) 462-4688; fax (202) 462-4689; e-mail: OVoiceDC@aol.com or ACAADC@aol.com or on the web: http://www.sover.net/%7Eschwcof/newshead.html

This alliance of survivors, supporters, child advocates, and health care and legal professionals works to educate the public, the media, and legislators. National resource line, legal referrals, and information on abuse, trauma, and memory.

Child Sexual Abuse Law Center, c/o Mary Williams, The Creamery Building, P.O. Box 1375, Point Reyes Station, CA 94956-1375, (415) 663-9202; fax (415) 663-1907.

Legal and scientific resources and assistance to attorneys working with victims of sexual abuse throughout the country.

Mothers Against Sexual Abuse (MASA), 503$^1/_2$ S. Myrtle Ave., #9, Monrovia, CA 91016, (626) 305-1986; fax (626) 305-5190; e-mail: masa@interinc.com or on the web: http://www.interinc.com/MASA

Offers public education, support for nonoffending parents, networking, legislative activism, and a newsletter.

Justice for Children, 412 Main St., Suite 400, Houston, TX 77002, (713) 225-4357.

Works to protect children when agencies fail to help. Operates a hotline, monitors court proceedings, conducts community forums, and educates elected officials.

The Family Dialogue Project, The Center for Contextual Change, 9239 Gross Point Rd., Skokie, IL 60077, (847) 676-4447.

Provides services to families seeking mediation as an alternative to legal action in response to allegations of sexual abuse.

BASTA! Boston Associates to Stop Treatment Abuse, 528 Franklin St., Cambridge, MA 02139, (617) 661-4667.

Workshops, support groups, consultation, advocacy, literature, training for professionals, resources, and referrals for people abused by helping professionals.

SESAME: Survivors of Educator Sexual Abuse and Misconduct Emerge: A Voice for the Prevention of Sexual Harassment of Students by Teachers and Other School Staff, 681 Rt. 7A, Copake, NY 12156, (518) 329-1265; fax (518) 329-0127; e-mail: sesame-w@taconic.net or on the web: http://home.earthlink.net/~jaye/index.html

SESAME works to increase public awareness, foster the recovery of survivors, encourage reporting, and promote a professional code of ethics.

The Linkup, 1412 West Argyle #2, Chicago, IL 60640; (773) 334-2296; fax (773) 334-0274; e-mail: ilinkup@aol.com or on the web: http://www.thelinkup.com

Works to prevent clergy abuse and empower its victims. Encourages religious institutions to prevent abuse, report it, hold perpetrators accountable, and treat victims with compassion.

The Center for the Prevention of Sexual and Domestic Violence, 936 N 34th Street, Suite 200, Seattle, WA 98103, (206) 634-1903; fax (206) 634-0115; e-mail: cpsdv@cpsdv.org or on the web: http://www.cpsdv.org

Serves both religious and secular communities, providing excellent literature, books, videos, trainings, conferences, and consultation, and is responsible for groundbreaking work on the relationship between the church and family violence issues.

The Safer Society Foundation (SSFI), P.O. Box 340, Brandon, VT 05733, (802) 247-3132; (fax) (802) 247-4233; referral line (802) 247-5141 (M, W, F 1:00–4:30 EST) or on the web: http://safersociety.org

This research, advocacy, and referral center publishes groundbreaking literature, audio, and videotapes, including the best resources for youthful sex offenders. They maintain a directory of agencies and individuals providing specialized treatment for youthful and adult sex offenders. Also sponsors Stop It Now, which challenges adults to confront abusing behaviors and offers a helpline for abusers who want to stop abusing: (888) PREVENT.

SurvivorShip: A Forum on Survival of Ritual Abuse, Torture & Mind Control, 3181 Mission St. #139, San Francisco, CA 94110-4515. (707) 279-1209; e-mail: survivorship@bigfoot.com or on the web: http://www.ctsserver.com/~svship

Provides resources, referrals, a pen pal program, email uselist, seminars, helpful booklets, and *The Survivorship Journal.*

NEWSLETTERS

The Healing Woman. P.O. Box 28040, San Jose, CA 95159, (408) 246-1788; fax (408) 247-4309; e-mail: HealingW@aol.com or on the web: http://www.healing woman.org

Intelligent and supportive, featuring self-help articles, interviews, creative writing, inspiring quotations, recent research, legal news, and book reviews. $30/year; $15/year low income.

For Crying Out Loud. The Survivor's Newsletter Collective, c/o The Women's Center, 46 Pleasant St., Cambridge, MA 02139.

This fine quarterly newsletter is by and for women with a sexual abuse history; $10/year.

Treating Abuse Today: Survivorship, Treatment and Trends. P.O. Box 3030, Lancaster, PA 17604-3030; (717) 569-3636; fax (717) 581-1355; e-mail: TreatAbuse@aol.com.

Refreshing in its political perspective, accessible language, and respect for survivors. Includes articles on treatment issues, interviews, and book reviews. Excellent coverage of "false memory" controversy. $39/year.

1. Sexual Assault Info Page
   http://www.cs.utk.edu/~bartley/saInfoPage.html
   Info on many topics including rape, law, domestic violence, men's resources, self-defense.

2. The Survivors Page
   http://www.sehlat.com/survs.html
   Extensive links to chat rooms, info on self-injury, pregnancy, and sexual harrassment in schools.

3. M.A.L.E.—Men Assisting Leading & Educating
   http://www.malesurvivor.org/index2.html
   Chat rooms, articles, and extensive links to a diversity of abuse-related resources (not just for men).

4. S.A.D.M.—Sexual Abuse, Dissociation & Multiple Personality Disorder Group
   http://www.golden.net/~soul/sadm.html
   Confidential e-mail listserv groups in which you can talk to other survivors. Great music and graphics.

5. Children: Abuse and Protection
   http://www.radix.net/~mschelling/children.html
   Many links to info on child abuse prevention, sexual abuse, abduction, foster care, parenting. Includes "scum" page with lists of sex offenders.

6. Partners and Allies of Sexual Assault Survivors Resource List
   http://idealist.com/wounded_healer/allies.shtml
   Resources for partners and allies of incest, rape, and sexual abuse survivors. Newsgroups, chat rooms, bibliography.

7. Canadian Online chat
   http://www.worldchat.com/public/asarc/welcome.htm
   Self-help support to survivors. Includes bulletin boards for survivors, therapists, partners, and family members.

8. Susan K. Smith, Attorney at Law—Civil Litigation and Claims for Victims of Sexual Abuse
   http://www.smith-lawfirm.com/resources.html
   Resources for lawyers and survivors considering civil suits, state-by-state information on statute of limitations, and links to lawyer referrals.

9. Help the Children (Pandora's Box)
   http://pages.prodigy.com/faulkner/help1.htm
   Advocacy for child abuse prevention, child protection, and resources for protective parents.

10. Discord's Abuse Survivors' Resources
    http://www.tezcat.com/~tina/psych.html
    Many links to newsgroups of interest to survivors, as well as general resources.

SEXUAL ABUSE AND HEALING

ABOUT SEXUAL ABUSE

Burns, Maryviolet, ed. *The Speaking Profits Us: Violence in the Lives of Women of Color / el Decirlo Nos Hace Bien a Nosotras: La Violencia en las Vidas de las Mujeres De Color.* Seattle: Center for the Prevention of Sexual and Domestic Violence (936 N 34th Street, Suite 200, Seattle, WA 98103, (206) 634-1903; fax (206) 634-0115; e-mail: cpsdv@cpsdv.org), 1986.

An excellent collection of essays about violence and racism in the lives of African-American, Latin, Asian, and Native American women. In Spanish and English.

Butler, Sandra. *Conspiracy of Silence: The Trauma of Incest.* San Francisco: Volcano Press, 1978, 1996.

A classic. Feminist analysis of child sexual abuse.

Fortune, Marie M. *Sexual Violence: The Unmentionable Sin: An Ethical and Pastoral Perspective.* New York: Pilgrim Press, 1983.

Written from a Christian and feminist point of view, this groundbreaking book explains why the church has ignored sexual abuse and rape and why and how it must deal with it now.

Herman, Judith. *Trauma and Recovery.* New York: Basic Books, 1992, 1997.

Brilliant, compassionate synthesis of our understanding of the impact of trauma including the experiences of battered women, sexually abused children, war veterans, and prisoners of war. Herman's *Father-Daughter Incest* (1981) was one of the first to deal with incest from a feminist perspective.

Rush, Florence. *The Best Kept Secret: Sexual Abuse of Children.* Englewood Cliffs, NJ: Prentice Hall, 1980.

A lucid feminist analysis of child sexual abuse from biblical times to Freud to the present. Currently out of print.

Wilson, Melba. *Crossing the Boundary: Black Women Survive Incest.* Seattle: Seal Press, 1994.

An African-American survivor writes a politically astute, warm, and accessible book.

SURVIVORS SPEAK OUT

Alleyne, Vanessa. *There Were Times I Thought I Was Crazy: A Black Woman's Story of Incest.* Toronto: Sister Vision, 1997.

A painfully honest memoir about surviving abuse and the denial of her family and community.

Bass, Ellen, and Louise Thornton, eds. *I Never Told Anyone: Writings by Women Survivors of Child Sexual Abuse.* New York: HarperCollins, 1983, 1991.

These personal accounts of childhood abuse will let you know you're not alone.

Claman, Elizabeth, ed. *Writing Our Way Out of the Dark: An Anthology by Child Abuse Survivors.* Eugene, OR: Queen of Swords Press (P.O. Box 3646, Eugene, OR 97403), 1995.

Fine poems, stories, and essays by women and men survivors of all kinds of abuse.

Cutting, Linda Katherine. *Memory Slips: A Memoir of Music and Healing.* New York: HarperCollins, 1997.

This concert pianist lost her ability to remember her music when she recovered memories of abuse. Gripping, beautifully written. The audio version is particularly compelling.

Silverman, Sue William. *Because I Remember Terror, Father, I Remember You.* Athens, GA: University of Georgia, 1996.

Award-winning memoir. Terrifying and heartening.

Wisechild, Louise. *The Obsidian Mirror: An Adult Healing from Incest.* Seattle: Seal Press, 1988, 1992.

A powerful description of healing. Vividly describes the process of remembering and connecting with inner children.

ON HEALING

Bass, Ellen and Laura Davis. *The Courage to Heal: A Guide for Women Survivors of Child Sexual Abuse.* New York: HarperCollins, 1988, 1992, 1994.

This groundbreaking book informs, encourages, and inspires. Written for women, but helpful to men as well. Available on audiotape and in an easy-to-read version, *Beginning to Heal.*

Bear, Euan, with Peter Dimock. *Adults Molested as Children: A Survivor's Manual for Women and Men.* Brandon, VT: Safer Society Press, 1988.

Excellent. A simple straightforward approach to healing for both men and women.

Engel, Beverly. *The Right to Innocence: Healing the Trauma of Child Sexual Abuse.* New York: Ballantine, 1989, 1991.

A recovery guide for adult survivors. Full of sensible, nurturing ideas for healing.

Gil, Eliana. *Outgrowing the Pain: A Book for and About Adults Abused as Children.* New York: Dell, 1983, 1988.

A good overview of the healing process. Cartoon illustrations and simple, clear text. In Spanish from Launch Press.

Levine, Peter with Ann Frederick. *Waking the Tiger: Healing Trauma: The Innate Capacity to Transform Traumatic Experiences.* Berkeley, CA: North Atlantic Books (PO Box 12327, Berkeley, CA 94712), 1997.

Based on the premise that the body holds the key to healing and that human beings, like all animals, have a deep and instinctual capacity to overcome trauma. Fascinating.

Maltz, Wendy. *The Sexual Healing Journey: A Guide for Survivors of Sexual Abuse.* New York: HarperCollins, 1991.

Helps survivors understand the impact of sexual abuse on sexuality and learn a new approach to intimate touch and sexual sharing. See Maltz's first book (with Beverly Holman), *Incest and Sexuality* (1987).

Wisechild, Louise. *She Who Was Lost Is Remembered: Healing from Incest Through Creativity.* Seattle: Seal Press, 1991.

A wonderful anthology, presenting the work of artists, musicians, and writers.

Wright, Leslie Bailey, and Mindy B. Loiselle. *Shining Through: Pulling It Together.* Brandon, VT: Safer Society Press, 1994.

An excellent, empowering book and workbook written especially for teenage survivors. Highly recommended.

RESOURCES ON MEMORY AND THE BACKLASH

In recent years, the validity of survivors' memories has been questioned repeatedly by proponents of the "false memory syndrome," the media, and the general public. A number of excellent resources have emerged which respond directly to this challenge. The books and web sites listed below provide a sane response to the continued attacks on the credibility of survivors and their therapists, while documenting the wealth of emerging research on memory and trauma.

WEB SITES

In an area of inquiry that is new and groundbreaking, the Internet is often the best source for information. The following websites provide current research and resources on recovered memory issues:

Jim Hopper's Page
http://www.jimhopper.com/
A comprehensive source of information about recovered memory issues, scientific research and scholarly resources.

Recovered Memory Page
http://cgi-user.brown.edu/Departments/Taubman_Center/Recovmem/Archive.html
Corroborated cases of recovered memory, related research, and publications on traumatic amnesia.

BOOKS

Falconer, Robert, et al., eds. *Trauma, Amnesia, and the Denial of Abuse.* Tyler, TX: Family Violence and Sexual Assault Institute, 1995.
     Articles about memory, abuse, and the current controversies by prominent professionals such as Judith Herman, Bessel van der Kolk, David Finkelhor, John Briere, David Calof, Karen Olio, and others.

Pope, Kenneth S. and Laura S. Brown. *Recovered Memories of Abuse: Assessment, Therapy, Forensics.* Washington, D.C.: American Psychological Association, 1996.

> One of the best resources on the topic. Brings together a review of the research, pragmatic guidelines for clinicians, and guidance on forensic issues.

Whitfield, Charles. *Memory and Abuse: Remembering and Healing the Effects of Trauma.* Deerfield Beach, FL: Health Communications, 1995.

> The most readable memory book for the layperson. Discusses remembering and forgetting personal history, delayed memory, and ways to sort out true from untrue memory. Analyzes the history, politics, and claims of "false memory" proponents and puts the backlash in perspective.

LEGAL ISSUES

Brent, Elizabeth. *Long and Mature Considerations: A Legal Guide for Adult Survivors of Child Sexual Abuse.* (Available for $12 from One Voice, P.O. Box 27958, Washington, D.C. 20038-7958), 1997.

> Essential reading for any survivor considering legal options. Explores the legal and therapeutic definitions of sexual abuse, the potential consequences of legal action, and activism as an alternative.

Myers, John. *A Mother's Nightmare—Incest: A Practical Legal Guide for Parents and Professionals.* Thousand Oaks, CA: Sage Publications, 1997.

> This valuable resource, written by a law professor, discusses the ways the legal system may fail mothers who are trying to protect their kids and explores the complexities of taking child sexual abuse cases to court.

SPECIAL TOPICS

ABUSE BY WOMEN

Elliott, Michele, ed. *Female Sexual Abuse of Children.* New York: Guilford Press, 1994.

> Addresses professionals working with both survivors and offenders; includes survivors' accounts of their experiences.

Evert, Kathy, and Inie Bijerk. *When You're Ready: A Woman's Guide to Healing from Childhood Physical and Sexual Abuse by Her Mother.* Walnut Creek, CA: Launch Press, 1988.

> One woman's story. A powerful resource for women molested by their mothers.

Rosencrans, Bobbie. *The Last Secret: Daughters Sexually Abused by Mothers.* Brandon, VT: Safer Society Press, 1997.

> Groundbreaking research, including testimony from 93 women. A significant and insightful work.

Wisechild, Louise. *The Mother I Carry: A Memoir of Healing from Emotional Abuse.* Seattle: Seal Press, 1993.

> Powerful, honest, beautifully written look at emotional abuse by a mother.

ABUSE BY SIBLINGS

Cole, Autumn, and Becca Brin Manlove. *Brother-Sister Sexual Abuse: It Happens and It Hurts. A Book for Sister Survivors.* Beccautumn Books ($9.95 from Autumn Cole, Range Mental Health Center, Box 1188, Virginia, MN 55792, (218) 365-5019), 1991.

> Validates the feelings, experiences, and healing needs of women who were molested by their brothers.

Wiehe, Vernon. *The Brother/Sister Hurt: Recognizing The Effects of Sibling Abuse.* Brandon, VT: Safer Society Press, 1997.

A guide to acknowledging and healing from sibling abuse, with a chapter on sexual abuse. Also see *Perilous Rivalry: When Siblings Become Abusive* (1991) and *Sibling Abuse: Hidden Physical, Emotional, and Sexual Trauma* (1990, 1997) which give guidelines for preventing and stopping sibling abuse.

ABUSE BY HELPING PROFESSIONALS

Gonsiorek, John C., ed. *Breach of Trust: Sexual Exploitation by Health Care Professionals and Clergy.* Thousand Oaks, CA: Sage, 1995

Current research, accounts by victims, legal perspectives, and prevention training.

Minnesota Coalition Against Sexual Assault. *It's Never OK: A Handbook for Victims and Victim Advocates on Sexual Exploitation by Counselors and Therapists.* Minneapolis: Minnesota Coalition Against Sexual Assault, (2344 Nicolett Avenue #170-A, Minneapolis, MN 55404-3352).

Excellent, clear and straightforward.

FOR MALE SURVIVORS

Grubman-Black, Stephen. *Broken Boys/Mending Men: Recovery from Child Sexual Abuse.* New York: Ballantine Books, 1990, 1997.

Full of first-hand accounts, this healing book written by a male survivor is simple, clear, and helpful.

Hoffman, Richard. *Half the House: A Memoir.* New York: Harcourt Brace & Company, 1995.

Beautifully written memoir about a working class childhood that included sexual abuse by a coach. This book led to the arrest of the perpetrator thirty years later.

King, Neal. *Speaking Our Truth: Voices of Courage and Healing for Male Survivors of Childhood Sexual Abuse.* New York: HarperCollins, 1995.

A moving collection of first-person testimonies.

Lew, Mike. *Victims No Longer: Men Recovering from Incest.* New York: HarperCollins, 1988, 1990.

Solid, clear, warm information and encouragement. This book helped launch the male survivor movement.

Sonkin, Daniel. *Wounded Boys, Heroic Men: A Man's Guide to Recovering From Child Abuse.* Holbrook, MA: Adams (260 Center Street, Holbrook, MA 02343), 1998.

A simple, straightforward guide. Especially good for men not versed in the language of feelings or recovery.

Wright, Leslie Bailey and Mindy B. Loiselle. *Back On Track: Boys Dealing With Sexual Abuse.* Brandon, VT: Safer Society Press, 1997.

Excellent, simply written. Helps boys (age 10 and up) recognize their feelings and take steps toward healing.

DISSOCIATION AND MULTIPLE PERSONALITIES

Cohen, Barry, Esther Giller, and Lynn W., eds. *Multiple Personality Disorder from the Inside Out.* Dallas: Sidran Press, 1991.

This helpful, hopeful book talks about MPD from the perspective of those who live with it. Everyone concerned with multiple personalities should have a copy.

Gil, Eliana. *United We Stand: A Book for People with Multiple Personalities.* Walnut Creek, CA: Launch Press, 1990.

A simple cartoon book that explains multiple personalities and dissociation.

WOMEN, WORK AND ABUSE

Murphy, Patricia A. *Making the Connection: Women, Work and Abuse.* Delray Beach, FL: St. Lucie Press (2000 Corporate Blvd. NW, Boca Raton, FL 33431-9868; (800) 272-7737; fax (800) 374-3401; e-mail: orders@crcpress.com or on the web: http://www.crcpress.com), 1993.

A vocational rehabilitation counselor looks at the way abuse undermines women's career choices and explores vocational counseling as part of the healing process. Also see *A Career and Life Planning Guide for Women Survivors: Making the Connections Workbook.*

FOR SUPPORTERS OF SURVIVORS

Davis, Laura. *Allies in Healing: When the Person You Love Was Sexually Abused as a Child.* New York: HarperCollins, 1991.

A comprehensive guide for partners who are struggling to take care of themselves and the survivors they love. Available on cassette.

Engel, Beverly. *Families in Recovery: Working Together To Heal The Damage of Childhood Sexual Abuse.* Los Angeles: Lowell House, 1994.

A straightforward guidebook for bringing families together and helping them recover from the devastation of abuse. Currently out of print.

Smith, Shauna. *Making Peace with Your Adult Child.* New York: HarperCollins, 1991, 1993.

A wise, compassionate book for parents who are struggling to heal painful rifts with their adult children.

FOR PARENTS

Adams, Caren, and Jennifer Fay. *No More Secrets: Protecting Your Child from Sexual Assault.* San Luis, Obispo, CA: Impact Publishers, 1981.

A fine practical guide.

Adams, Caren. *Helping Your Child Recover From Sexual Abuse.* Seattle: University of Washington Press (P.O. Box 50096, Seattle, WA 98145-5096, (206) 543-4050; fax (206) 543-3932), 1987, 1992.

Practical guidance for parents, including sample conversations and activities for parents and kids to do together.

Gil, Eliana. *A Guide for Parents of Children Who Molest.* Rockville, MD: Launch Press, 1987, 1995.

Clear, simple, and compassionate. A must.

Levy, Barrie and Patricia Occhiuzzo Giggans. *What Parents Need to Know About Dating Violence.* Seattle: Seal Press, 1995.

Straightforward advice about abusive dating relationships.

Matsakis, Aphrodite. *When the Bough Breaks: A Helping Guide for Parents of Sexually Abused Children*. Oakland: New Harbinger Publications (distributed by Varied Directions, 18 Mt. Battie Street, Camden ME 04843, (800) 888-4236; fax (207) 236-4512; e-mail: Joyceb3955@aol.com), 1991.

A compassionate guide written by a therapist whose daughter was sexually abused.

Note: An excellent mail-order source for hard-to-find abuse-related books is Full Circle Books in Albuquerque, New Mexico. For their extensive annotated catalogue on healing from sexual and family violence, access them online at http://www.bookgrrls.com/fcb. For a printout of the catalogue, send $10 to Full Circle Books, 2205 Silver SE, Albuquerque, NM 87106, or call (800) 951-0053.

ABOUT THE AUTHOR

Laura Davis is a nationally recognized expert on healing from child sexual abuse. She is the co-author of *The Courage to Heal* and *Beginning to Heal* and author of *Allies in Healing: When the Person You Love Was Sexually Abused as A Child.* She also publishes a monthly parenting column and is the co-author of *Becoming the Parent You Want to Be: A Sourcebook of Strategies for the First Five Years.*